Can dreams be nothing more than a confusion of the mind?
A No-Man's Land of nonsense . . .
When we leave the world behind
Pursued by terrors we explore an unfamiliar place
And live the drama of a life, all in a moment's space.
Are dreams the crazy images of a blurred and senseless thought?
I sometimes think that when we dream, some part of us is caught
between two worlds, the earthly and the realm of the unseen.

Anonymous

Also by
Angela Thompson Smith, Ph.D.

Remote Perceptions

DIARY OF AN ABDUCTION

A SCIENTIST PROBES THE ENIGMA OF HER ALIEN CONTACT

ANGELA THOMPSON SMITH, PH.D.

Cover design by Steve Amarillo

For information write:

Hampton Roads Publishing Company, Inc.
1125 Stoney Ridge Road
Charlottesville, VA 22902

Or call: 804-296-2772
Fax: 804-296-5096
e-mail: hrpc@hrpub.com
www.hrpub.com

If you are unable to order this book from your local
bookseller, you may order directly from the publisher.

Call 1-800-766-8009, toll-free.

Library of Congress Catalog Card Number: 00-109655

ISBN 1-57174-201-8

10 9 8 7 6 5 4 3 2 1

Printed on acid-free paper in Canada

Acknowledgments

The writing of this book has taken over thirteen years, although the material contained in the book goes back over fifty years. Starting in 1986, I began keeping journals of my experiences. These were supplemented with files of material I gleaned from the scientific and anomalies communities. There are so many people who helped me along the way.

Special thanks are due to my good friend, Mariah Folger, who helped me understand that I was not alone with my experiences. She bravely shared many of her experiences with me. Special thanks are also due to my other special friend, Barbara Flick, and her commonsense attitude to the abduction experience. She helped me laugh when things were tough.

I would also like to thank Hampton Roads Publishing Company, and especially Richard Leviton, for having the courage to publish this book.

Table of Contents

Introduction

> "Contact is the recognition of, and the coping with, the other, the different, the new, the strange. It is not a state we are in or out of . . . but an activity. I make contact on the boundary between me and the other. The boundary is where we touch and at the same time experience separateness. It is where the excitement is, the interest, concern and curiosity or fear and hostility, where previously unaware or diffuse experience comes into focus, into the foreground as a clear gestalt."
>
> —Laura Perls, "Conceptions and Misconceptions of Gestalt Therapy," in *Voices*, 1978, 14, 31–36.

This is a true story. Although it reads like a novel, all the events have actually happened. There is a very real phenomenon, currently called alien abduction, that is experienced by thousands of people around the world. However, the experience has become confounded by the many theories and suppositions that surround it, by myth and fabrication, and by downright denial by the media, science, and the government.

I think of the alien abduction phenomenon as an enigma. An enigma is something that is hard to understand or explain. There is no platform—either scientific, secular, or religious—to explain human contact with the Visitors. Nothing in our present society prepares us for the experience of alien abduction. This book is an attempt to understand, and perhaps explain, the phenomenon. However, to explain something, to make it plain or understandable, demands a common ground between the phenomenon and the perceiver. There is very little common ground between the Visitors and us. So as a final chapter, I have gone to the Visitors themselves to seek some answers.

I am a scientist trained in neuropsychology and the cognitive sciences. Over the past twenty years I have worked with many individuals, research groups, and organizations, trying to understand how people think and act. In 1986 I came across a phenomenon called alien abduction that seemed at first to be beyond my comprehension. I had no terms of reference in which to place this distressing and invasive set of experiences. As I listened to what the abductees had to say, I became suspicious that I, too, had been involved in similar experiences.

Using data contained in personal journals, files, and records covering eighteen years of research, I have uncovered new facts about the phenomenon known as alien abduction. This has been a difficult book to write. It holds no punches. It states facts as they are. Related in journal format, *Diary of an Abduction* tells of my quest as a scientist for answers to some deeply disturbing questions.

Diary of an Abduction contains graphic descriptions of abductions that are remembered as "real dreams"; it uncloaks shadowy characters lurking on the fringes of the UFO and parapsychology communities, who are themselves caught up in the machinations of the phenomenon and who announce their wish to "derail the train"; it describes technical apparatus and medical equipment remembered from abduction experiences, and the alien and human characters involved in these events. Writing *Diary of an Abduction* has been healing for me on many levels. The alien abduction scenario remains a virtually taboo topic in many fields of scientific investigation. Therefore, many people referred to in this book have been given pseudonyms to ensure their anonymity. However, the story remains a true one.

As a teenager, I had some unusual personal experiences that both were unique in themselves and initiated a sequence of mystifying events that have generated many intriguing questions. The search for answers to these questions has taken me across international, social, and cultural boundaries; into bookshops and libraries, universities, and colleges; into research and support groups; and to seminars and conferences. I now have many key pieces to the puzzle and can start to see that the picture on the puzzle box is one that has been seen by many thousands of experiencers. That picture is of a small, gray humanoid with large dark eyes, pointy face, and overlarge cranium.

In 1961, when I was sixteen years old and my brother Alan was thirteen, we moved from Bristol, a seaport, to Wimborne, a rural market town in Dorset, England. My father worked locally at Herne airport in engineering maintenance, and my mother served in a Wimborne bakery. I started work that year as a trainee hotel receptionist, while my brother still attended the local high school at Ferndown. We lived out in the countryside, in an area called Stapehill. The house had a large, long garden, mostly meadow, and at the bottom of the garden was a stand of old elm trees, a tiny brook, and beyond that more rough meadows. Alan and I had separate bedrooms at the back of the house.

One night in the spring of 1962, at about ten, our rooms were lit up with an intensely bright light. My brother looked out of his bedroom window and said that a flying saucer had landed in the meadow beyond the brook. I was very frightened and hid under the bedclothes, but I could still see the light. Alan continued looking and said that people had come out of the flying saucer and were moving around. Later, the light went out as suddenly as it came on, and it was totally dark. The next morning neither our parents nor anybody else in the neighborhood mentioned seeing the light. Following that night, I suffered from terrifying nightmares in which I would be squeezing through small spaces before arriving at a long gray room. There, at the end of the room, was a boxlike table, and I would experience the most incredible terror. I would wake from these nightmares in panic, but I could not find a reason for such terror and tried to forget them.

In the years that followed, I trained as a nurse and social worker, worked in hospitals, nursing homes, and children's homes in England, and for two years at an orphanage in Colombia in South America. Returning to England, I went back to school and received my B.S. in psychology from Cardiff University in Wales and my M.S. from Manchester University in England. I was married and divorced and emigrated to the United States, where I worked as a scientific and medical researcher at some of the most prestigious universities on the East Coast of America. During all of these active, interesting years, strange events continued to haunt me.

During the weekend of June 2 to 4, 1988, I went to Cornell University to attend the seventh annual meeting of the Society for Scientific Exploration. It was an exciting three days, with talks that included physics, neurophysiology, UFOs, interspecies communication, Eastern philosophies, parapsychology, critical thinking, and many other interesting topics. One of the invited speakers was Carl Sagan, who stressed the need for critical thinking in science.

During the reception, I told one of the presenters, Dr. Richard Haines, about the experience that my brother and I had had in

England twenty-six years earlier, and he told me that this was about as close as a lot of people come to having alien contact. Richard Haines is one of the top people in his field, an ex-NASA psychologist, and a well-respected researcher, but I was conflicted about his interpretation of my experience. Haines and other researchers, including Budd Hopkins, Dr. John Mack, and David Jacobs, claim that people who have been abducted experience episodes of missing time, are subjected to medical examinations, and are caused to suffer from an amnesia that hides their experiences from themselves and others. According to these investigators, hypnosis may uncover these hidden memories and lead to an understanding of the phenomenon.

At one of the conference meetings, Richard Haines showed the group a series of slides of drawings of aliens he had collected. Sitting in the corner of the room, I watched the slides with an increasing nervousness that developed into a full panic attack. My heart started thudding, I could not breathe, my legs were shaking. I felt giddy and wanted to run out of the room screaming. Part of my mind was denying the panic, saying "This is all nonsense. There is absolutely no need to feel this way. It is all imagination." Another part of me, amazingly even calmer, was telling me that I had better take notice of these feelings, because there could be something here that needed to be explored. David Jacobs lectured the group on the abduction phenomenon and cautioned the audience about starting an investigation with an abductee until they were sure they really wanted to open, as he put it, "a can of worms." As I left the meeting room that night, I thought my ordeal was over, but little did I realize that there was much more to follow, including an episode of possible missing time.

The next day I left Cornell about eight A.M. with a professional colleague named Jim to drive home to New Jersey. We talked about the conference and listened to the radio and to a Paul Winter tape we both liked. I was watching the sky and fantasized about seeing a UFO and what I would do if I did see one. I remember seeing a strange, small, black car in the distance behind us, except its outline didn't look like a normal car. Jim also saw it, but we could not remember passing it. At about the same time, a wind sprang up, whipping the treetops along the road, and Jim remarked that the wind seemed to be traveling along the road at the same speed we were. We thought there might have been a helicopter above us, but we did not see or hear one. About this time, I also had a strong urge to go to sleep.

My next solid memories are that we were still going along the road, passing a brewery, signs for a college, and an unfinished bridge. We got into road construction and were passing between concrete roadblocks in single file with other cars. I somehow felt that it was important to remember landmarks. Jim remarked that he thought we were going in the wrong direction and stopped the car to look at a map. We were miles out of our way, and Jim, who knew the road well, commented that he could not understand why we had made a wrong turn. As we passed the landmarks I had seen earlier, he said he could not remember passing them. We both began to feel confused and anxious.

We drove on and eventually saw signs for the exit we needed, but again we missed it and ended up in southern New Jersey. We wandered around for about half an hour until we finally got onto the road that eventually brought us to our destination. On the last lap of the journey, we were both exhausted and very anxious to get home. As we passed signs to our hometown, our anxiety decreased considerably. During the drive, we both had been very quiet and Jim kept opening and closing the sunroof. It would get warm inside the car and he would open it. Then suddenly he would close it. We kept the windows closed even though the sun was shining and it was warm outside. We didn't think this strange at the time. I felt dissociated and kept getting the urge to close my eyes and go to sleep.

We arrived at home at 3:15 P.M., over seven hours after leaving Ithaca, which was a four-hour journey at most! I felt spaced out and very tired. I mentioned to my housemate, Emily, that I felt it was possible we had experienced some missing time. I felt very conflicted about the reality of the experience. I slept for a couple of hours but awoke with my heart racing and feeling very hot, and I felt extremely lethargic. I went back to sleep and slept through to the following morning.

The next day I felt a lot better physically but I was very irritable. That evening I talked with Emily and told her the strange story of our journey, and she was able to reassure me that there was probably a perfectly good explanation.

The next five years was a period of decision making. While I was determined to understand my experiences, I was also determined that I did not want to undergo hypnosis. I did not want someone else determining what was real or not about experiences that were intensely personal and that I desperately did not want to be real. I decided that I would gently explore my inner self through dream recall; through a personal memory search; through meditational journeys, journal keeping, sharing, and networking with other people who had similar experiences; and by reading everything related to the subject. I was committed to face the phenomenon, to steal its thunder, whether it turned out to be a new undiagnosed form of psychosis, an interface with another dimension, an unknown manifestation of group consciousness, or a nuts-and-bolts reality.

On June 25, 1988, I gave my subconscious permission to look for any hidden memories I could possibly associate with being abducted. If no such memories existed, then I would expect my subconscious mind to tell me so. If there were such memories, I instructed my subconscious to reveal them in dream form, where I could deal with them, and I would document the results in my journals. This proved to be a successful method at bringing up repressed emotions and evoked many dreams. The next day I wrote the following in my dream journal:

> Last night revealed a flurry of dreams and I awoke feeling quite shaken! What they mean and if they are actual trace memories is uncertain. What I can record is that the dreams took on an increasing feeling of reality as they progressed throughout the night and into the early morning. I went to sleep about one A.M., which is late for me. I didn't awake until ten A.M. this Sunday morning, although I was aware of thunderstorms and rain outside.

And on the next day:

> The first dream was one of anxiety. I was scheduled to go on vacation and had my bags packed. I and several other people were writing our names on a strip of paper, which was supposedly the ticket to get on the bus. The bus came and somehow started, but I did not have my luggage. It was locked inside the house along with keys, tickets, and so forth—everything I needed on my vacation. I was very upset and anxious. I was embarrassed as the bus had to stop and go back. I was also angry at myself, because I had locked the house with my luggage inside, so it would delay the bus even further.
>
> I feel this dream symbolized my anxiety about my dream project and was throwing delaying tactics into the process.
>
> In the second dream I was playing a computer game. I had won quite a lot of gold pieces and came upon a room that contained all twenty-six of the monsters in the game.
>
> Two further dreams were very similar and consisted of being outside and looking at the moon. To the right side of the moon

> was a smaller disc. In the second dream I remember asking why the moon had another moon by it. In both dreams this smaller disc came rapidly toward me. It got bigger and bigger and engulfed me each time.
>
> The last dream was bizarre to say the least! I awoke feeling very shaken. I dreamed that I was asleep in my bed at home. I was a child again and I was lying curled up on my right side. I could see a crack of light coming under the door from the landing outside. I heard someone say my name, "Angela," but it did not sound like my parents or my brother. I pulled the sheet partly over my head. I had enough space to continue looking at the door to see if anyone would come in. Then to my surprise, I felt someone very light sitting at my back and pulling back the bedclothes. I turned so that I was looking at whoever was there and came face to face with what I can only describe as a "creature." To be honest, and without deluding myself, I must say he looked very similar to the pictures of "aliens" in the current literature. I gazed at him for some time, and my anxiety lessened. He had a rounded head but narrower than in current illustrations; also he was much smaller and slighter in build, almost fragile. The eyes were slanted but not as exaggerated as the common illustrations. He did a strange thing. He was kissing my left hand very gently. I asked him, "Are you well?" He said, "What is well?" I said, "Are you happy? Are you healthy?" He said, "Yes." Then I awoke.

These were scary dreams but I considered them a good start: an indication to me that I was on the right path to uncovering information about my experiences.

During the following five years, I joined several professional organizations such as the Mutual UFO Network (MUFON), the Center for UFO Studies (CUFOS), and the Fund for UFO Research (FUFOR), that seemed dedicated to understanding the UFO abduction phenomenon and got caught in the cross fire between pen-battling investigators and therapists, who were intent on destroying each other's reputations. I got caught up in the paranoia of suspecting governmental authorities of being actively involved in UFO abductions and read everything publicly and privately written about the three-letter government agencies and UFOs. For example, that the CIA had been reported as having a "weird desk" that followed up on UFO stories.

I queried abduction researchers on the state of the field, but the terminology they used (abductions and aliens) assumed that the phenomenon was negative. I decided that I would refer to my experiences as Interfaces and to the entities as Visitors. Until I could understand their intentions, I could not assign a negative or positive quality to the Visitors' interactions. I explained it this way: if a wild animal wandered into my house at night, I would try to get it outside again without too much agitation. However, if a person entered my house at night with the intention of stealing or hurting me, I would be furious. I felt that the Visitors' intentions fell somewhere between the two examples.

When I finally decided to tell people about my experiences, in the late 1980s, I found that I was ignored. This was a relief, as I thought I would be outcast, ridiculed, and maybe even fired from my job. It was also sad, because as a competent researcher and experiencer, I could perhaps help throw some light on the subject. I continued to read the many, often ridiculous, theories surrounding the phenomenon, to monitor the infighting between groups supposedly helping abductees, and to watch the exploitation of abductees.

Since 1988 I have been adding data to the information pool, finding new pieces to the jigsaw as new information links with old. I have gone through intense pendulum swings of belief in the phenomenon, ranging from outright denial to full acceptance of its personal and global importance. At this point in my search, I am intent on stealing the thunder and power from the experience itself, from the negative researchers who have monopolized the field, from the media that have sensationalized and trivialized the topic, and from the authorities who have ridiculed and denied the experience. With the fear removed, it will be easier to understand this phenomenon.

A 1991 Roper Poll determined that more than 2 percent of the American adult population has had experiences very similar to those claimed by abductees. I believe that this population varies in its reaction to the experience. Like any random population, there will always be a small percentage that copes poorly. Very often, experiencers will present to clinical professionals symptoms that are diagnosed as "post-traumatic stress disorder syndrome," a psychological reaction to an intensely traumatic situation. There will also be another small group whose members bring good coping mechanisms to bear on their experiences.

I have been very fortunate in belonging to a nationwide support group of professional people who are well established in their own fields and who have found ways to integrate their abduction experiences into their daily lives. Between these two groups is a huge body of people for whom no provisions have been made. Once the thunder has subsided and the clouds clear, I advocate that we take a fresh look at the abduction phenomenon and ways to understand it. This fresh look will entail looking at the phenomenon without fear.

I continually add information to the *Diary of an Abduction* database. This information is then shaken down through my "reality filter" to see what drops out and what matches up. It is surprising what "noise" can be filtered out in this way and what elements link up.

Diary of an Abduction recounts how artifacts are often left behind by whoever is monitoring the abductions. I have used the artifacts to trace these activities to various government contractors employed in medical research and development. *Diary of an Abduction* will not provide all the answers to this perplexing phenomenon, but it will give researchers a place to start looking.

For many years I did not have a name for my experiences. While researching this phenomenon, I discovered that the late J. Allen Hynek of the Center for UFO Studies had come up with a categorization to describe contact with the Visitors. He termed these CE1, CE2, and CE3.

CE1, or Close Encounters of the First Kind, occur when a UFO is seen at close proximity, within roughly five hundred feet. Next, CE2, or Close Encounters of the Second Kind, is defined as a UFO leaving evidence of its passing, including ground markings, or interfering with auto engines and radio signals. Lastly, CE3, Close Encounters of the Third Kind, occurs when one or more nonhuman entities, or extraterrestrials (ETs), are observed. Stephen Spielberg's movie *Close Encounters of the Third Kind* focused on this third category. The movie even included a cameo appearance by Allen Hynek. You can see him in a blue suit, pipe in mouth, gazing up at the UFO in the final scenes.

A few years ago, Jacques Vallee, a UFO researcher, came up with two further categories: CE4 and CE5. When a human has an involuntary interaction with a nonhuman entity or ET, including abduction and paralysis, this is considered to be a CE4, or Close Encounter of the Fourth Kind. CE5, or a Close Encounter of the Fifth Kind, occurs when a human has voluntary interaction with an ET, including communication. The last two categories, CE4 and CE5, are the most frequently reported experiences in this book.

In this book, I have reviewed CE4 and CE5 reports from other abductees and the effort of scientists to debunk their accounts, and to make sense of all this material, I have included my own remembered abduction from 1962. The urge to make sense of this very personal event led me to research the entire field of abduction. I do not claim to provide all of the answers, but I would like to point researchers in directions that might provide answers to this enigma.

The book is written in journal form, with dated entries that span the time frame from 1988 through 2000. My recorded dreams and recovered memories serve as a guide back to the abduction experience. Throughout this book I have tried to chart the confusing layers of hysteria, misinformation, distortion, paranoia, delusion, and obfuscation in the field and my efforts to work my way through it to some kind of truth.

Very often, individuals who have interacted with the Visitors remember their experiences in memory flashbacks or in dreams that seem incredibly real. Many times, these same individuals may try and make some sense of their experiences by keeping journals and recording their dreams and memories. The self-inquiry process I developed, where I collected pieces of evidence from memory and analysis of dream recall, is something new to the abduction process. It opens up a new model of dream theory, which I call "real dreams," in which events that seem to have happened, in what Carlos Castaneda called the "second attention," are recalled during sleep and remembered as dreams. Real dreams of alien contact, including medical intervention, are often accompanied by physical signs such as wounds, abrasions, and puncture marks the following morning. They indicate Close Encounters of the Fourth Kind.

Over the course of a dozen years, through the process of real dreams, I was able to reconstruct some very strange, troubling events. I have remembered dreams, childhood events, some including my family, colleagues, and friends, and even some deliberate meditatively induced encounters with the grays, which were Close Encounters of the Fifth Kind.

When I began my quest, my intent was to prove the reality of my suspicions to myself and to extract some kind of rational explanation for these weird details and memories. As I progressed through the journey, the original quest was not forgotten but was subsumed by an interest in the actual process. The fear was replaced, at first by concern and confusion, and later by a mixture of intrigue and excitement, as I began to realize that many other people had experienced the same thing. My emotions came full circle, to be replaced again by fear, as I realized that there were human agencies tracking these phenomena. The pendulum has now swung again and the fear is gone. I have nothing to hide, so there is nothing to fear.

Glossary of Terms

Some of the following terms have become commonly known and associated with the field of alien abduction: that is, missing time and alien-human hybrids. Some are less well known, such as my definition of a real dream. The definitions are included here as an introduction to the contents of the book.

ABDUCTEE(S): Term given by researchers and therapists to individuals who have reported a specific set of experiences in which they have encountered nonhuman entities. The term is seen as a negative one by some experiencers, as it assumes that the person was taken against his will. In some cases this may be true. However, some experiencers feel that, at some point, they gave permission for the contact to take place. There is a wide response to abduction. The response of abductees depends on the circumstances of the abduction, the support they receive, and their individual coping skills.

ABDUCTION PHENOMENON: Another term for the matrix of events that surround the abduction experience. Abduction is referred to as a phenomenon, because within the current scientific paradigm, there are no hypotheses that totally explain the experience, and the experience cannot be replicated at will.

ABDUCTIONS: Refers to the events in which an individual experiences contact with nonhuman entities. Experiencers often refer to the abductions by other terms such as "interfaces."

AKASHIC LIBRARY and **AKASHIC RECORDS**: Outside of the Western scientific paradigm and seen as only a belief down through the centuries is the concept that there exists a repository of all information of the past, present, and future. It is also believed that this information can be accessed through various mental tools. Remote viewers, for example, refer to the Akashic Records as the "matrix" and teach that it can be accessed through remote viewing methods and protocols.

ALIEN(S): In the abduction phenomenon, this is any type of nonhuman but humanoid entity; the term usually refers to the small grays, tall grays, tall goldens, and so forth. A reptilian type of entity has also been reported. The term alien assumes that the entities are from another place, strange and unnatural, repugnant, and not belonging here. The term in itself is negative and encourages xenophobia. More neutral terms that have been used are the Visitors or Visiting Others.

ALIEN ABDUCTION: The act of abduction by the Visitors. The term is a negative one in that it assumes forced abduction against the individual's will. Many experiencers report that this is not always the case. Some experiencers state that they have chosen to have contact with the Visitors.

ALIEN CONTACT: An early term for contact and interaction with nonhuman entities. It used to be thought that alien contact might occur in the far future. Then in the 1970s individuals reported conscious and ongoing contact with entities that were visiting the Earth. Unfortunately, the most vociferous of the contactees formed tight-knit social groups that took on the appearance of cults.

ALIEN-HUMAN HYBRID: From the early abduction literature, it has been assumed that the main reason for Visitor contact is to replenish the alien's damaged DNA and to produce alien/human hybrid entities. This is a hypothesis that is still under consideration.

ALPHA: A measurement of brain wave activity and a term used to describe an altered state, when the person is experiencing alpha brain wave activity. Most people experience the alpha state when they close their eyes and calm their thoughts. In most people, hypnosis, meditation, certain sleep states, and daydreaming appear to take place in the alpha state.

ALTERED STATE OF CONSCIOUSNESS: An altered state of consciousness is any mental state that differs from an individual's normal waking state. Sleep and dreaming are two of the most common altered states of consciousness. Borderline states of consciousness are the hypnogogic state, just before sleep, when the individual may experience vivid, visual imagery. Another borderline state is the hypnopompic state, which occurs upon waking, when the individual may experience physical paralysis, even though her mind is awake and alert. Most individuals cycle through varying states of consciousness throughout the day and night. Hypnosis consists of eliciting an array of changing states of consciousness.

AVIARY: The Aviary is a term, coined by the conspiracy communities, to designate individuals who may have a secret and important role in the hiding and denial of UFO and abduction information. The supposed members of the Aviary are given bird names: Hawk, Dove, and so forth. They have been accused of spreading disinformation. Most of the identified Aviary members have denied their involvement in the cover-up of the UFO and abduction scenarios.

BABY DREAMS: Many abductees report baby dreams. Sometimes these may involve the appearance of Visitor infants or hybrids. These babies and children are typically very frail looking with absent or dry, wispy hair. They appear to be a hybrid mix of alien and human characteristics.

CONSPIRACY COMMUNITIES: Subgroups within the UFO and abduction communities that believe the government and military are conspiring against the general population to keep it from knowing the truth about UFOs and abductions.

CONTACT: The act of interacting with a nonhuman entity, either by mental means or physically.

CONTACTEE: Another name for an abductee, and a term that was popular during the 1970s.

CROP CIRCLES: Geometric shapes that have appeared in fields of ripe grain. Originally, they took the form of concentric circles but have developed over the years into complex and elaborate designs. Many of these can only be appreciated from an aerial viewpoint. Some human designers of crop circles have come forward to claim their work, although many elaborate crop circles remain unexplained.

DATA DOWNLOADS: Experienced by abductees, data downloads or data dumps are altered-state experiences during which experiencers perceive that streams of visual and auditory signals have entered their field of consciousness from an outside source. The visual signals are often perceived as known and unknown symbols that may scroll across the visual field. Auditory signals may take the form of electronic-sounding beeps, which may occur in numerical series. Sometimes the downloads occur as factual information, much of which was previously unknown by the experiencer.

DRACOS: The name given to a reptilian type of entity that has been reported by some abductees. Within the abduction community, the reptilian type of entity is viewed as having negative intent and negative interactions with abductees.

DREAM TEACHING: Many abductees report that during their dreams they perceive themselves to be in a classroom or learning situation with the Visitors. There is a great deal of sharing of information. In the morning, most of the teaching has been forgotten, although the memory of the teaching situation remains. The teaching appears to be subliminal or just below the threshold of consciousness. The experiencers feel unrested, as if they have been awake during the night.

EXPERIENCERS: A term coined by Dr. John Mack and other abduction researchers as a replacement for the abduction term.

EXTRASENSORY PERCEPTION (ESP): Following interaction with the Visitors, many experiencers develop heightened paranormal abilities. It may be that individuals who are more intuitive may perceive the Visitors easier than others. Another theory is that interaction with the Visitors is so traumatic that dormant survival faculties are activated, which take the form of heightened ESP abilities.

EXTRATERRESTRIALS (ETs): It has been generally assumed by some that the Visitors originate in some distant place in the cosmos: extraterrestrial, as in outside the Earth. There has also been speculation that the Visitors have bases on the Moon, Mars, and other nearby locations. Other theories are that the Visitors reside in some alternative dimension.

FLYING SAUCERS: An early term for a circular, unidentified flying object (UFO). The term is still used by debunkers to ridicule sightings of UFOs.

FOCUSED ATTENTION: A mental state of selective attention. It has been hypothesized that selective attention might facilitate interaction with a single entity. A diffuse or unfocused attentional state appears to be conducive to interacting with a group of entities.

FREE ASSOCIATING: A mental tool for accessing hidden memories. Individuals relax in a comfortable, undisturbed place, then let their mind wander back over their life in general, or to a specific situation. There is no effort to remember specific events and no prompting from another individual. In this relaxed, searching mode, memories become more accessible to the individual; memories from twenty or more years ago may come to consciousness. Free Associating is a form of self-hypnosis.

GANZFELD: A type of methodology in which extrasensory perception (ESP) is tested. The method entails putting subjects into a state of partial sensory deprivation in a relaxed state in an isolation booth, listening to "white noise" through headphones, and having their visual input blocked with opaque eye covers lit by a red light. The rationale behind this method is that when external sensory input is excluded, subjects can focus better and pay attention to their inner, intuitive perceptions.

HIDDEN MEMORIES: In normal, waking consciousness, individuals have selective attention and selective memory retention. We would be overwhelmed by sensory information if we were to pay attention to and remember everything we perceive. Normally, we do not remember everything and our memories fade and degrade over time. In traumatic situations, immediate, short-term memories may not be transferred to long-term memory. Many abductions occur in an altered state of consciousness and may be accompanied by other fearful or traumatic events. Memories of these experiences may become hidden to waking consciousness. Sometimes, these abduction memories may be recalled during dreams and as flashbacks during waking consciousness. Hypnosis may be helpful in uncovering hidden memories, but this should be carried out in a therapeutic setting with a trained hypnotherapist.

IMAGINAL: A term employed by Dr. Kenneth Ring and

Dennis Stillings to indicate that certain experiences, such as abduction, may originate within the mental processes of the individual rather than be caused by external events. They are not saying that the experiencer purposefully imagines the events, rather that the experiencer's own internal mental processes generate the experience.

IMPLANT: An implant is a small device placed under the skin often for therapeutic purposes, such as insulin pumps for diabetics. However, many abductees report that they have perceived implants being placed in their bodies without their permission. Implants have been reported as being put in eyes, ears, in the skull and brain, in nasal and sinus cavities, and underneath the skin. The purposes of these implants include: as tracking devices, the delivery of electromagnetic impulses, and as microwave signal transducers.

INFORMATION LOADING: See **DATA DOWNLOADS**.

INTERFACE(S): A neutral, alternative term for alien contact and abduction.

LITTLE PEOPLE: There are theories that mythological beings such as dwarves and elves may have been early interpretations of Visitor contact. Much of our knowledge of these beings stems from the sixteenth and seventeenth centuries.

MAGICAL THINKING: In early childhood, children believe they can make something happen by thinking about it. They have a belief system that they are the cause of events. Magical thinking is also involved in the "invisible friend" reports from childhood. Some researchers feel that magical thinking is used by some adults in their belief that the Visitors are interacting with them. However, magical thinking is generally only observed in preschool children.

MANDALAS: A series of intricate and colorful circular designs seen in the artwork of many cultures. These forms of artwork have religious and spiritual meaning. Jung wrote that the designs contained ubiquitous shapes and designs that had deep psychological meaning.

MEMORY RECALL and **MEMORY SEARCH**: See **FREE ASSOCIATING**.

MISSING PREGNANCY: During a woman's reproductive life, she may experience signs of pregnancy but not produce an infant. There are several medical conditions that can lead to this state, including disorders of the pituitary gland. However, increasing numbers of women are claiming they are experiencing missing pregnancies in connection with interaction with the Visitors. Before pregnancy there is an interface, with another one several weeks or months later, when the woman experiences the loss of the pregnancy. In between these two interfaces, the woman may feel she is pregnant and may even have positive pregnancy tests. The woman does not abort a fetus—it just disappears. Some women have gone full term only to find that their uterus contains a placenta but no fetus. Some abductees report being shown hybrid infants and children, during subsequent interfaces, and being told that these children are theirs.

MISSING TIME: A term given to an experience during which one or more individuals cannot account for a period of time. For example, individuals may commence a journey at a designated time, that usually takes one hour to complete. During the journey, they experience a break in continuity. They may find themselves many miles down the road, or on a different road, several hours later, with no conscious memory of the intervening distance or time.

NIGHT VISITORS: A neutral, alternative term to alien. However, not all interfaces occur at night; they may just as easily occur during daylight hours.

OBSERVER PHENOMENON: A psychological state in which the individual or experiencer perceives some part of herself as an observer to her everyday activities. It is a form of detachment. This occurs normally on an occasional basis to most people. However, if it becomes pervasive and persistent, or attributed to a malevolent outside source, it may be diagnosed by the medical profession as a form of emotional disturbance. However, not all observer phenomena are distressing or caused by mental disorders.

PHANTOM PREGNANCY SYNDROME: See **MISSING PREGNANCY**.

PROBE (ALIEN): See **IMPLANT**.

PSYCHOKINESIS (PK): A form of paranormal activity in which human consciousness may interact with the physical world.

Many people believe that we are all composed of the same atomic structure, just arranged in different ways, and that we are all connected; therefore PK is acceptable. Psychokinesis is not acceptable within the current, materialistic, scientific paradigm.

REAL DREAMS: There are many types of dreams. During dreams, some people can become temporarily conscious and these are referred to as lucid dreams. The dreamer, however, knows that she is dreaming and can direct the course of the dream. There is another type of experience—a real dream—where the individual has been dreaming, then becomes conscious, but knows that she is no longer dreaming. A real dream is different from a lucid dream, as the individual knows that she is awake and not dreaming. The events that occur during real dreams are remembered as vivid, and sometimes frightening; the dreamer knows she has little control over them. The experiencer enters a deep, often dreamless, sleep after the real dream. In the morning, the real dream is remembered as being "more real" than a dream. There are often physical marks present on the body, such as needle punctures, scratches, and bruises, that correspond to the real dream activity.

REAL-TIME EVENTS: Abduction or interface activities are often clouded by the fact that memories of the events are lost or hidden in the subconscious. However, if an interface occurs, accompanied by a real dream, and is followed by the finding of trauma the following morning, this indicates a real-time event happening. That is, that the interface most probably happened that night. More often, an individual may awaken with physical trauma, feel very tired, and have the feeling that she had a "busy night" with no memory of an interface. The memories may surface a few nights later in a dream or seep into conscious memory as flashbacks. These are delayed memories of a recent interface. Individuals may also have dreams of interfaces with no remembered physical trauma and no feelings of tiredness the following day. This may be dream memory of a much earlier interface. However, dreaming of the Visitors and interfaces does not mean that an interface has occurred at all, but that the dream may be a dream!

REMOTE VIEWING: The trained ability to access information about people, events, places, and things that are shielded or hidden from ordinary means of perception. This used to be called clairvoyance, or second sight. The term remote viewing was coined by Ingo Swann.

RUNES: Several types of ancient symbols or glyphs that were used both as an early written language and as a divination tool. The runes were rediscovered and became popular in seventeenth-century Europe.

SELECTIVE AMNESIA: See **HIDDEN MEMORIES**.

SELECTIVE ATTENTION: See **FOCUSED ATTENTION**.

SENSORY DEPRIVATION: See **GANZFELD**.

STAGED TABLEAU: Experiencers have reported that, during their abduction experience, they are required to view a type of virtual reality scenario, sometimes on a video screen or through a window. These staged displays often portray a cataclysmic event or the future of the Earth. Experiencers have reported that they have ostensibly met departed relatives and friends, only to realize that the entities have staged the event. Staged tableaus mean different things to different experiencers.

THETA: A measurement of brain wave activity and a term used to describe an altered state, in which the person is experiencing slower brain waves than in the alpha state. Most people experience the theta state when they are daydreaming and become unaware of their surroundings, or just as they are falling asleep. Brain wave measurements of astronauts in zero gravity in space show a lot of theta activity. The theta state is useful for guided imagery and memory recall work.

UFO: Unidentified Flying Object. This is an older term now used mostly by debunkers of the UFO and abduction phenomena.

VIRTUAL ROOM: In contact experiences with the Visitors, it appears that a mutual meeting place is generated that is compatible with both . Sometimes this can be a natural scene, such as a woodland, or it might be an enclosed space that can contain the participants. In some cases, the room may be furnished with incongruous furniture.

VISITOR(S) and **VISITING OTHER(S)**: Less negative label given to the aliens or entities involved in the abduction scenario. The term implies that the Visitors are our neighbors in the cosmos.

1

A Strange Restlessness

"When the long awaited solution to the UFO problem comes, I believe that it will prove to be not merely the next small step in the mark of science, but a mighty and totally unexpected quantum leap."

—Dr. J. Allen Hynek, scientific consultant
for Air Force Project Blue Book,
The UFO Experience: A Scientific Inquiry: 1972.

September 7, 1986

Since coming back from my vacation in England, I have been watching a series on New Jersey TV called the "Omega Factor." The series outlines various adventures into the paranormal by a psychic who uncovers various government conspiracies. Apart from enjoying the series for its content, I have become aware that my basic knowledge in parapsychology and the UFO field is rather sketchy. So I plan to do some serious study on the subject.

For the past three years, I have had a special friend: Dr. P. There is a twenty-year age gap between us (he is older than I am), but we get on well together and talk about everything under the sun. I met Dr. P in 1983, while I was working as a legal secretary for some lawyers in West Orange, New Jersey. At first I was seeing Dr. P on and off, and he told me he was also going through a divorce. Dr. P was a commissioner for the Federal Mediation and Conciliation Service (FMCS). Before his twenty-five-year service with the FMCS, he worked for air force intelligence and with the OSI, a forerunner of the CIA. Now, after three years of knowing him, I feel a psychological rift in our being together. He is attentive and great fun to be with, but he is disinclined to spend time with me. The ancient, animal part of my mind enjoys the physical aspect to our relationship, while the modern, upper part reminds me of the serious differences between us, particularly his disinclination to commit to the relationship. The time has come to make some major changes in my life.

September 17, 1986

Last January I received a copy of a report from a local university that is exploring a topic called remote perception—the ability to access hidden information from a remote geographical location, using something other than the known five senses. I was impressed by the report's scientific thoroughness.

Today, I wrote the laboratory to express my interest in their research, and I briefly mentioned some of my own experiences. I also read today about another researcher, who is director of the Psychophysical Research Laboratories (PRL), a facility that is not connected to the university. I will write to him as well and see if I can participate in their parapsychological studies.

September 23, 1986

I received a packet of materials from the psychophysics laboratory regarding their parapsychology (psi) research. It included a questionnaire, which I filled out and will mail tomorrow. The packet also contained some interesting literature about parapsychology and the director of the laboratory.

October 18, 1986

Yesterday, I went down to visit the psychophysics laboratory for my introductory session, and I want to record my impressions. The big computers were "down," so I could not take part in any of their remote-perception experiments, but I did take part in some of their psi computer games. The laboratory described their research as a parapsychological process "in which people are shut off from normal sensory input and then tested for psychic ability. In the typical test, the subject, or 'receiver,' sits in a soundproof room. He wears padded headphones that broadcast a static-like 'white noise' and translucent goggles that reduce everything to a uniform pinkish blur. Seated in another soundproof room is the 'sender,' who tries to mentally project a target image, usually a picture that he views on a video monitor."

My initial reaction was that the psychophysics laboratory was a modern research facility and the staff went out of their way to be friendly and helpful, even to the point of picking me up at the railway station. I had an initial interview with Helen, one of the researchers, and, with another subject, I watched a videotape about their research. We were shown around the laboratory and saw the meat locker-like room in which the subjects attempted to receive psi influences under conditions of sensory isolation. The room felt a little daunting but also exciting.

Several odd things have happened since my visit to the laboratory. My intuitive abilities appear to be heightened. Several times I called Dr. P at home, just as he was calling me. The night following my visit to the lab was strange. As I was waiting to fall asleep, I began to visualize very weird, negative images. Some were scenes out of Dante's *Inferno*: devils and demons and cowled figures without faces. At the same time, Dr. P, who was staying the night with me, seemed to be having a nightmare and was kicking and groaning in his sleep. Each time I stroked his back or hugged him, he would stop moaning and my visualizations subsided, but as soon as he went back to sleep, they returned as vividly as before. Maybe I was picking up his nightmare and it was being revealed as hypnogogic imagery in my tired mind? Dr. P dashed off this morning, so I was not able to ask him about his nightmare.

October 24, 1986

I talked to Helen and have made an appointment to go down to the paraphysics lab on November 7 to take part in their current experiments. Helen has expressed an interest in us getting together to do experiments with some techniques to look at past lives. Helen also encouraged me to keep a dream journal. Since my discussion with her, I looked at my old dream journals and found many dreams that were precognitive. One foreshadowed the death of a college friend in Manchester; and there was a dream about my marriage to my now ex-husband Randolph, before we even met. I have begun having dreams about UFOs and aliens. The dreams are disjointed and do not contain any persons I know in my waking life.

November 7, 1986

I visited the paraphysics lab to take part in their experiments. Helen picked me up at the train and we traveled together to the lab. We discovered that there were electrical problems with the equipment, so after getting wired up for the study, I sat for about half an hour listening to music tapes. Helen said that these would relax me. Another participant "sent me an image" from where she was seated in another soundproof room, watching a randomly selected picture on a monitor. She could hear what I was saying, but I could not hear her. During the following half hour I talked about what was going through my head, such as visual impressions. At the end, I had to choose between four static video images and say which one I thought the sender was watching. I chose the right one!

November 8, 1986

This has been a positive period in terms of psychic experiences, and on several occasions there have been strong instances of synchronicity. I have also felt a strange restlessness and excitement for no apparent reason. I am writing this down because I am puzzled by this feeling and I am not sure what it means.

I have been feeling disappointed with my relationship with Dr. P. I asked him if we could spend more time together. His answer was negative and he has not been around since then. I had decided that if he did not get in touch by the middle of December, I will end our relationship. Anyhow, we are supposed to be having dinner on December 16.

I have been having lots of vivid dreams lately, mostly related to being in authoritarian, military-like situations, where I have to resolve the situation by escaping from it. I have also had several instances of feeling "enlightened," of being at one with the universe and understanding what life is all about. The feeling is similar to when you find the missing piece to a jigsaw or see the connection between many things at once.

December 27, 1986

Over the past few weeks I have been having some unusual

dreams about infants and birth. Symbolically, for me these types of dreams mean the emergence of a new aspect of my personality or consciousness.

In one dream a child was born to me underwater in a swimming pool and emerged smiling. It was able to swim, and was symbolic of the emerging of a new year.

January 18, 1987

I watched Shirley MacLaine's film *Out on a Limb* and I was entranced. While I was watching the enactment of her relationship with the politician, I recognized comparable aspects in my relationship with Dr. P. He is charming and a gentleman, but I am here at his convenience. So I have decided that the next time he calls, I will be busy. I do not feel that I can be here at his beck and call forever.

I have been experiencing strange sensations in the solar plexus area (the stomach chakra), indicating changes within myself and in my life.

March 3, 1987

Recently, after Helen and I had supper together, she commented that she had seen a movie called *Starman* at a friend's house. We discussed the probability that extraterrestrials exist. Helen recounted a meditation of hers, in which she decided to meet some ETs. In her imagery, she went with some aliens to their home world. However, she could not remember how they or their world looked. She remembered their craft coming down between her house and the neighbor's and hearing her name whispered in her left ear, but that was all she could remember.

I told Helen how my brother and I had an experience in our youth that was possibly extraterrestrial in origin. Helen and I both commented on the popularity of ET-type films over the past decade and how exciting it would be to do some sort of research to locate or communicate with ETs. However, we never got around to doing any research that I can remember.

2

"You Have a Lot of Power"

"I can assure you that flying saucers, given that they exist, are not constructed by any power on Earth."

—President Harry S Truman. April 4, 1950,
White House press conference.

March 15, 1987

Helen has taught me the I Ching, which is an ancient form of Chinese divination using three coins. I have decided to keep an open mind about these techniques until they have proved themselves, and I have been working with them for about a month. I consulted the I Ching on several major issues, including my job. It seems that I am due a change, sometime around December or January of next year. I feel the urge to go into parapsychology research. However, the reading indicated a time of waiting until the time is more appropriate.

I have never learned the Tarot, another form of ancient divination, using symbolic cards, although I have been fascinated with its wonderful artwork. Helen is proficient at the Tarot and she did a reading for me. It revealed the same state of waiting for major changes in the work field and the sorrow of parting from Dr. P.

Pennies seem to be materializing in my apartment. Periodically, I go through my drawers and cupboards and gather up all the pennies. Each time I empty my purse, I gather up all the pennies and put them in a glass container. However, I still find pennies around the apartment. For example, about once a week I sweep and wash the kitchen floor. Then, a day or two later, I will find a penny on the floor and I know that I did not drop one. Yesterday, I opened up the storm windows, which had been closed up since last October. In between the inner sash window and outer storm window was another penny. I remember that before I closed up the storm windows last fall, I swept out the space of debris, so I wonder where these pennies are coming from? I wonder if someone, somewhere, is missing pennies?

I have asked Helen if she will obtain printouts for me of my computer games at the psychophysics lab. Finding out about my psychokinetic, or PK, ability is the same feeling as if I suddenly discovered that I could play the piano well.

The only dreams I can remember lately are related to the pennies. In the dream, I am with Helen and looking at piles of pennies. The piles of coins are growing and decreasing, and Helen and I are wondering where the coins are traveling to and from.

March 18, 1987

I was thinking today about the various ways that are available to us to access hidden knowledge. This hidden information is often referred to as the Akashic Record, the Source, or the Library. There are many ways of obtaining the material contained within the Source. Also, there are two possible locations for the knowledge: it might already lie within our own mind and, although we are not consciously aware of it, we can access it through various means; or the Source is external to our minds. Some people think the Source is God, while others believe that the knowledge exists on another plane of understanding. Whatever its location, this knowledge can be accessed through a variety of tools such as meditation, the I Ching, Tarot, runes, channeling, and so forth.

Underlying all of these methods or tools must be a "key"—a principle or main concept. It seems that whatever the type of practice, the information retrieved appears similar. For instance, I Ching, Tarot and rune readings, for a particular situation, give very similar answers. What is this key or concept that underlies all these tools?

March 19, 1987

I awoke remembering two major dreams. The first was about being pregnant. I suddenly discovered that I was thirty-six-weeks pregnant! I saw a written record attesting to the fact. The information was written on a wall (the writing on the wall—a warning?) I was comparing the size of my abdomen with that of a work colleague who was also pregnant. I was not very big and could understand how some women could be pregnant and not know it. I knew that I only had a month to go and wondered what the contractions would be like. It was an awesome experience.

Maybe this dream symbolizes a new phase that is opening in my life: the possibility of a new research job in parapsychology and interesting new projects with Helen.

The second dream was about a magical show taking place in England. The show was in a small theater in a department store. The theater was very modern, with tiers of flat, cushioned seats. There were mostly children in the audience. The magician/wizard looked like one of the visiting foreign researchers at the psi lab. He was picking out children to stand with him on the stage. I almost flew down into my seat, leaping over the cushions, as if there wasn't much gravity. I sat and watched the proceedings. Then the wizard saw me and took me to the stage to stand by his side. He said to me, as we held hands, "You have a lot of power." I replied, "Yes, I know." Then I woke up.

I think that this dream symbolizes my growing awareness of my psychic abilities, which have been awakened by my visits to the psychophysics lab. The visiting parapsychologist was symbolized in my dream as a wizard, because I see him as a mystical figure and he looks a bit like a wizard.

March 20, 1987

Helen has suggested that I let her hypnotize me to see if this facilitates my psychic abilities. I am keen to do away with some of the tools and props of the psychic world and wonder if there is some direct way to access hidden information. It will be an interesting venture.

March 22, 1987

Helen took me through two hypnosis sessions to see if I could improve or facilitate my ESP ability. The first session took me to an alpha state and I was able to visualize freely. The second time I got down to a deeper theta level and I was able to access information at a more concise, nonvisual level. At the theta level, I needed very precise questioning, whereas in the alpha state, impressions were more fluid and general. I talked to Helen and we discussed the possibility that there were even more hypnosis levels to explore. We planned to try some of these levels at a later date.

March 23, 1987

A few weeks ago I answered an ad in the *Psychic Guide*. The ad looked interesting and promised news of a society that was doing alien research. I was intrigued but disappointed in the flyer they sent, so I wrote for more information. This evening I had a phone call from the guy who runs the organization, and I was even more disappointed. He made vague references to aliens: that there was to be a supposed landing in Arizona in a few months; that he had a channeled contact with the aliens; that alien knowledge was being passed down via the gene pools of North and South American Indians.

The bulk of his information had to do with North American Indian teaching, which he distributes to interested students. He was very involved with the teachings, but I think he was disappointed that he did not convince me to become enrolled in his courses. I told him that I might subscribe to his magazine but that I was not interested in taking his course. I feel that I am very firmly on my own Celtic path.

April 2, 1987

Helen made me copies of the relaxation tapes that are played before the sessions at the lab. She said that these would be helpful in developing my psychic abilities. I decided to play one before my usual bedtime. This particular tape was relaxing, and I stayed somewhere in the alpha state.

When my visualization began, I found myself on top of a hill, which I eventually recognized as Glastonbury Tor in England. The tower was behind me and I was facing east. I varied my position from standing to sitting on the grass with my back supported by the tower. As I watched, the stars were shining and moving very fast overhead. It took about half a minute for the starry night sky to race overhead and then the sun rose very quickly in the east and day began. The day began very bright and also took about half a minute to pass overhead. Then, a constant succession of days and nights raced overhead while I watched. It was awesome.

April 12, 1987

Have been having dreams four nights in a row about a young man, Randy, whom I met at the psychophysics lab. In the dreams, I have been talking with him, traveling in a car, and in another dream watching him from another room.

April 14, 1987

Told Helen about my dreams of Randy. Told her that this is very different from my usual patterning of dreaming, where I rarely dream of the same thing twice, let alone four times in a row. Helen felt that Randy was causing the dreams to happen—possibly he was attracted to me. I learned that he works as a computer consultant for a government "think tank" in California—something super secret.

June 14, 1987

I have continued to go to the psychophysics lab and have participated in several studies both as a receiver and as a sender. Helen and I have spent time together working on developing my psi abilities. She has hypnotized me on several occasions, and I have accessed information for her from the past and the future. The lab has made their library available to me as well as a computer to use. I am exploring the idea of a career in parapsychology.

Recently, I have had a surprising increase in my psi abilities: I think about people and predict when they will call me; there have been many instances of synchronicity, lots of déjà vu, lucid and precognitive dreams, and precognitive events during my waking hours when I think that something is about to happen—and it does.

June 30, 1987

All this last week I have had vague nightmares, but in each dream I was able to overcome what was bothering me. I am not sure what is causing the nightmares, but I seem to be coping with them and they haven't affected my day-to-day functioning.

Something else that is bothering me is an irregular heartbeat. I normally have a regular heartbeat, but I have been experiencing my heart racing and skipping beats. If it persists I will see a doctor.

At the lab, Helen has suddenly become very distant and unfriendly, and I cannot understand why this could be. I don't think I have done anything to hurt her feelings. She seems preoccupied, and I have decided to cut down on my visits to the lab and not to do any more psi sessions. However, after I had made that decision, I had a weird dream.

I dreamed that I was down at the lab and met a tall, distinguished man with white hair and expensive clothes, a man with power and charisma. He talked with me and persuaded me to continue going to the lab. I wonder if I will eventually get to meet him?

July 12, 1987

Helen continues to be unfriendly, even rude, and I am not sure what the problem is. I decided to keep going to the psychophysics lab, because I was learning so much from the other staff and the lab's library. Helen did say a while back that she was under a great deal of personal pressure. I have been wondering what to do about the situation. It is possible that Helen is depressed. If that is the case, there is not much more I can do other than what I have been doing, which is being friendly and supportive. On the other hand, if Helen is being deliberately rude, a reasonable alternative would be for me to cut my losses and quit my participation at the lab. However, I enjoy attending the lab and participating in the studies. What to do? I have decided not to let Helen's rudeness affect me. I decided to send Helen loving and healing thoughts through meditation.

July 21, 1987

I woke yesterday morning after having an interesting dream about being at the psychophysics lab. I was talking to one of the male researchers about magic. We were playing with a device made from bamboo. When you stick both fingers into the hollow tube and pull, your fingers get caught. There is a trick to getting your fingers free. When I awoke I thought about this dream and likened it to life. Very often we get caught in situations and the more we struggle, the more tightly we get caught. The trick is to relax and you can get free!

October 19, 1987

Called the lab today and chatted with Helen. I told her that I had been visiting another parapsychology laboratory for the experience. She seemed pleased. I shared with her my acceptance of my growing psi abilities and how I have become more confident of the positive psi results that I have been experiencing. Helen said that I should come back to their psi lab and work on some of their computer games that measured psychokinesis. She said that I could do as well as a famous English psychic who had recently visited their lab. It seems that the psychophysics lab is closing down because of lack of funding, and that may be the reason for Helen's unhappiness. Have made an appointment to go on November 6 to participate in a psi session and will keep going on Wednesdays until they close.

October 31, 1987

I woke with a heavy nosebleed from the left nostril. I have never had nosebleeds before. Just before I awoke, I was dreaming about flying saucers. In the dream, I was at home in England, where I grew up. I was looking out of my bedroom window, looking toward Wales, and over the horizon came several flying saucers. They came one after the other, then more came. I called to my family to come and look, but they would not listen to me. Weird dream!

November 4, 1987

Over this past six months, I have continued to explore my psi abilities, especially PK within a controlled laboratory setup. It has been both exciting and reassuring to be able to test my abilities in this way. I have always known I had some natural talent, but in attending the psychophysics labs, I have been able to explore and expand my abilities.

November 14, 1987

I have been spending my days off from my regular research job at the two psi laboratories. It has been a great adventure. Had an interesting dream about capturing a gentle giant. I think he was a symbol of my psi abilities, but when I captured him, I was the one being chased, and this dream refers to my fear of my abilities being misused. My new motto is "There are no limits."

November 22, 1987

I had lots of dreams over the weekend. The gist of most of them was the taking of risks and chances, but being able to cope and handle unusual situations.

In one dream I was in an elevator, riding up the outside of a building. The door of the elevator swung open and the elevator tilted, almost tipping us out. I was able to take control and close the door. I was anxious but not frightened. In another dream, an Oriental man dressed in Eastern clothes told me to go with him, as he had a lot to teach me, but I had to go "straightaway." I lingered for a moment, doing what I was doing, then decided to go with him. I wish I could remember what he taught me.

November 30, 1987

There was an interesting article in *OMNI* this month on UFO abductions. The article contained a questionnaire about abductions. While I don't claim that I am a contactee or abductee, I thought it would be interesting to fill in the questionnaire. I mentioned the sighting that my brother, Alan, and I had in Dorset, England, when we were teenagers. The questionnaire also asked about UFO dreams, so I recounted some. Most of my UFO dreams have had one main theme: I see UFOs in the sky and try to show other people in the dream, but they either do not see them or they do not believe me. The *OMNI* article discussed the possibility of alien babies. My stand is that UFOs are a possible reality but there are also a lot of misguided ideas and a lot of people who have jumped on the UFO bandwagon.

December 4, 1987

What a frustrating day. I went down to the psychophysics lab and spent almost all day there. I participated in another Ganzfeld session but picked up information from all four of the targets and ended up choosing the wrong one. Also, the other experiment was locked up and nobody but the lab director could get into it. It was a wasted day as far as I was concerned. Lots of talk at the lab about their lack of funding and that they will soon be closing down.

December 14, 1987

Had people over for a holiday party and some of the folks from the parapsychology laboratory came up. After most of the guests had left, I was talking with the manager of the parapsychology lab and was offered a part-time position. Positions in parapsychology are extremely difficult to come by. I am so fortunate.

3

Looking at Past Dreams for Incidents of Contact

"Because of the developments of science, all countries of Earth will have to unite to survive and make a common front against attack by people from other planets. The politics of the future will be cosmic, or interplanetary."

—General Douglas MacArthur,
October 1955, the *New York Times*.

January 1, 1988

1987 was a year of self discovery. With Helen, I have learned how to get into a trancelike state to access information about the environment. Unfortunately, the psychophysics lab is closing down because of lack of funding, and my connection with it has gradually declined. However, my participation with the parapsychology lab has increased to the point where I will be starting work with them later this year. I will be a research assistant and will work with the lab manager. There will be lots of changes ahead as we go into 1988.

January 3, 1988

Last night I had many dreams, most of which I forgot upon wakening. However, one dream stayed with me and is probably the most important. What is interesting is that I analyzed the dream as it was unfolding.

I dreamed that I was making my way to visit a factory. To get there I had to climb and scramble over high mounds of rubble and debris from demolished buildings. I was aware that under my feet were layers of rusted chicken wire that could give way. Underneath those layers were the demolished remains of buildings into which I could fall. In the dream, I became lucid and realized that this was an anxiety dream. I reminded myself that this type of dream symbolized anxiety in my life and that I could overcome the anxiety. I also reminded myself of my new motto, "There are no limits." I was able to gain confidence and climb down off the ruins and get to my destination.

The ruins represent the defenses that I have demolished in allowing myself to accept and acknowledge my PK and other abilities. It had taken me years to build up these defenses, first in a critical childhood environment, and later in a skeptical, scientific environment. I no longer need those defenses.

January 4, 1988

What a terrible, terrible day. The director of the cognitive science research program, in which I am currently employed, got my resignation letter today and reacted badly. I spent the day very upset. He was angry that I was leaving and angrier that I had not talked to him. When I tried to explain that he had not been around to discuss things with me, he got even angrier. Things went from bad to worse. However, we parted fairly amicably even though he was still angry and I was still upset. During the day, I learned how compassionate people can be as the rest of the staff showed their concern. How can it be that a person so committed to freedom of inquiry can get so upset that I am leaving to pursue a career investigating human potential? I guess this area of concern causes some very deep-seated feelings to be aroused?

January 12, 1988

Last night I had several vivid symbolic dreams with two main themes: breaking down walls in a house to reconstruct the space within; and being naked. I feel that these dreams are symbolic of my continuing growth and adjustment to my PK talent. The nakedness in the dreams reflects my anxiety about revealing my abilities to others. The rebuilding of the house is the ongoing adjustment to all the new changes in my life. In my final dream I was walking through woods and pointing out that it was finally springtime and green leaves were sprouting on the trees.

Today was a strange day. Maybe because I am completing my time at my neuroscience job, or maybe because I did not have a lot to do, time seemed to stand still. An hour seemed like all morning.

February 1, 1988

The last three months have seen some interesting personal changes and more changes are in the offing. My participation at the psychophysics lab has dwindled to a halt and, because of its lack of funding, it will probably be closing. I told Helen that I would come down for one last visit, but I really do not think I will have the time. My participation at the parapsychology lab has increased and, at Christmastime, the manager brought up the possibility of working with them. This tentative offer resulted in a definite job offer, and I start today, February 1. My job position is as a technical assistant. I will move closer to the parapsychology lab at the end of February.

My first full day at the parapsychology lab was quite stressful. I suppose every first day is like that. I spoke to my friend Emily and she agreed that I could live in her house while I am working at the lab. All in all, this has been an exciting time of life with the promise of more exciting times ahead.

February 4, 1988

This has been my first full week at the parapsychology lab and it has been both tense and exciting as I undertake new activities and duties. There has been some consternation in the parapsychology lab concerning a critical paper written by a colleague (Gregory) from the psychophysics lab. Tonight, Gregory called me to ask how I was doing at the parapsychology lab. He was concerned what the staff thought of his research methods paper. I told the lab manager that Gregory had called and she was very amused.

February 11, 1988

I had a dream that I was at the parapsychology lab and the walls were covered with spiders. I was not afraid of them, only intrigued. When I tried to show them to my colleagues, the spiders disappeared.

I pondered on this dream and the symbolism of spiders. In mythology, spiders are generally considered to be lucky and teach lessons in patience and perseverance. I will heed this lesson myself.

March 6, 1988

It has been a month now since I started working full time at the parapsychology lab and it has been an interesting four weeks. Everybody who is anybody eventually visits the lab. There have been some interesting new people to meet and lots of new things to learn.

April 6, 1988

We spent the day at the parapsychology lab (which I have decided just to refer to as the lab) working on the program for an upcoming conference. The abstracts for the conference deal mainly with anomalies from various fields such as physics, neuropsychology, psychology, and astronomy. On the way home from the lab, Bev (a colleague) and I experienced an anomaly of our own.

Bev and I left the lab about 7:30 P.M. as it was getting toward dusk. We had put in a full day and were feeling tired, but we were awake and alert. We stopped for take-out Chinese food, and we were laughing and joking on the way home about a situation that had occurred at the lab.

As we approached Emily's house, we saw a strange thing: a small globe that appeared to be reflecting silvery light. Bev said she saw it as faceted. It moved along the side of the road, about a foot to eighteen inches above the surface. It bobbed up and down but did not roll, and it did not touch the road surface at all. We both said, "What is that?" At first I thought it was a large soap bubble, but it was more substantial than a bubble and perfectly round.

As we watched it, the globe made a ninety-degree turn up a driveway. It deliberately stopped, waited a few seconds, then made another turn toward the house. Bev and I "high-tailed" it out of there. We had no idea what it was. Some of our colleagues in the UFO field said that we might have encountered an alien probe of some kind.

What is interesting is that just across the road from the sighting are the Princeton-based offices of the Defense Advanced Research Projects Agency (DARPA), a government agency. Could the globe have been one of their "toys"?

April 7, 1988

We had a strange sequel to yesterday's appearance of the silvery globe. After lunch, I was telling another colleague at the parapsychology lab about the incident, when we heard a sound as if someone had dropped a ball bearing on the floor above us. It went "plink, plink, plink, plink" as it hit a hard surface several times. Later, when Bev and I went upstairs to the bathroom, we found a palm size, glass ball on the landing halfway down the stairs. The plinking sound must have been made as it fell down the stairs. It seems strange that the sphere should appear at the same time I was telling my colleague about yesterday's incident. Where did it come from and who does it belong to?

June 7, 1988

Lately, I have been hearing from several colleagues about the alien abduction phenomenon and the UFO field. I have been remembering stories told me by my parents about their sightings in England. Although I cannot claim to have seen a UFO, I have had lots of dreams about them. Starting in 1978 for about three or four years, I kept a dream diary as a form of getting to know myself. I documented almost all of my dreams for a year, then the important ones over the following years. I have kept the two journals in which I recorded these dreams, and looking through them now, I find that several of these dreams refer to strange situations that might be related to UFOs and aliens.

> *December 1, 1978*: In my dream someone was teaching me a hand sign-language, and we spelled out the letters K,O,M,P, L. "K" was formed by intertwining the fingers of both hands, with the fingers in the palms; "O" was made with the two forefingers and two thumbs meeting, making an O; "M" was made with the left hand clenched as a fist, but with the fingers straight not curled; "P" was made with the left hand, the thumb and first finger making a circle, the wrist stretched and the other fingers curled into the palm; "L" was made by stretching the thumb away from the hand at an angle, while stretching the other fingers straight up and close together.

> *January 10, 1979*: It was Christmastime and I was a child again. My parents said they had something that they wanted to tell me, which was that there wasn't really any Santa Claus but that the presents were brought by flying saucers. I did not want to

believe them, but they told me to look out of the window. I could see four lights darting around: two white, one red, and the other green. Then I experienced a very strong feeling, part excitement, part fear. We went into the garden where one of the spacecraft had landed. A tall man stepped out, his arms were full of parcels. Dad and the spaceman started walking together up the path to the house. Instead of walking all the way on the path, they were walking on ice. It started to crack, but they were unaware of it. I called to Dad to warn him of the cracking ice as it was dangerous.

January 20, 1979: I had a confused dream and most of it was forgotten when I awoke. I had a task to do. It was a sort of mathematical puzzle, but I am not mathematically inclined. The task went like this: I had four elements and my job was to find four matching elements to complete the first four. The addition of the second four elements, when added to the first four, did not make eight, but only made the first four elements more whole, so they remained four elements.

When I awoke I puzzled over this for a while. Then I understood the answer to the problem. The first four elements must have been incomplete figures or numbers less than one. The first elements needed to have something added to them (the second four elements) to make them whole and yet still remain four elements.

February 21, 1979: Two very inventive dreams. In the first, I had discovered a new type of mass communications system based on a closed-circuit television system but much more efficient. I was explaining the system to a group of people. In the second dream, I invented a color analysis statistical program in which I saw a pictorial way of looking at correlations and differences between groups of scores, very like chromatography. Two sets of figures would have to be printed in different colors, then displayed on a screen, and a computer scan of this would calculate a score depending on the mix of colors.

March 12, 1979: I had a dream about an old man who was going to turn off the electricity supply to the world. I was trying to persuade him not to do it, but I knew that he wouldn't listen to me.

March 17, 1979: I was talking with some people about technical and medical aids. Someone produced a silver tube about six inches long with a black top. It was a pulse and temperature gauge. All you had to do was put your finger on the top and it took recordings.

April 3, 1979: In my dream I was talking to a college friend and we were recollecting time we had spent at Cardiff University. We saw lights in the sky, first flashing blue, then green, then they became flying saucers. They shot across the sky, getting closer and closer to us. She was amazed. She is a strict Christian and the sighting shook her beliefs. She said she hadn't believed in flying saucers before, but she did now.

April 16, 1979: People living in the West Country of England (Somerset, Gloucester, and Wiltshire) had been hearing a "hum" at all hours of the day and night. Nobody had come up with a decent explanation and lots of ideas about it abounded. Just before I woke up on the 16th, I heard the "hum" distinctly in my dream.

Whether these dreams have anything to do with the abduction experience, I do not know. But, as I read them, I have a gut feeling that they do.

June 26, 1988

I received news this week that my position at the lab has been made permanent. It is five months now since I started at the lab. This was a position that was made for me.

At the lab I have been experimenting with a theta brain rhythm tape. I listened to the tape today and discovered that the theta rhythm is very similar to a cat's purring. The lab manager commented that this maybe tells us something about people who own cats: they may enjoy the theta rhythms cats produce when purring.

Late last year I answered a questionnaire put out by *OMNI* and Bud Hopkins regarding possible abductions and contact with aliens. I sent in the questionnaire relating details of an experience that my brother Alan and I had as teenagers in England. I also sent details of some UFO dreams that were followed by nosebleeds. Today, I heard back from Dr. M, who was responding for Budd Hopkins, an abduction researcher. In response to their suggestion that I might have had an abduction experience, I have begun an exercise to look at my dreams and memories to see if there have been any incidents of contact or abduction in my past.

I have been looking at my dreams, out-of-body experiences, family anecdotes, and memories from my childhood. I have given myself a dream task. I have instructed my subconscious that if there are any hidden memories, these will be brought up in my dreams. Also, that if there are any contact dreams, they will also be made apparent in my dreams.

June 27, 1988

Last night was the first night I did the dream exercise and I remembered five dreams! The first two were basically anxiety dreams, the second two were about the reflective bubble, but the last one really shook me. It involved a meeting with a strange creature sometime in my childhood.

July 9, 1988

Last night I had a strange symbolic dream:

In the dream I found a strange animal. It looked a bit like a possum but was fatter and had three eyes. I was trying to show it to some people, but they would not accept the animal as real. The animal was fierce and bit, but I was able to hold it securely and closely, and it did not bite me. One person tried to direct me up to a children's zoo on the roof. He said that my animal was not real but was imaginary, like a children's story. I tried to get people to look at the animal's three eyes to show them how it was unique. But they still would not accept it. So, I said, give me a knife and I will kill the creature. I took it outside to a wooded area and let it go. I decided for its safety to let people think that I had killed the creature.

I think this dream relates to my current interest in the abduction phenomenon. It is a scary topic, and many of my friends and colleagues are concerned that this new interest will "bite" me, and perhaps them. So for now I have decided not to tell too many people about my new quest.

July 22, 1988

I had a beautiful, lucid dream. In the dream, I was watching the parapsychology lab manager in a wonderful, almost Oriental setting. There were hanging brocades, silks, and jewels. She was dressing in a beautiful sari made of gold leaf, her hair was in small braids decorated with jewels, and she was covered with other gold jewelry. I asked her if I could be a part of her dream and she agreed. I decided to wear a long, floaty dress of a silvery, papery material, which fell in many folds and falls. I also wore lots of jewelry. We wandered around enjoying the surrounding scenery.

In this dream, I feel, I was recognizing the lab manager's power and potential and my wish to be a part of the world she is part of. There are two aspects that I respect: her professional life at the lab and her vast knowledge of myths and mysteries. I recognize and identify with both of these areas.

In another lucid dream, I was playing with a soccer ball-size piece of blue clay, which was taking shape as I molded it. It was like the toroid of three-dimensional physics—like a doughnut. I kept the outside rounded while I was trying to invert the top like a bowl. I had a sudden revelation regarding my abilities and talents. At that breakthrough, the ball of clay imploded and collapsed. I realized that I had been trying to adapt myself to other people's expectations. Now that I have recognized my abilities, I don't need the clay ball.

September 3, 1988

I have just returned from a trip to England. After getting over several days of jet lag, I had a full night of dreaming: many weird and wonderful dreams, probably compensating for the dreamless sleep of the past few nights. One dream involved a new colleague in England, Robert, who was very interested in the work of the parapsychology lab.

In the dream, I received a package from England. It was from Robert, our colleague in England. When I opened it, it contained some papers and books, and a heavy, black silk robe. It was a wizard's robe. I felt pleased as, in the dream, Robert had told me to look out for the package. The robe was black but very old and faded. It had esoteric symbols woven into the material. It had a high collar and buttons down the front. It had long, wide sleeves. In some places the material had worn right down to the threads. I put on the robe and felt powerful.

In the morning, I told Emily about my dream and she told me that she had been awake during the night and was reading a book that featured a wizard's black robe.

September 8, 1988

While I was at home in England, I thought it would be interesting to ask my mother Dr. M's UFO questions and see if any of her answers tied in with mine and Alan's. Mum is very critical of anomalous events, including UFOs, and I was surprised that she agreed to complete the questions.

Mum saw a UFO in 1953 at about eleven at night. It was a small, orange light, bigger than a star, moving fast across the sky. There was no noise and no clouds. The light looked near and then it suddenly vanished. She went in to call my father, who was interested in UFOs, but it had gone. There was no missing time associated with this sighting. I questioned her further, and I found that she has a fear of sitting in a small, dark, dirty toilet, and of putting her hand out of bed into the dark in case someone touches it. She has no scars relating to weird dreams, but she has had dreams of flying through the air. She said that both my father and I had reported UFO sightings to her. My father had reported seeing a UFO shaped like a light bulb. My mother used to read about UFOs but not now; she considers it all fiction.

On August 19, 1988, I visited my brother, niece, and sister-in-law in Kent, England. When we were teenagers, Alan and I shared an experience (which I have already documented) where a UFO landed in the field behind our house. Dr. M supplied me with an extra UFO questionnaire and I took it with me to England to get Alan's answers.

Alan has had four UFO sightings. The first three took place in Dorset, and the fourth in Kent. The first sighting was when he was thirteen years old. His room was lit up by a red-orange light, but there was no sound. He looked out of his bedroom window and saw an intense light descend into the field at the bottom of the garden, beyond the trees. Alan related that he had commented on the light to me; I was in the next bedroom. Suddenly, the light went out and he has no memory of what happened after that. He may have fallen asleep. Our parents and neighbors never commented about the light, even though it was intense.

The second sighting occurred when Alan was sixteen. He was on his way to a youth group meeting and while waiting at the bus stop saw a very bright star. He did not take too much notice of it at the time and the light was very, very high up. This sighting took place out in the countryside, and there were no street lights. Coming back from the meeting, Alan got off the bus near our home and the light was in exactly the same position. However, five seconds later the light shot off at high speed and was gone.

A third sighting took place about ten thirty at night when Alan was twenty-six. He was lying in bed with his wife. The bedroom curtains were open. Alan said the night sky was cloudy. They saw a streak of light cross the sky very fast. Alan commented to his wife, "I saw a UFO." It went past several more times, as if it was circling, then stopped still in the clouds, six or seven hundred feet up. Alan said it was cigar shaped. It stayed for about five seconds, then accelerated away. The sighting was reported in the local paper the next day and explained away as Marines using searchlights. Alan said, "No way!" Friends of Alan's, who were out fishing in the bay, saw the same object come over the Purbeck Hills, and hundreds of people also reported seeing the object over the Dorset area.

In 1987, when Alan was thirty-eight, he had his fourth sighting in Kent, England. He was out walking at night at about ten thirty, with his daughter, aged ten. They were walking up a road and looking at the sky, when they saw a bright light. It was not flashing and there was no noise. The light stopped still for a few seconds, then moved on.

Alan recalls that during these sightings there was no missing time or gaps, as far as he could recall. He has no fears of places or stretches of highway and has not experienced any displacement as to time or place. He says there have been no strange figures in his bedroom, no strange wounds or scars, and no recurring dreams of UFOs.

However, he was frequently lost as a child and thinks of himself as a "wandering kid." He had no fear of strange places or people and was always wandering off. He has no intense phobias or fears and no recollection of meaningless words that come into his mind. Also, he has no unexplained medical problems, is not a sleepwalker, and does not hear voices in his head. An exception to this last response is that he has heard his name called, such as when he has been sitting quietly and he hears a voice call his name. He has described it as a soft, male voice. Once he experienced this at night. He says that he usually ignores the voice; he had forgotten about these incidents until I asked him these questions.

His opinion is that UFOs are probably only misidentified real objects, but he accepts the possibility that some of them might be extraterrestrial and that at least some of the abduction accounts seem genuine.

Alan is a casually curious person who has maybe read a book or two and a few articles on UFOs over the past few years; his reaction to the questionnaire was one of intellectual curiosity. Alan is amazed that so few people admit to having seen UFOs, and he wonders why he has seen so many. He is also amazed that UFOs can come to such an abrupt stop after traveling so fast, then shoot off again at incredible speed.

September 9, 1988

Since June I have become increasingly interested in the UFO controversy. I have been reading the literature and looking at various experiences in my own life that may be related to the UFO contact or abduction phenomenon. It is hard to sort out what is wishful thinking, fantasy, or imagination from reality. I intend to remain open-minded. I have also decided to attend a UFO conference in Connecticut to see if I can unravel any more of the mystery. I have continued to correspond with Dr. M. She has been helpful in giving me names of people who might share transportation and accommodation at the conference.

September 11, 1988

It is now over eight months since I started full time at the lab and a whole year since my first visit to the lab. It has been an exciting, productive year, and I feel I am at the right place at the right time in my life.

Lately, I have been hearing some criticism of the abduction scenario, with the critics attributing the experiences to magical thinking. I looked up "magical thinking" and found that it is a behavior attributed to children, between four and seven years of age, and is characterized by allowing for any possible relation between a number of things, rather than a critical search for factually consistent relationships between events. After reading this, I don't think I apply magical thinking to the abduction problem. I have been quite critical in my evaluations.

September 18, 1988

The following is from my memory search, which could account for some missing time about four years ago:

In the summer of 1984, I went with a friend to a singles group in Morristown, New Jersey, which was held at the Unitarian Church. We stayed until about 11.30 P.M., then a group of us went to a local bar to dance and talk. Jane and I left the bar at about one A.M. to drive back to West Orange, which was about a thirty-minute drive away. Jane was familiar with the route, as we had been to the Morristown singles group before. We started off in good spirits. Jane had met someone and set up a date. After about an hour of driving, she announced we were lost and that she had no idea where we were. We found a telephone booth to find our location and discovered that we were still in Morris County, but west of Morristown. We called the local police for travel directions and they directed us to a nearby major highway.

We eventually found the highway and started driving again. However, this time we found ourselves near Perth Amboy, way past Orange, and we had to backtrack. Eventually, Jane dropped me off at my apartment, and when I looked at the clock it was 5:30 A.M. The sun was rising, and I was puzzled how we could have been driving for four and a half hours. The distances we had driven didn't account for the time spent. I was so exhausted that I went straight to bed and slept through most of Saturday. When I related the tale to other friends they were puzzled that Jane and I could have been driving around for such a long time. They asked if we had needed to stop for gas, which we hadn't, and the whole incident was so bizarre that I let it go.

September 19, 1988

There is some discussion that early childhood dreams are symbolic of actual events that have occurred in the child's world. Major recurrent dreams or nightmares can reveal hidden conflicts and anxieties in the child's environment. There is anecdotal material that abduction events occur early, sometimes as young as at five years of age, and that these events, although not recalled consciously, may be revealed in dreams. Some may be strong enough to be remembered long into adulthood. There are several childhood dreams that I still remember and that seem as fresh today as when I dreamed them so many years ago. These dreams contain symbolism that could possibly be recognized as referring to UFOs, aliens, and possible encounters.

The most obvious of these, in UFO terms, is a recurrent dream in which I see a UFO or a fleet of UFOs from my bedroom window. The house in the dream is the one in which I grew up in Shirehampton, the suburbs of a large city, Bristol. Although we were surrounded by residential neighborhoods, we could see the Welsh hills and countryside from my bedroom window. In my dream I would be in my room and see the disks fly over from the Welsh hills and over our house. I would call to my parents or people in my dream to come and see. I was very excited and could not understand their reluctance to come and look at the flying disks. When I could finally get them to come and look, the disks would be gone and the people in the dream would be angry at me for calling them to look at nothing.

These dreams occurred during my early childhood years between ages five and eight. I also had strange fantasies about aliens. During the waking time before going to sleep, I would lie in bed and worry about aliens landing and coming into the house through my bedroom window. I would think, "Now they are coming up the garden path; now they are climbing up the wall of the house; now they are just underneath the window sill"—and at that point I would dive under the bedclothes. It was probably a silly childish acting out of anxiety, just as some kids had fantasies about monsters in the closet. In addition to these dreams, I remember another frightening dream in which a female applied a hot iron to the small of my back. It hurt terribly and I was very confused as to why someone would do this to me.

September 21, 1988

Tonight I attended a local UFO club and heard a woman, whom I will call Betty-Sue, talk about her UFO and contact experiences. She mentioned how she had visited the psychophysics lab that I had attended and had been hypnotized by Helen and that she felt very strongly that more had happened than she remembered. Betty-Sue felt that it had to do with UFOs and aliens.

In her recollections, Betty-Sue remembers a dream about a white-haired, older male, whom she calls "Destiny Man." In her dream she was taken to Washington, D.C., and met Destiny Man, who took her to meet the president of the United States. I remembered that I also had dreams of a white-haired man during the time I was visiting the psychophysics lab. At the time, I was considering not visiting the lab because of Helen's rudeness to me. The white-haired man in my dreams urged me to continue attending and participating in their experiments.

Following her dreams, Betty-Sue attended the psychophysics lab to participate in their psi experiments. Following one session, she was asked to the conference room, where several visitors were gathered. One was the prince of a small European country, who has funded UFO and parapsychology ventures. The other man, she was shocked to recognize, was Destiny Man from her dreams. She became rattled and asked the researcher, Helen, who Destiny Man was. From her accounts, Betty-Sue related that Destiny Man appeared to know her well, even knowing her nickname. After the meeting, which left Betty-Sue in a deep state of shock, Helen urged Betty-Sue to contact Destiny Man.

Following these events, Betty-Sue was in contact with Destiny Man, who seemed to know what she had been doing and even called her before her major UFO sighting. When she confronted Helen, the researcher told her she was right about her misgivings. Betty-Sue threatened to have Helen and the psychophysics lab investigated. Helen responded that she would not be around to be investigated. At that point, Helen broke off her friendship with Betty-Sue. It was at that time that Helen also broke off her friendship with me.

This has left me with some very disturbing questions. For example, was I also involved in clandestine research that was not part of the psychophysics lab directive? Things have somehow been put into perspective, but more questions have been raised than answered.

September 24, 1988

These have been a disturbing few days, because I have been trying to piece together the strange information that surfaced at the UFO club regarding my participation at the psi lab last year and my hypnosis sessions with Helen. These new concerns have surfaced since my visit to the UFO club last week and hearing Betty-Sue talk about her experiences. This has prompted me to look back through my journals to try and piece together this complex situation. The questions I am asking are:

During the hypnosis sessions was there any experience I was not aware of, such as questioning under deep hypnosis? Did this questioning concern UFOs? Were there any posthypnotic suggestions made by Helen? I realize all of this sounds paranoid, but it is something I have to follow up.

September 25, 1988

After reading back through four of my journals and writing fifteen pages of notes, I am convinced that "something" was happening at the psychophysics lab other than the standard parapsychology studies. While I have absolutely no proof, I feel it had to do with looking for information, via hypnosis, about UFO contact and psychic experiences. Why? I don't know.

In the journals, I recorded: my visits to the psychophysics lab; discussions with Helen about UFOs and aliens; disturbing nightmares involving the staff; an irregular heartbeat throughout the whole period; feelings of depression and anxiety; the fact that I had visited the lab and left whole pages unwritten (with no memory of the visit); strange comments by Helen regarding my possibly being an alien (which I shrugged off at the time); notes about our frequent hypnotic sessions, some of which left me very disoriented; and dreams of aliens. Of particular interest was a note in which Helen had commented on how exciting it would be to do some research to locate and communicate with aliens. I do not remember ever doing any abduction research with Helen.

The experience is behind me now, and I have no further contact with Helen. It seems pointless to attempt to uncover anything more, especially as the psychophysics lab has closed down, and maybe I don't want to know. I have discussed this with Emily, who feels that Helen was probably doing something she should not have been doing and backed off when Betty-Sue threatened her with an investigation. Emily feels that Helen was doing this on her own and that other members of the psychophysics lab were not involved.

I still feel concerned about the hypnotic part of the experience and asked a psychologist friend for advice. He told me that any material covered during very deep hypnosis would not necessarily be remembered. However, my consciously negating any possible posthypnotic suggestions could neutralize them, even if I did not know what they were. This is reassuring to hear. To function with a clear mind, I have to put all this behind me and go forward.

September 29, 1988

Last week I decided to send some of my notes of possible abduction memories and experiences to Dr. David Jacobs, an abduction researcher, and to Dr. M in the hope that they could give me an honest, professional appraisal of the contents. I have not yet heard from Dr. M, but Dr. Jacobs called me today to tell me he thinks that I have had some genuine abduction experiences. He suggested further investigation under hypnosis to uncover more about my experiences, but I declined. After the psychophysics lab business, I am reluctant to let anyone hypnotize me. I let him know that I wanted to continue my own search in my own way: through my dreams, diaries, and memory search.

September 30, 1988

I have been using the time when I walk to work as a time of meditation. I have been working on memory recall, particularly any memories relating to my current project. This morning I dredged up a strong memory regarding a visit to an air force office when I was a little girl. I have asked my mother about this memory several times and she does not remember it. However, my memory is very strong. It occurred when I was about three or four and my brother Alan was still a baby. I went with my parents and my younger brother to a center in Bristol that I think was used, at that time, by the Royal Observer Corps. My father was a dispatch rider in the war, and I have always been under the impression that he was returning his uniform.

The corps was situated in a series of Quonset-type huts, as was common after the war when so many buildings had been bombed in Bristol. While we were there, we were shown into a small movie theater, where we sat on fold-down seats. I had been to the cinema to see cartoons and was expecting to see cartoons in this theater. Instead, we were shown films of planes. I don't have a strong memory of exactly what planes we saw.

I do remember that my mother wore a slim, blue suit and a little hat with a veil. I had the feeling that it was important for us to watch the films and that I should sit still and watch. I have no idea why we were there (and neither does my mother) or why we had to watch the films.

October 1, 1988

I did some more memory search and remembered the time my brother Alan and I spent all day at a local beauty spot called Blaise Castle. There could have been missing time. We had gone to Blaise Castle in the morning and did not get back until late at night. Our parents were very worried and angry at us for staying out. We were in our early teens. I remember on the way home we were trying to think of excuses to give our parents as to why we were so late.

Also, when I was in the junior school, I constantly fell asleep at my desk in class. My parents and the school were concerned and took me to a doctor, but there was nothing physically wrong with me.

October 2, 1988

This morning I went for a massage, and while I was walking there, I remembered a dream I had a few years ago. I think that the pleasurable anticipation of the massage prompted the memory. The dream would have taken place about 1986.

In the dream I was in a small, white, brightly lit cubicle, lying on a table. I was feeling cold, anxious, shivery, and confused. A woman in a blue overall came in. She wore the kind of overall that beauticians wear. She covered me with a warm, very soft, light, blue blanket. She tucked it around me and I felt warm and safe. She left and told me to sleep. I remember that when I awoke, I wanted to return to the experience. I remember that the table I had been lying on was a sort of shelf at the rear of the cubicle.

I have been going over and over my old journals, trying to make some sense of my worries about the psychophysics lab and Helen, and getting nowhere. I copied down twenty pages of notations, which made me feel more unsure than ever. What to make of all this? Basically, it's a record-keeping exercise, looking for possible answers to what was happening. What I will do with it I have no idea.

I thought I could be supportive of Betty-Sue and her similar dilemma, but she seems intent on suing the lab and Helen, and I do not want to go to those extremes. I plan, however, to meet Betty-Sue at the UFO Conference next weekend in Connecticut.

During the time period that I was visiting the psychophysics lab, I did several visualization exercises to try and contact aliens. Whether this was my own decision or whether it was influenced by Helen via hypnosis, I do not remember. However, I will record two of them here. I did not record them at the time that I did them, as they seemed too weird and impossible.

In the first visualization, I asked myself to imagine an alien ship and what it was called. I recall that I gave it the name "Tau" or "Tao" and that it meant something like "home" or "mother." At this remembrance, I felt a great emotion welling up in me and tears came to my eyes. The emotion was one of nostalgia and great sadness. I could not continue with the visualization. In the second visualization, I attempted to visit the ship again. I saw small "men" at the controls with their backs to me. They did not seem to be aware of me.

This intense emotion welled up again recently when I was telling Emily about my experiences with Helen and my worries. Emily advised me to put the experience into a mental "subdirectory" and forget about it. I did a mental exercise to put this experience into some perspective and had the realization that the UFO experience had caused me a great deal of unconscious grief.

October 6, 1988

Yesterday afternoon at the parapsychology lab, I was alone doing paperwork and fell into a reflective state. I sat back and closed my eyes for about ten minutes and used the opportunity to do a general forgiving and healing meditation around the Helen dilemma. I used an affirmation of confidence and faith in myself and my abilities and forgave all those who had caused me to have anxious feelings during the past couple of weeks. As thoughts came to mind, I affirmed them, until the whole experience left me calmer and with a sense of inner peace.

This morning I remembered a dream I had while I was living in Dorset, England, between the years 1962 and 1967: In the dream I was looking out of the front window and saw a very big, long, cigar-shaped spaceship land on the grassy common across the road. People were being collected from their homes and led to the spaceship. I had the urge to hide during the dream.

October 7, 1988

Talking with Betty-Sue and getting to know about her emotional problems made me worry how abduction might affect people. I became curious about whether abductees might be emotionally disturbed.

I received a copy of a report published by the Fund for UFO Research (FUFOR) entitled "Final Report of the Psychological Testing of UFO 'Abductees.'" The authors are Ted Bloecher, Aphrodite Clamar, and Budd Hopkins, and it is dated January 1985. Nine individuals who had abduction experiences were extensively tested and the following was found:

1. They were all of relatively high intelligence, with a concomitant richness of inner life.
2. They had relative weaknesses in the sense of identity, especially sexual identity.
3. They were vulnerable in the interpersonal realm.
4. They showed a heightened orientation to alertness, hypervigilance, and caution.

I recognize many of these traits in myself: I am of above-average intelligence; until I was in my thirties, I was incredibly shy and reserved; I have been married twice; I've always felt the need to be alert and aware of my surroundings. I always thought these were personal traits engendered by the society in which I was raised (working-class, postwar England), but perhaps they are a result of something I have shared with numerous other people, the abduction experience?

Another paper I came across was written by June Otillie Parnell, Ph.D., and was entitled "Personality Characteristics on the MMPI, 16PF, and ACL of Persons Who Claim UFO Experiences." The paper was part of her Ph.D. dissertation for the University of Wyoming in 1986. Dr. Parnell found that:

> The participants in the study exhibited a high level of psychic energy and a tendency to be questioning authority or be subject to situational pressures or conflicts. They can be seen as self-sufficient, resourceful, and preferring their own decisions. These characteristics were evident for all participants in the study, across each level of each category considered. Mean scores also indicated the following general characteristics among participants: above average intelligence, assertiveness, a tendency to be experimenting thinkers, a tendency toward a reserved attitude, and a tendency toward defensiveness. Participants were honest persons and no overt psychopathology was indicated.

These findings appear to support and complement the previous study. Finally, I found a third paper entitled "Preliminary Data on Eighteen of Thirty Subjects Reporting UFO Abduction," authored by Jo Copeland Stone, M.F.C.C., of Sherman Oaks, California. This is what she reported in her paper:

> The graph on Descriptive Self-Report suggests this group perceives themselves as honest, sensitive, loyal, trustworthy and hard working. They identify themselves as intelligent, worthwhile and having a good sense of humor.

The graph on Behaviors indicates that these subjects practice meditation on a regular basis. It is interesting to note that even so, fifty percent of the eighteen subjects report insomnia.

While the graph on Feelings shows a group of apparently happy, optimistic, energetic subjects who consider themselves to be hopeful most of the time, they also report being anxious, restless, and conflicted.

Another memory surfaced today. During the time I was married to my ex-husband and we were together as a family in the Poconos in Pennsylvania, we may have experienced some missing time. During the week beginning June 12, 1981, I spent a week alone at a mountain cabin, the home of friends in the Poconos. My marriage had been going through troubling times and I needed a breathing space. It was beautiful in the mountains; I walked, slept, meditated, read, studied, and tried to work on some of the marital problems. At the end of the week, my then husband, Randolph, and his two young children came to take me home. They spent the night before we went back the next day.

The night they arrived Randolph decided we should go out after dark and go down to Deer Trail Lake to look for deer. We went down to the lake at about nine o'clock and sat by the water on an overturned canoe and waited for the deer. It was quite chilly even though it was June. The children got restless and played at the lake edge.

We were looking at the stars and saw a round, silvery object in the sky, very high up. It did not move and was much bigger than the stars. We watched it for some time. We seemed to have been at the lake for a long time, and there could have been some missing time involved. We looked at the silvery object later on and it was in the same position that we had seen it earlier. I thought it was a UFO, but Randolph was highly skeptical and said it was a weather balloon. I felt that if it had been a weather balloon it should have changed its position during the time we had been watching it. We didn't see any deer and the children were disappointed. We were at the lake, which is five minutes from the house, for several hours, ostensibly just sitting by the water, waiting for deer.

In my quest for answers to my own experiences, I started looking at memories of UFO interest in my immediate family. The following recollections are not in chronological order, but as I have remembered them. My parents had an interest in UFOs. When we went out for rides into the countryside around Bristol, such as to Gloucester, Somerset, and Wiltshire, we would look for UFOs. When we went to Frome in Somerset to visit relatives, we would pass Clay Hill, which had a reputation for UFO sightings, and we would always look for them. There was a particular hill in Somerset called Crooks Peak, which we always climbed to pick heather. However, my father would never climb that hill with us and would never give us a reason why.

When we were living in Dorset, England, my brother and I would pass the time while we were waiting for buses by scanning the night sky. We searched for flying saucers. We had the understanding that even if you put all the universe that we could see with our eyes in a box, there would still be space outside the box, and if you put all that space outside the box into a bigger box, there would still be space outside that box, ad infinitum. We had discovered the unboundedness of space.

While I was thinking about past experiences with my family, I got to thinking about another factor that is associated with the abduction phenomenon. Some UFO abductees have claimed they have scars they could not explain. Most of my scars have remembered origins. For example, I remember having a large sheet of iron fall on my foot when I was a little girl and I still have a small scar on the front of my left foot. There is one scar on the inner aspect of my right ankle that takes the shape of a white half circle. It looks as if it could have been quite deep, and would have bled, but I don't have any recollection of ever cutting myself there. The OMNI questionnaire asked about scars, but I had forgotten about the one on my ankle, and I didn't mention it.

There have been many illustrations in the literature about what the aliens look like. Generally, they have very large heads and small, slight bodies. Their eyes are large, oval and dark. When I was working in Manchester, England, during the 1978–80 period, part of my research job was to evaluate premature infants, who were part of a project to determine whether they would be right- or left-handed. I felt very strongly at that time that these premature infants, with their large heads, large eyes, and small, slender bodies, looked very much like aliens. The general opinion in the UFO literature is that the aliens have very rounded heads. My feeling is that they are slightly flattened at the sides.

Around 1975, before I went to Cardiff to do my undergraduate degree, I was working at a residential children's community home near my parents' house. At night, after a day off, I would walk the mile or so from my parents' house to the home. The road went up a hill and down the other side, and the down side faced the Welsh hills. As I walked, I would watch the sky and say, half-jokingly, "Here I am, where are you?"

I remembered several more things over the weekend.

During the period of 1971–72, I took a practical course in residential social work at Ruskin College in Oxford. Part of this course was spent at a children's home in Henley-on-Thames. During my month there, I went camping with one of the staff members and eight children from one of the family groups. One morning just as the sun was rising (about five) there was a terrible sound, like thousands of people screaming, and it was getting closer and closer. I felt tremendous fear and thought the end of the world was about to happen. In contrast to my usual behavior, which would have been to go to the children, I could not get out of my camp bed. I lay wide-awake and shaking. The noise got still louder then faded away. When the noise had ceased, I was able to get out of my bed, but everything in the camp was okay. Nobody mentioned the early morning noise.

When I was at home in Bristol during the late 1970s, there was an occasion when I was sitting out on the back step and noticed a house up on a hill to my left. It looked as if it was on fire. I called my father and mother to come and look. The house, as far as we could tell, was lit with a bright orange light. It was late afternoon in the summer and the sun did not set until much later. We got my father's binoculars and we all took turns looking. The house seemed bathed in an intense orange light. It seemed at times as if the light emanated from the inside of the house, but it must have been intense to be noticed from a distance on a bright day. We watched it for a while; then abruptly there was no light anymore and the house was back to normal. We watched the television news, but there was nothing to explain the light. The house had definitely not been on fire.

There is a great deal of anecdotal material regarding the possible reason why humans are abducted by aliens—to provide genetic stock. In the UFO literature, there are stories of women who have been given gynecological examinations, whose eggs have been harvested; there is even the idea that fetuses have been implanted in them and harvested. These women have experienced baby dreams, where they feel they have been in contact with the result of this genetic experimentation. Whether all this is true is another matter.

Over the past years I have had many baby and pregnancy dreams. It is possible that, in my case, the dreams were merely wish fulfillment, as I have never given birth and would have liked children when I was younger. Now the possibility of my becoming a mother is remote, and I have adjusted to this new status. The longing for a child, which was strong in my thirties, is gradually waning as I proceed through my forties.

October 10, 1988

This past weekend I attended the UFO Conference at North Haven, Connecticut, and had an interesting time. The interaction was on several levels: attending lectures and hearing accounts of sightings, abductions, and investigations. On a personal level, I found it very interesting to talk to some of the abductees about their experiences. All in all, it was an interesting conference.

Dr. M was able to match me up with people to share rides and accommodation. I shared a room with MK from Maryland, whom I learned later was there "undercover." The company that she worked for (Science Applications International, Corporation [SAIC]) is a government think tank, and her branch in McLean, Virginia, was involved with Star Wars applications. In fact, her initial letter to me regarding sharing a room was written on SAIC letterhead. However, MK was very worried that her colleagues and the attendees at the conference would find out who she was. I was intrigued and kept my mouth shut. I noticed that she talked to many of the abductees at the conference.

My ride to the conference was shared by an army doctor and his young wife, a schoolteacher. The doctor, who had been working with Dr. David Jacobs, was training to be an army psychiatrist. The ride was very stormy, and we joked all the way about missing time.

The lectures were a mixed bag: some were excellent, others were an insult to the audience. I bought a cute T-shirt that read "I got abducted by aliens and all I got was this lousy T-shirt!"

One of the abductees, Kathy Davis, got up and talked about her experiences to the audience, but I felt that she had been pressured into doing so. She was very tearful and shaky. I noticed one abduction researcher in the audience with his arms around the shoulders of several young girls. At the conference I got to talk to several abduction researchers, but I never found Betty-Sue.

October 11, 1988

This weekend conference on UFOs has caused a batch of memories and dreams to surface. Some seem directly connected to the topic, while others have a tentative connection, if any at all. But I am recording them. They are not in any order—that will come later—and they are listed as they were remembered:

Many of the UFO "mother ships" have been described as fish-like. Since my childhood, I have had dreams and fears of swimming in very deep water and of a large fish swimming alongside and brushing itself against me. The memory of the dream itself sent fear down my spine. In 1975 I decided to allay this fear and swim in very deep water. On vacation I went out to a point on the coast where there was deep water and swam in to the shore. It was scary, but I did it and had no further nightmares. In 1981 I was able to go snorkeling in deep water in the Dominican Republic on my honeymoon with my now ex-husband. It was an exhilarating experience, and I had no fear.

My brother and I were always making "hiding dens," where we would stock up on comics, apples, flashlights, and water. Maybe lots of children do this, but we chose strange places. We had dens in a small broom cupboard under the stairs, in an empty coal bunker, and in an abandoned air-raid shelter. We would play that we were isolated from the rest of the community and had to take enough supplies to last. Unfortunately, my mother always found us and did not approve of our play areas, particularly the coal bunker. What or who were we hiding from?

I had many childhood dreams of flying and being able to breathe underwater. My brother also had these dreams. I have told other people about these dreams and they have expressed surprise, because they have never had them.

As a young child I had a fascination with injections. I would play-act being given injections, which never hurt. When, at age eight, I got sick with an infected knee, I had real injections and was greatly disappointed that they hurt. I also played games in which I would cut out small squares of paper and imagine that a doctor was placing these all over my body. I would do this in bed and remember that I did not want my mother to see me doing this. When I heard her coming up the stairs, I quickly rubbed them all off. I was disappointed that the bits of paper dried up too quickly and fell off. I had the feeling that they should stay put for a while. Was I play-acting actual experiences?

When my brother was two years old (I would have been five) he had to have a badly infected tooth removed. I was told that the dentist would "put Alan to sleep," and I visualized him being wrapped in a blanket and placed in a shelflike bed in a wall recess. When I was taken to the dentist at a later age, I was surprised to not see this bed alcove. Where had I seen such a bed?

I have always felt a great yearning for the stars and space. I watched Carl Sagan's television documentary "Cosmos" several times and felt compelled to sit up close to the screen, so as not to miss anything.

At the UFO conference, I learned that an insignia often worn by aliens is a flying snake, serpent, dragon, or phoenix. I have had a fascination with all of these elements, and my personal favorite is the phoenix, which has inhabited my dreams since I was a little child.

I have been thinking about the hand signals for the alphabet that I dreamed a few years ago. I have been trying to remember the other letters of the alphabet. I have remembered "A." It is formed with the hands together as in prayer, then opened so that the first two fingertips of each hand are still touching. The other fingers are spread open. The two thumbs are placed on top of each other, sort of interleaved. I will get my artist friend to make some sketches when I have the alphabet complete.

October 12, 1988

This afternoon, even though I had a full night's sleep, I felt a great urge to sleep and took a six-and-a-half-hour "nap." I had three major real dreams.

In the first dream, I awoke to hear someone downstairs, whom I assumed to be Emily. I was ashamed at being in bed when I should have been working on a newsletter. I could not move at first, then only with extreme lethargy. I turned off the TV, which had come on while I slept. This took a great effort. The person who had come into the house came up and down the stairs several times and went into the room of Emily's grown son, Sydney. His room was across the hall. I still could not move. Then I found myself in the bathroom between Sydney's and my room, sitting on the floor with my back to the tub, behind the door. I felt ridiculous sitting there but could not move.

I slept and dreamed again but could only remember the word "Phoenix" from the dream. I awoke after this dream to answer the phone. I told Emily I was still working on the newsletter, which I fully intended to do, but then went back to bed and back to sleep.

I dreamed that I was a child again in Bristol. I was playing in the street with two little friends. It was summertime and warm. It was midevening and the sun had started to descend. One of my little friends was younger than I was and had her hair in braids. We were lying in the deserted roadway, drawing with chalk. We were talking about flying saucers.

To our horror, a fast-moving "motorbike" with two riders rode past us, almost hitting us. The "bike" was a maroon color but had some sort of superstructure attached to it. The riders both wore large red helmets. The bike and occupants looked "new." We screamed, shut our eyes and clung together. We were on our knees in the roadway. I was the eldest and felt obliged to comfort the other two, even though I was scared to hell.

Then we decided to go home. I got up and started walking. The little girl with braids ran on ahead. I was walking with the other girl, holding her hand. Then I looked up and saw three, very large, red, cigar-shaped UFOs. They hovered in the air and underneath hung what looked like cords or ropes, but what could have been some sort of vapor trails.

I remembered that the strange "motorcycle" had been silent and we did not hear its approach on the road. The "bike" only stopped to observe us, then sped off. The next thing I remember in the dream was that I was walking in a village near my home. I saw signposts for Shirehampton and decided to walk the mile or so home.

While I was writing down these dreams, I remembered another part of last night's dream. In the dream, I was talking to a white-haired man about UFOs and I was having some sort of emotional spasm. The white-haired man was concerned and asked if I was in pain. The spasms were mostly facial, and I don't recall any pain.

October 13, 1988

Today, I came across some record books I had been keeping last year. Helen had taught me the I Ching. The book recorded our questions about jobs, relationships, and future education. One page records two questions: The first mentioned "A UFO Venture with Helen?" The I Ching answer had been that "work was needed before completing a topic," and that we were "inexperienced and needed a teacher." The second question asked "Do extraterrestrials exist?" The I Ching answers had been "temptation, coming to meet, harmonious, in accord with the universe."

Other questions involved the use of psi, major changes, and the friendship between Helen and myself. However, I cannot remember ever agreeing to participate in a "UFO venture" with Helen, although we did question whether extraterrestrials were real. This inability to remember these details adds to my uneasiness about the venture. I remembered that sometime in 1987 was probably the last time Helen visited my home. During her visit, I developed an intense migraine and had to vomit while she was visiting. I had forgotten about this visit until today. I feel that I was under intense pressure and stress at that time.

During a dream, I recall having my hands restrained and biting the restraints to get them off my hands. I was also aware at one point that my heart rate was very slow.

Today, I have been having the words "chemical restraint" going through my mind, but I have never heard this phrase before and do not know what it means. But it sends chills up my spine.

October 14, 1988

There were two dreams last night related to UFOs.

I dreamed that I was in an encounter with Randy, again. I had met Randy, who worked for a government contractor, at the psychophysics lab.

In the second dream, I was talking with Dr. David Jacobs, the UFO researcher. He told me that he had been reading my notes and was convinced that I had experienced genuine abductions. I found his words hard to accept, and yet I was relieved that I had not been fantasizing.

October 16, 1988

During these last few weeks, I have felt another increase in my psi abilities. It could be a "practice effect" as I have been working at the parapsychology lab. I have had "psychic flashes" almost every day, where I seem to access information about events that are about to happen. This increased ability could also have resulted from my continued acceptance of my talents and abilities.

Last night I played a computer game using the name of "Andromeda." I have been thinking about why I like that name and why I use it for computer games. This brought up memories from my early teen years when we first had a TV. At that time, there was a show called *Andromeda*, which we watched weekly. Most kids in their teens adopt role models from TV. I adopted the character from the *Andromeda* show. She was an alien in the form of a young woman. She had long blond hair and blue eyes and possessed supernatural abilities, which she had to hide from the world to live a normal life. I realize now that I identified with the *Andromeda* character, as I also had to hide my abilities, both natural and supernatural, in order to function in the everyday world.

October 19, 1988

I had a long dream in which I was present at some sort of press conference. There were a stage and a seated audience. At the front were a blackboard and a map. The audience consisted of men, women, and children. The general impression was that we were in Japan, although the audience consisted of both Asians and Caucasians.

Three aliens appeared at the front of the audience and were applauded. The aliens were giving a show to get to know people. They were going around cutting marks into people's programs. I noticed that most people held out their programs with the right hand. I wanted to be different and to be acknowledged by the aliens, so I held my program out with my left hand. The alien cutting my program stopped to ponder this, looked at me closely, and went by. I felt I had been recognized. The aliens were acknowledging photos and cards that had been sent to them as welcome greetings. They were giving prizes to the children consisting of slips of paper that could be redeemed for real prizes. The aliens were taller than me, as I was seated, but they had the classic large eyes, large heads, and thin body and limbs. Overall, they seemed very friendly.

I received a letter today from Dr. M, the psychologist. She had finally read the notes I had sent to her before the UFO conference. She comments: "I've read your manuscript very carefully and would think that you did have an abduction-type experience." She added, "You seem to be integrating it nicely via your dreams. Some scary parts remain. Keep dreaming!" She asked if she could use some of my notes (with an alias) in her writings. She also suggested that we talk on the phone.

This is an interesting confirmation. It is also an encouragement of my own method of looking at my own experiences via my dreams. I have decided to let her use some of my quotes under the pseudonym of Andromeda.

October 20, 1988

I called Dr. M and we chatted for about an hour this evening. We discussed ambivalent feelings and emotions about abduction experiences and she commented, again, that I seem to be integrating my experiences via my dream and memory recall.

October 21, 1988

I had a very disturbing dream relating to Betty-Sue, from whom I have not heard in a long time. This was the woman who had claimed that the psychophysics lab and Helen had done some sort of hypnotic experiments on her without her consent. I had the feeling that she was angry with me for not being more supportive and talking to her about my own experiences. This dream seems to symbolize my guilt at not being willing to share my experiences with Betty-Sue and a recognition of her anger.

October 22, 1988

In a dream I sat in a large auditorium, listening to a man talk about a UFO that had landed in the desert. There was a large map on the wall. A tall, fair-haired girl in the audience got upset, as she had some connection to the crash. She ran to the front, looked at the map, and fled from the room in tears.

I am not sure about the interpretation of this dream but could the fair-haired girl have been me?

Several times since the end of August I have thought about writing down the following incidents but each time I "forgot."

When I first moved to Princeton and moved into Emily's house, there was an unusual occurrence that we could not explain. Emily and I both woke up to find that some large "insect" had bitten us on the front of the throat and left a bloody scab measuring a couple of centimeters wide. When the scab came off after a few days, it left a small, red depression, which gradually healed. It looked like the kind of scar that is left after an intravenous drip needle has been in place for a while. This happened last February or March, and there were no flying insects around at that time. Emily's bedroom is downstairs, mine is upstairs, and our rooms are at opposite ends of the house. The question remains: why did we both get the same "bite" in the same place on the front of the neck? I remember we joked about vampire bats and giant mosquitoes, and we casually dismissed the incident.

November 30, 1988

Over the weekend, Emily and I both discovered a strange, oily liquid on the furniture, that smelled like tree sap or resin. I found some on my dining table. It had soaked into a piece of paper and was sprayed on the lamp base. I wiped up approximately one quarter ounce of it off the table top. The soaked paper turned translucent, then the oil eventually evaporated off the paper.

Emily found a spot under her jewelry box that was making a mark on the wood. She said it looked oily and smelled resiny. There were no plants nearby. I thought that the cat had sprayed, but the liquid was too high up under the lampshade for that to be possible. Also, Emily's finding of the oily liquid was underneath her jewelry box. Emily thought it might be related to UFOs or ectoplasm. We decided to look out for it should any more appear.

November 31, 1988

I had a disturbed night. I awoke in the middle of the night as my phone rang. There was nobody there. I found that my radio had come on and I could not turn it off at the switch. I turned the volume down very low and went back to sleep. However, I remember feeling scared and anxious. Maybe I was dreaming and PK'd the telephone and clock. I had been dreaming before waking, but I do not remember the dream content.

I have been reading about ETs, who they may be, where they might come from, and why they are interacting with us. I came across the following paper by Martyn Fogg, who is a researcher in astronomy and geology associated with the Extraterrestrial Department of London University. He also is a fellow of both the Royal Astronomical and British Interplanetary Societies. His research interests include planetary formation, cometary impact cycles, and SETI (Search for Extraterrestrial Intelligence). One of

Fogg's current projects is the study of the possible origins of life early in the history of the universe. Fogg recently wrote an interesting article for Analog Science Fiction/Science Fact on something he calls the "Extraterrestrial Intelligence and the Interdict Hypothesis." He asks:

> What would an extraterrestrial intelligent life form look like? How would such an alien think? What would it be like to be one? How could alien races interact with humanity? These are just some of the fascinating questions that have stimulated the writing of some of the most entertaining science fiction. However, in order to speculate realistically one essential question must be slotted in ahead of the rest. Do extraterrestrial intelligent beings exist? . . . It now seems that the existence of alien civilizations can no longer be taken for granted, even though our galaxy contains over a hundred million stars, many million of which are similar to our own sun.
>
> Some of my recent research on galactic colonization has led me to conclude that there may be an 'Interdict Hypothesis' with implications regarding the abundance and distribution of intelligent life which go beyond even the speculations of Carl Sagan and Frank Drake. Civilizations may be numbered in not millions, but in billions, nearly all having originated from a mere handful of racial progenitors born when the Earth and solar system were nothing but dust drifting in the star lanes. . . . If ETs exist and interstellar space travel is practical, then life and intelligence must be very abundant. The galaxy must be largely settled.

Fogg concludes in the words of T. B. Tang, "Absence of evidence of ETs may make little sense, but absence of ETs makes no sense at all!" Is Fogg so way out? What is the official stand on the search for extraterrestrial intelligence? I came across a paper published in 1987 entitled "Space: 30 Years into the Future," by James C. Fletcher, NASA administrator. While talking primarily about our options as a space-faring people, Fletcher states that finding other intelligences in the universe is vital to our efforts to explore space. He writes:

> Rather than dwell on where we have been, I'd like to look ahead—30 years into the future—at two priority subjects that NASA has thought a great deal about. I believe that these subjects deserve priority attention from all of us in the years ahead because of their profound implications for our civilization. The

> first is philosophically profound. It is the necessity to put real effort into the search for extra-terrestrial intelligence, or SETI, for short. The search is intimately related to the second subject: the inevitability of venturing beyond Earth, not only to explore the solar system, but to exploit its resources in an economical way for the benefit of humanity.

Fletcher speculates that by the 1990s, the budget for the search for extraterrestrial life should exceed the total sum of all previous searches. He also speculates about plans for this search being extended to be conducted from the far side of the Moon.

4

Only Stray Psychokinetic Energy?

"We have indeed been contacted—perhaps even visited—by extraterrestrial beings, and the U. S. government, in collusion with the other national powers of the Earth, is determined to keep this information from the general public."

—Victor Marchetti, former special assistant to the executive director for the CIA, in an article written by him for *Second Look* entitled "How the CIA Views the UFO Phenomenon," vol. 1, No. 7, Washington, D.C., May, 1979.

November 2, 1988

This is the seventh journal in this series that I started in 1978, and a great deal has happened over the past ten years. At Halloween this year, I chose Mary Poppins as my costume. The Mary Poppins character has been my facade for many years, maybe to cover my psychic abilities and skills. Wearing the costume at Halloween was symbolic of recognizing this facade and allowing my inner self, and its abilities, to be free.

During this past year, I have seen a gradual strengthening of my psychic abilities and skills. My participation at the parapsychology lab has allowed me to push the boundaries of my abilities and explore new areas. One of these new areas has encompassed the possibility that some of my anomalous experiences could be explained by the UFO abduction scenario. To explore this area, I have given my subconscious permission to bring into consciousness any hidden memories related to this dilemma. I hope any hidden memories will come into dream consciousness or even into actual memory. I have talked to psychologist, Dr. M, on this matter, and she feels I am on the right track doing my memory search this way.

Emily and I have a very dear friend who was a Hungarian countess. She and her husband fled from the Germans and Russians during the Second World War and came to the United States. This lady is now quite elderly, an inventor and scientist, very intuitive and with a wealth of knowledge. I shared my interest in the runes with her, and she loaned me a book on Swedish history and runes. Among the illustrations of large standing stones bearing runes was another intriguing picture. The carvings show several boats and spirals, as well as a procession of figures that runs across a large, fallen stone. There are twenty figures in a line, proceeding from left to right. One of the figures, which stands about a third taller than the others, is being led by a rope or device around its neck. The nineteen other smaller figures have large round heads and small bodies. They appear to carry something that protrudes in front of them. If the taller figure was, say, six feet, the smaller figures would have been about four feet in height. According to the illustration, the artifact is located somewhere in Hallstad or Halsingborg. Was this an early depiction of the grays?

November 3, 1988

Back on October 14 this year, I recorded several dreams about a professional colleague named Randy. I met Randy at the psychophysics lab last year, when we were participating in parapsychological experiments. One of the researchers, Helen, had told Randy I was interested in him, which was true. Yesterday, I had a letter from him in which he said he would be in the New Jersey area over Thanksgiving and wanted to get together with me. As he works for a government contractor, I want to ask him if he knows anything about the abduction phenomenon. I also want to ask him if he let Helen hypnotize him, too, and if she had ever talked to him about alien abduction research.

November 8, 1988

We have had another appearance of the mystery fluid that we discovered around the house. My housemate, Emily, found some of the resiny, oily liquid on a bookshelf, in the downstairs dining room. It was the same oily, volatile, resinlike substance that she found on her dresser the other day and that I found on my table, but we have no idea where it comes from. Emily mopped up the liquid on the bookshelf with a tissue, which still retains the characteristic resin smell.

November 18, 1988

I received an interesting article from Dr. M comparing abduction and nonabduction dreams. Dr. M quoted a "noun-verb" rule, which basically states that nouns of people and things in dreams can generally be interpreted as symbolic, but verbs like "pursue, capture, or probe" are generally what they appear to be. Here is a quote from her paper: "The Noun/Verb rule has an axiom. The objects seen in the dream, i.e., nouns, are ALWAYS symbols and cannot be taken literally . . . to discriminate the abduction dream from an abduction experience check out the level of anxiety, fear, awe, and other feelings . . . to evaluate the dream as a sign of abduction versus no abduction, separate the verbs and nouns . . . dreaming of abduction actions is a positive sign that an actual abduction could have taken place."

Reading this article brought to mind several recent dreams:

> I was screaming. I was being chased. I ran into a large barn or hangar and, with great difficulty, closed the large doors. Several people were trying to push open the doors from outside. I had my body wedged against the door to keep it from opening. I started screaming but realized (in a semilucid state) that other people in the house would be awakened if I screamed too loud. So, I was screaming with my mouth open but no sound came out.
>
> When I awoke, I realized that this dream related to my horror that I might be experiencing alien abduction, my efforts to keep the door on the subject closed, and to keep these experiences out of my conscious mind. There was another dream related to my pursuit of the truth about abductions and that reflected my continued reluctance to go deeper into my dream psyche.
>
> I dreamed I was at a hotel that had been converted to a student's dormitory. The rooms were wood paneled, and various

craft items, like weaving looms, stood around. I opened a basement door, descended some stairs, and found myself on a ledge overlooking a huge lit cavern. There were lots of people walking over the stone slabs of the floor. The walls and floor were smooth like huge rounded pebbles. I felt frightened and scared to jump down into the cave (my subconscious), as it seemed a long way down. Someone gave me some encouragement and I made the leap to the floor. I found to my horror that huge monsters were roaming the floor of the cave. They stalked and chased me. I found refuge with a cluster of people who were reassuring me that there was safety in numbers and that we did not have to face the monsters alone.

November 19, 1988

I recently received some communication from the University of Connecticut from Professor Kenneth Ring, who is carrying out a survey of people who attend UFO conferences. The project consists of answering questionnaires that seem fairly innocuous, and I sent off the reply card to say I would take part. In Ring's words, he believes that "the findings will provide insights which will aid our understanding of the significance and implications of UFO encounters." Kenneth Ring, Ph.D., is professor of psychology at the University of Connecticut and cofounder and past president of the International Association for Near-Death Studies (IANDS). He is the author of two books on the near-death experience, *Life at Death* and *Heading toward Omega*, and many articles dealing with the same subject.

November 20, 1988

As a possible explanation of my preoccupation with extraterrestrial encounters, I would like to mention here three occasions on which my brother and I were almost abducted by humans. It is possible that my preoccupation with alien abduction is centered around unresolved issues related to these events. The first two occasions happened when Alan and I were about five and eight years of age and the third when I was about thirteen and Alan would have been nine years old. The almost-abductions took place in the countryside at isolated places. It is possible that memories and fears generated by these experiences have been translated over into dreams of extraterrestrial origin.

December 9, 1988

It seems that we have developed some poltergeist activity at the house (centered on the room of Sydney, Emily's son) and at the lab, consisting of loud bumps and noises, footsteps on the stairs, doors creaking and opening. These noises may be connected with the appearance of the anomalous resinlike liquid that has appeared three times on wood surfaces in the house.

We think that the poltergeist phenomena may be caused by Sydney's out-of-body experiences (OBEs) when he visits home in an out-of-body state. The disturbances started when we were burgled and Sydney may have wanted to check home and see if all was okay. The disturbances usually follow a set pattern: the sound of the front-porch door squeaking, heavy footsteps on the stairs, sometimes heavy footsteps in the living room downstairs; noises from Sydney's room like drawers being pulled out. Emily and I have heard these noises independently. Another colleague, TJ, heard them when both Emily and I were out. Also, we ruled out the cats as the source of the disturbances, because they were not in the rooms when the noises were evident. This has been happening for several months now and may possibly fade away as Sydney's anxiety decreases.

December 25, 1988

I have had several dreams with a medical theme that involved needles.

A male colleague, SO, was having several large needles put into the roof of his mouth to numb it for some sort of examination. I was watching with horror and wondering if I would have to have the same thing done to me, too.

This dream may be related to events that occurred when James and I experienced some missing time back in June on our way back home from a conference in New York state. I told James about the needle dream and his comment was that he "hated needles," and that "they were invasive and went too deeply into my body." He reacted as if he was experiencing anxiety as I related my dream to him.

In a second dream, a small person was putting a needle into my right hand, into a vein. Then I was given a device to insert a shot into my left forearm. Neither the needle nor the shot in the forearm hurt at all. I lay waiting for the effects of the shots, wondering what would happen.

I drew the needlelike device. It had a gray plastic outer casing, stood about three inches tall, and its edges were rounded. It felt heavy. It was somehow spring-loaded and delivered a medication through a needle when pressed against the skin. It made a sort of popping sound and needed little pressure to activate it. I have never seen anything like this used in regular medical practice.

As I write this, I remember that about a week ago I noticed a small triangular-shaped puncture wound to the skin on my left forearm. It looked like the sort of trauma that results from an IV needle used to draw blood or give fluids. It healed in a day or two. The trauma did not hurt. I do not remember getting scratched by the cats on that arm. Anyway, cat scratches look different. Maybe last night's dream reflected a memory of an interface which resulted in skin trauma?

December 26, 1988

I dreamed that I was down at Lake Carnegie in Princeton, New Jersey, watching rowing crews on the lake. I was with my boyfriend from California, Andy. I suggested that we go up onto the bridge to get a better view. As we started up toward the bridge, we saw construction scaffolding through which there was a tunnel running up to the bridge. As we neared the bridge, the tunnel roof began to drop stones and rubble onto us. Andy and I turned around to go back down the tunnel, which now resembled a church nave with a high roof and stained glass windows. I was lucid and knew that I was dreaming. I knew that the falling stones would not hurt me and that I would get out of the tunnel alive. Andy broke a window and got out on one side, but the window became double panes with plastic. I had to kick out a window on the opposite side of the nave and managed to get to safety.

This was a strange dream and probably relates to my growing relationship with Andy. We are living far apart, and coupled with my reluctance to marry again, it may have fueled this symbolic dream. It could also reflect my anxiety as to how I can share my abduction research with Andy without sounding too weird.

December 27, 1988

I dreamed that I met psychologist Dr. M and that I traveled with her by train to Westchester on Long Island. There she showed me some film that at first she claimed was of a UFO. As I watched the film, the unfocused object that at first looked like a cigar-shaped UFO was revealed to be a life-size model of the space shuttle. Dr. M admitted that this model was used for the promotion of real-estate sales in New York State.

I realized how easy it is to be fooled by appearances in a dream. What does this tell me about my impressions of Dr. M? Maybe not to take things too seriously before looking more closely?

I also dreamed that during the night Emily shouted up the stairs that she could hear strange noises. However, it was a vague dream. I was also discussing with someone a way to try and communicate with aliens. One way was to write questions on a piece of paper and tie it around my neck. I commented to my dream companion that the aliens were still trying to decipher the symbols on the amulet I used to wear at night.

I stopped wearing the amulet, because I always found it on the floor in the morning. Also, one morning I awoke to find my nightdress neatly folded at the bottom of the bed!

December 29, 1988

My dream of two days ago turned out to be precognitive. I had a letter today from Dr. M, which was written on the 27th. In her letter she mentions that she wants to include some of my UFO dreams and experiences as part of a book she is writing. My dream was telling me to examine things a little more closely and not to look at surface appearances. I have decided to write and tell her my decision that I do not want any of my dreams or experiences used in her publications. This is because I feel very uncomfortable with her doing this. I originally sent my notes for her professional opinion, but now I feel that my writing could be open to misinterpretation. I am still not convinced I was ever abducted. As soon as I made my decision, earlier this evening, I felt a lessening of anxiety and knew that my decision was the right one.

December 31, 1988

Later this evening while Emily and her boyfriend, George, were out having a meal, I heard a thud sound downstairs and the creak of a door in the house. All the cats were outside. I was not sure if it came from Sydney's room or from downstairs. Initially, I felt scared but reminded myself that the noises were only stray psychokinetic energy.

Psychokinetic energy, or PK, relates to the ability of certain individuals to be able to move things with their minds. Spoon bending and poltergeist activity are two examples of this type of mind-matter interaction. In the general population, the incidence of PK is widespread but the effects are often small and associated with emotion. For example, two lovers could be holding hands at a Mexican restaurant. Between them on the table sits an aluminum bowl of chips. As their eyes meet and they talk excitedly to each other, the chip bowl starts to spin. Neither one of them has physically touched the bowl. As soon as they notice the spinning chip bowl, it stops spinning.

Some labs, like the parapsychology lab in New Jersey, have been studying controlled PK, but the majority of PK remains uncontrolled. Many teenagers and young adults show evidence of "stray PK" when phenomena break out in their homes, such as lights switching on and off, strange noises and smells, and objects moving around. The phenomena usually cease as the young person matures.

5

Symbols and Paradoxes

"The day will come, undoubtedly, when the phenomenon will be observed with technological means of detection and collection that won't leave a single doubt about its origin. This should lift part of the veil that has covered the mystery for a long time. A mystery that continues to the present. But it exists, it is real, and that in itself is an important conclusion."

—Major General Wilfred de Brouwer, deputy chief, Royal Belgian Air Force, *"Postface" I SOBEPS's Vague d'OVNI sur la Belgique—Un Dossier Exceptionnel*, Brussels: SOBEPS, 1991.

January 1, 1989

1988 was a momentous year of personal growth. 1988 began with a major move and changes, both in terms of living and working arrangements. Last Christmas I was offered a position at the parapsychology lab and I readily accepted. I moved permanently, in February of 1988, and found lodging at the home of Emily and her son, Sydney. The lab and my personal life seem intertwined; it is not definite where one ends and the other begins, and there have been some major personal changes taking place.

For many years, I have maintained an exterior facade of order, possibly to be free to be chaotic inside, to dream, to fantasize, to have psychic experiences. Now I am at a point in my life where it feels okay to be a little chaotic on the outside too. In the past, I had to hide my abilities, both my high intelligence and my psychic abilities, because of nonacceptance by parents, teachers, work. Now, having found a place of acceptance at the lab, I can use all of my abilities to their full potential, free from restrictions. At the lab, I have been given the opportunity to explore my full potential.

In October I attended a conference on UFOs in Connecticut, met some very interesting people, and heard some fascinating talks. My motivation for attending the conference was my growing awareness that many of my anomalous experiences correspond to those described by individuals claiming to have experienced alien abductions. I have been exploring these relationships through my dreams and memory analysis. I am still not convinced of the reality of the abduction scenario and my role in it, but I will continue my explorations.

New friends have figured prominently during this past year, particularly colleagues at the lab who have given me the freedom, both professionally and personally, to explore my abilities and my self. This New Year, I have made only one New Year's resolution: not to make any New Year's resolutions!

January 5, 1989

When I awoke I had the feeling that the dream I had been having was connected with my UFO dream research but I forgot the dream. However, when I was getting ready for work I remembered a real dream that had a medical theme.

I was at a medical facility and I was lying on a narrow examination table. There was a row of such tables, but there were no curtains for privacy. I was experiencing some stomach pains. I felt very alone. A "doctor" came and gave me a shot of yellow dye. It hurt and stung. I asked her why she had done that. It turned out that there was a mix-up over my identity, and I had to convince them who I was. They were wanting to do some kind of procedure, but I insisted that it was my stomach that was the problem. As the dream continued, I was getting up, dressing, and trying to find my way home.

January 7, 1989

All this week I have been thinking about times during the last few years when there may have been dreams and experiences related to a possible abduction. A particular occasion came to mind several times during the week, one that I would forget soon after. This seemed strange, so as soon as I remembered the occasion again today I decided to write it down.

The occasion took place back in 1978 in my last year at Cardiff University. One day I remember feeling very strange, anxious, and unsettled—it is hard to find the right words. I wandered around the university, looking for someone or something, not knowing what or who I was looking for. I felt very alone, even though I had many friends, and felt as if either something momentous had happened and I could not remember it, or that something momentous was about to happen. It was a weird day and totally unexplainable.

Further memories have emerged as I extend my memory search. When I was about eight years old I went through a period of drawing people with very large eyes. The eyes dominated the faces of these drawings and the heads were unusually large for the bodies. They resembled, in these respects, the reported characteristics of the gray aliens reported by abductees. This was in 1954, long before the current popularization of drawings and descriptions of the grays. Later, in my teens, I wrote a lot of poetry and prose. Some of the poetry I wrote was about feeling alone and vulnerable at night. Did these poems reflect the anxiety, sense of aloneness, and helplessness of the abduction victim or just a young teenager exploring ideas and feelings?

January 8, 1989

As I was drifting off to sleep last night, another incident came back to me, but I was too tired to get up and write it down. I remembered it again when I awoke this morning. The incident relates to an acquisition of information that researchers of alien abduction call information loading.

When I was about sixteen or seventeen, I was walking from where I lived in Dorset, England, to visit some exotic bird gardens. The walk was about two or three miles. During the walk I was mulling over several philosophical questions, mainly about life in general. Suddenly, as if my mind had opened up, I experienced a flow of information. Some of this answered my questions, but the bulk of it I did not even understand.

The information flowed in for several minutes. I was a deeply religious person at that time and thought that God had sent me this wisdom, even though I could not comprehend its content. I felt very blessed, chosen, and happy. Nobody has been able to fully explain it, but I have met several people who have had the same or a similar experience. It is possible that I tapped into what the ancients called the Akashic Library (which contains all the information that ever was, is, and will be). Another alternative that has been suggested to me was that the information had an alien source.

My friend B called me yesterday, and we talked for a while about abductions. She mentioned that she has a friend who has possibly had these experiences. The friend has written down many symbols she has remembered from her experiences. I mentioned to B that I had a long-term interest in symbols and that my current study of the runes stems from that interest. B said she would send me some of her friend's drawings. I remembered that MK, one of the people I had met at the Connecticut UFO conference, had mentioned that she too had been interested in ancient symbols from a young age. Does this fascination with symbolic language have any correlation with the abduction scenario?

Looking back at my own past and possible symbols that have had some meaning for me, I can think of several, as well as the runes. These have encompassed crosses, spirals, and mazes; bell shapes; divided circles of all kinds, especially the yin/yang symbol; and curved signs like the treble clef and the English pound sign.

Last night I had several dreams that were not overtly UFO-related, but one seemed very interesting. It centered around a white-haired man I have met several times at scientific conferences, whom I will call X. I was at the train station waiting to meet X, my enigmatic friend from Washington, D.C. It was raining, quite a storm. Several people were there, but I was able to recognize him.

I was trying to identify him as the white-haired man who has appeared in several other abduction dreams, but I was not able to come to any conclusions. X has an active interest in UFO research and has conducted animal studies as a preliminary to possible alien communication. . . .

I remembered a dream from December 19th in which I commented to Emily that the aliens were still trying to decipher the symbols on the amulet I used to wear at night. I decided I would start wearing it again and would try to decipher the symbols myself.

The amulet consists of a circular pewter medallion I bought at a Renaissance Festival last summer. The amulet seems to be relevant to my current life and learning. Its stated function is an aid to "communicating with animals" and it contains Celtic, Chinese, Arabic, Judaic, and astrological symbols.

January 9, 1989

Early this morning before I went to work, I got a call from Betty-Sue from the UFO club. She was the woman who felt Helen had messed with her mind. She wanted to know if Helen, who had since left the psychophysics lab, had given me her address. Betty-Sue said she wanted to return a book. I did not feel comfortable giving her this information, and I said I would let her know if I found it, which was true, because I did not have Helen's address handy.

I have taken a preliminary look at my dream journal marking verbs, using Dr. M's noun/verb rule. She says that certain verbs may indicate an abduction experience.

These are, as dated:

<u>1988</u>

June 26:	shaken, anxiety, upset, embarrassed
August 8:	high state of panic
September 14:	chasing
September 28:	instructing, poking
October 3:	shivering
October 6:	urge to hide
October 10:	tremendous fear
October 11:	fear down my spine
October 13:	restrained, biting, hitting, screaming, crying, walking
October 14:	very frightened
October 15:	hovering, floating, observing, chased
October 17:	flying
October 19:	aliens appearing, cutting, looking, acknowledging
October 21:	probing, tracing
October 22:	alking, crying, fleeing, hurrying, catching, lifting, choosing, objecting

As yet I have not looked at any earlier dreams and I am not drawing any conclusions. After all, Freud said, "Sometimes a cigar is just a cigar!"

January 11, 1989

Today I have been trying to remember dreams that have contained an element of great fear and terror. One came to mind that I experienced three or four years ago. Dr. M states that the emotional content of dreams can indicate actual experiences, and may be abduction experiences.

In the dream, I am visiting a house. It has a lower story, all one long room with windows. The lower room is empty, like a barn. There are stairs up to a higher room, which is also one long room, except that up at one end is a raised floor, like a stage. As I approach this area, I see that it has a boxlike structure on it, and this causes me to experience indescribable terror.

This dream has stayed with me and I have tried to analyze the fear by doing a visualization exercise to look at the box. In the exercise, I approach the box and it becomes a coffin. Inside the coffin lies a dead nun. I am still not sure what the dead nun symbolizes and why it should cause me such terror. I am quite familiar with the dead, having prepared many dead bodies as part of my nursing duties in England. To me, nuns symbolize spirituality and celibacy. Is the box actually a table upon which I experienced the end of my innocence at the hands of some alien medics, causing me to experience such terror?

January 12, 1989

I have decided to take a further look back at the dream diaries I kept from 1978 onward to look for elements of extreme emotion according to Dr. M's theory:

<u>1978</u>

November 25: anxious and worried
November 30: bewildered and frightened
December 1: frightened, appalled, running away
December 11: frustrated and angry
December 14: shocked and hurt and angry at a doctor
December 18: panic and alarm
December 21: anxiety, feelings of inadequacy, panic, fright

<u>1979</u>

January 1: confused and angry
January 7: nauseated and unpleasant
January 13: anxious and uneasy
January 19: anxious and frightened

January 20:	anxious and insecure
January 26:	crying and yelling I panic
January 27:	very anxious
January 28:	resentful, hurt, and angry

This is just a small section from the end of November 1978 to the end of January 1979, but I am amazed at the feelings repeated over and over again: confusion, anxiety, anger, fear, frustration, which outnumber the positive emotions of confidence and pride. The diaries were written during a relatively stable and happy time of my life. I had an interesting research position at Manchester University in England, interesting friends, and a reasonable standard of living. It seems strange that these negative dream emotions should be so prevalent.

The purpose of the 1978–79 dream diaries was for personal growth. At that time, I was doing daily meditations of "letting go" via imagery and symbolism of unnecessary "mental blockages." Maybe as I was consciously "letting go," my subconscious was also able to let go of unpleasant associations. I pursued the dream diaries and found references to relief at being released from some situation, being distressed, being chased and caught, and the deep sense of loss over the death of an infant.

So the emotional content of the dream diaries goes on. I must have been blocking the emotional content of the dreams because I was under the impression that my dream diaries were fairly neutral, on the whole. It has surprised me greatly that I have revealed such negativity within my dreams of that time. What it all means, I am not sure. I am also planning to go back through my regular diaries from 1972 to see if I can reveal any answers to these questions.

January 13, 1989

As far back as I can remember, I have been an "observer of life," watching nature and people. I have had an insatiable curiosity about everything. I have always wanted to know what makes people tick, what makes the flowers grow, why things are. I have recognized that part of my personality could be called the "observer." I always thought I was unique in this respect. However, over the past few months I have met several women, who like me, have been puzzling over the abduction question. They have also recognized the "observer" phenomenon.

Since I was a child, I have had dreams of a phoenix-like bird, which I have come to recognize as my spiritual nature. Recently, at the UFO conference in Connecticut, I learned that the phoenix and flying dragon are symbols that are often reported by abductees under hypnosis. The symbols are seen as badges and emblems worn by the aliens on their clothing.

The phoenix symbolizes something that rises from the ashes or destruction of something else. For me, the phoenix symbolizes the spiritual side of my nature, which has had to undergo several major metamorphoses during my life. In dreams in which I fly, I literally become the phoenix. I cannot remember reading about the phoenix when I was very young, so my early phoenix dreams could be an archetype. It was interesting, however, to learn about the phoenix symbol in regard to aliens.

January 14, 1989

Tonight, I did a session of free associating, a method that I find helpful in looking at partially hidden memories. As far back as I can remember, I have had flying dreams, have dreamed of the phoenix, and have felt very attached to butterflies. For me, butterflies have symbolized the power to fly and escape the confines of the physical body.

More free association: as a young girl, between the ages of ten and sixteen, while we were still living in Bristol, England, I had a strange incident. I had a very bad habit of sitting in my bedroom window after I had been put to bed and reading by the dying light. I would read anything, even the cereal box at the breakfast table. I was hungry for words and information. I would read until it got so dark that I could not read any longer. I had gotten hold of a book of horror stories and was avidly reading it. The memory of the event is patchy, but one horror story I was reading became very real and I seemed to live the story. I do not remember the actual story, but I remember a picture of a man awakened from sleep by some monster of the night. I must have fallen asleep and maybe dreamed the horror story. When I awoke it was dark and I climbed into bed and went to sleep. However, the images that remain with me are of large eyes, the horror-stricken, awakened sleeper, and the large eyes of the monster. The recollection of large eyes ties in with the abduction scenario.

I have discovered that if I open a blank page of my journal and let my mind roam, it throws up all sorts of lost or forgotten memories. I have been using this free-association method to look at situations that could have some bearing on my UFO memory and dream search. I have been doing this exercise for the past week, and it has yielded a lot of interesting memories. Whether they have anything to do with the abduction phenomenon I am not so sure.

When I was about ten years old in grade school in England, we had Friday afternoon craft classes. We could choose painting, music, orchestra, or puppetry. One year I decided to try puppetry. We made glove puppets out of papier-mâché over clay, which we painted and dressed. I remember that my puppet had a large head, large eyes, and I decided to leave it bald. That would have been my choice, but the teacher persuaded me to put cotton hair on the puppet's head.

During those early years, we were encouraged by the headmistress to write and produce our own plays. I produced one about a girl who was kidnapped and had to be rescued. Shades of abduction or too many fairy tales?

Connections have been made in the UFO literature between angels, fairies, and aliens. I thought I would look at my own history in light of this. In grade school, I was always given the part of the Archangel Gabriel in the Christmas play. I was never Mary, a wise man, or a shepherd, but always the chief angel. I feel the choice was made because I was tall, blond, and slim, just as Phillip, the only black child in the school, was always cast as one of the wise men.

However, from such early role casting, I have had an ongoing affinity with the idea of angels. I like the quotation attributed to Saint Augustine, who saw Anglo-Saxons sold as slaves in early England. He is reported as saying "Not Angles, but angels!" because he was taken by their beauty.

Historically, angels have been considered higher beings of light who function as messengers. The Greeks called them angelos; the Hebrew called them Malach; and in Arabic, they were called Malak. Another category of beings known to the Arabic world was referred to collectively as Al-Jinn. According to Arab history, this term is derived from the root-verb Janna, which means to "hide or conceal." Jinns (sometimes spelled Djinn) were thought to have originated from a distant location, perhaps even from some other space dimension. Historical references exist from the Orient that indicate that some Jinns were fully physical entities. There is speculation whether the Jinns were good or bad. Some of the Jinns were considered to be devils or Shaytans, while in other records, particularly in the Qur'an, they were considered benevolent. The following characteristics of Jinns have been collected by Gordon Creighton, in his *Angels, Men and Jinns. The True Nature of UFO Entities* (Kent, U.K.: FRS Publications, 1983):

1. In their normal state, they are not visible to ordinary human sight; however, they are capable of materializing and appearing in the physical world.
2. They can alternatively make themselves visible or invisible at will.
3. They can change shape and appear in any sort of form, large or small.
4. They are capable of appearing in the guise of animals.
5. They are known to lie and deceive.
6. They are known to abduct and kidnap humans.
7. They are known to attempt sexual liaisons with humans.

Creighton emphasizes that in Islamic cultures, the existence of the Jinns has always been accepted and, even today, it is accepted by Islamic law. He gives us more information about the Jinns:

1. The Jinns were known to snatch up humans, teleport or transport them, and then set them back down miles from where they were picked up.
2. Sometimes these abductions took place outside the limits of our knowledge of time. For example, the transportation would take place instantaneously, or "in the twinkling of an eye."
3. According to Arabic tradition, there have always been some humans who have worked in league with the Jinns. Some humans were thought to have an unusual alliance with the Jinns.
4. The Jinns have been known to empower some humans with psychic abilities following their interaction.
5. The Jinns were said to possess telepathic powers, and to be able to entrance humans.

Are the gray aliens the modern equivalent of the Jinns?

Janary 20, 1989

Today, my colleague B came to visit Princeton. She brought with her some drawings that were done by one of her friends. B is a psychotherapist, and she felt that her friend may have experienced an abduction. The friend's drawings consist of symbols that she felt compelled to draw. They do not correspond to any commonly known symbolic language. I told B I would look at them, compare them with the runes and other symbols that I know, and give her some feedback.

While I was looking at the symbols (which felt very familiar to me), I got to thinking about the time in college (between 1975 and 1978) when I was doodling and "thought up" a numerical system using lines only, no circular shapes. There was a seven-element system and a ten-element system. The numbers one through seven in the seven-element system were represented by gradually evolving pyramid shapes. In the ten-element system, the numbers one through ten were represented by gradually evolving box shapes with lines radiating from a cross-hatched box. Where did these concepts come from?

Looking at B's friend's drawings, I saw correspondences with my number system but her drawings also had circles and curved representations. I noticed definite runic symbols in her drawings, such as Gebu, a runic X that indicates union, partnership, and gifts from the gods. Europeans use the X symbol to signify kisses and put them on personal letters. I also noticed the rune symbol Kano, an open <, which indicates light and opening, and is associated with the Goddess cult of Nerthus. There was Othila, a diamond shape, interpreted as property, or land, a person's native home or land, as well as the rune Sowelu, shaped like a lightning bolt, symbolizing wholeness, the life force, and the Sun's energy. Lastly, there was Eihwaz, a rune shaped like a long letter I with fish-hooks on each end, facing in opposite directions. The runic interpretation of Eihwaz is defense and powers to avert. I have also noticed some of these same rune symbols in the depictions of crop circles.

January 23, 1989

While Emily and George were away in Hawaii, there were some strange occurrences, possibly psychokinetic in nature, at Emily's house. I perceived these as dark, peripheral shadows. Also, Emily's alarm clock (which she says she never sets) kept going off at various times, day and night, and eventually I had to unplug it, because it was bothering me.

January 25, 1989

The real dreams have been quiet these past few weeks, but last night there were various medical dreams that seemed very real.

These dreams portrayed a gynecological examination (which I did not want) that involved a needlelike instrument and a painful, punching action to take "samples." The "biopsy needle" was attached to some kind of flushing system. It was very painful and I felt faint. One person was performing the procedure. She was short and plump. There was some sort of video device through which I could view what was happening inside me. The monitor display was in color. After the initial procedure, there was another procedure to put a needle through the abdomen wall, but I do not think this was completed. When I awoke in the morning (later than my normal time), I was bleeding.

February 11, 1989

About a month ago, Emily and I were discussing a colleague, Mariah Folger, who had experienced some abductions. Mariah Folger is a pseudonym this colleague uses to talk about her abduction experiences. Emily had asked Mariah if I could read her manuscript of her experiences, and she had agreed. In turn, I agreed to send Mariah some notes on my own experiences, which have grown to a large manuscript. I received a long letter back from Mariah, which basically confirmed that we had shared a great number of similar experiences. Mariah asked if she could share my manuscript with X.

I received a call from Randy, whom I had met at the psychophysics lab, and we had a long telephone visit. Randy is currently working as a computer security consultant for the government and was off to give a talk in London at the end of the week. He told me that he had recently interviewed for a job at a computer security think tank.

I am fascinated with X. It is interesting that he has appeared in the dreams of other women who have had abduction experiences. Later, these same women have met him in waking reality. I met X for the first time last year at a conference in New York, where he talked about his paranormal work. This January there was a small piece in a New Age magazine about his work, and it seems his goal is to locate a sunken UFO.

Yesterday, I sent a letter to Mariah to affirm that it is okay for X to look at my manuscript. X also called the lab, and I confirmed to him that he could read the manuscript. It seems that he and Mariah are long-time friends and colleagues.

During this past six months, I have heard firsthand from two women who believe that they were pregnant but that their pregnancies suddenly ended without any product: no miscarriage and no fetus. The pregnancies were accompanied by dreams of alien visitation, examination, and other anomalous phenomena. One of the women had a previous hysterectomy but had all the symptoms of pregnancy. Looking back at my own history, there have been occasions when I have missed several periods but never got into pregnancy. I felt that I was immune from the UFO pregnancy syndrome because I was never pregnant long enough.

However, the other evening I was watching a TV program on cattle insemination and breeding in which fertilized ova are taken from the wombs of incubating cattle and are transferred to the wombs of other cattle to be carried to term. The scientists involved in the process said that the optimal time for transfer of the ovum was seven days past fertilization. If the aliens are following this sort of procedure, as some say they are, it may happen that a woman could have her period a week or so late and still have been pregnant.

When I consider my own menstrual history of a forty-day cycle, rather than the usual twenty-eight to thirty-one days, it might be possible that my dreams of gynecological intervention indicate an insemination, fertilization, and harvest of fertilized eggs. My logical mind rejects this scenario as unrealistic.

February 12, 1989

I seem to have developed a fairly substantial correspondence in the UFO and abduction field and met some fascinating people. I had a longer letter back from Mariah and a letter yesterday from MK from Maryland. Mariah had some interesting ideas. She feels that negative terminology, such as abduction, abductees, and aliens, needs to be changed to visitation, participation, and Visiting Others, or VOs.

Mariah has developed a Rule of Six, which means that all experiences and occurrences have at least six, possibly sixty, and maybe six hundred alternative explanations. Mariah and I have shared many similar experiences, and these match the experiences of many other women. Mariah felt that the reflecting bubble, seen by a colleague and me as we returned home from the lab, was a marker or sensor for something larger. Mariah also had a white-haired man appear in her dreams.

Mariah feels that I will eventually remember what I have learned from my experiences. Mariah has also experienced selective amnesia and feels that my dreams of the dead nun represent the loss of my virginity in an almost celibate, medical context. The real dream, in which I felt a "hot iron" applied to the small of my back, was also experienced by Mariah's son. Mariah felt this "hot iron" application was a common practice of the Visitors.

Continuing with the comparisons between Mariah's and my experiences, she feels she has had problems with having to identify herself, because during interfaces, wrong procedures are about to be performed on her. Mariah believes she has an implant in her right eye and that this might explain the observer phenomenon.

I had another letter yesterday from MK in Maryland. The letter was vague and courteous. Maybe she feels that she went too far in telling me about her own experiences and wants to keep her distance. In my last letter, I had asked about her UFO dream symbols, but she said she had passed on my request to Dr. M. She did not say whether she had contacted X, who lives in her neighborhood. She had asked me about him the last time she wrote, and I passed on his phone number. MK suggested that I read Ruth Montgomery's *Aliens among Us*.

February 15, 1989

I awoke late, because I had forgotten to set my radio alarm. Before I woke, I was having a dream that made me very anxious.

It was night and I found myself outside of a building. I knew that was where I was working but did not recognize it on waking. I found myself locked out, without money or keys, and no memory of how I got outside the building. Then I found my wallet with the card section and knew that, somewhere in there, was a magnetic card that would open the back door. I walked around the building, trying to find the card in my wallet. I was very anxious that the wallet would get stolen, because it was a dark and isolated spot. The back door turned out to be the back door of the cooperative store in the village where I grew up. I was fumbling with the card, when along came a calm, serene woman who had a key. It was Mariah. She opened the door. I told her I had a magnetic card, and she answered, "But you don't know if it works." We went up several staircases and I reached another closed door, but it was not locked.

I awoke this morning with very stiff muscles, a headache, and a small, itchy blister on the inside of my left upper arm. The dream before the locked-out dream was a medical one. I was helping to splint a man's arm because it was thought to be broken. I feel these dreams reflect my anxiety about the abduction process and my hope that Mariah will help me find some answers. Perhaps she has the key?

February 16, 1989

Dr. M sent me a photocopy of a document that was supposed to be a script found on a crashed flying saucer found at Aztec, Arizona. The script was eventually turned over to Dr. William F. Friedman and Lambros P. Callihamos for study and interpretation. I will call Dr. M to find out more details. After I excluded obvious terrestrial symbols, such as numbered paragraphs, brackets, and inverted commas, there still remained an intriguing residue of unusual symbols. Many of these symbols resembled the Viking and Germanic rune glyphs.

The first symbol I noticed as runelike was Uruz, which represents strength. The symbol, seen as both a triangular shape standing on its base and an inverted V, was dominant throughout the script. According to Ralph Blum, an authority on Germanic and Scandinavian runes, Uruz was one of the precursors to our modern letter "U." The traditional Viking interpretation of this glyph stood for the species of wild ox called auroch. The auroch was sacrificial animal (to the gods and goddesses) and signified strength and energy.

Another rune glyph that appears frequently in the script is Sowelu, a lightning-bolt-shaped symbol representing the sun. Sowelu was the precursor to our modern letter "S." The traditional interpretation was the sun. A similar glyph, occurring a little less often, is the symbol Laguz, representing water. This symbol, looking like a hook-shaped staff, may be written in any one of four positions and may originally have given directions. Laguz was the precursor to our modern letter "L." Also seen was a runic, fish-shaped symbol called Othila, representing hereditary lands, possession of lands and home. It represents our modern letter "O." The rune Naudiz occurs frequently in the text and represents need or necessity. It is represented as a straight or slanted line with another slanted line running through it and was the precursor of our letter "N."

Several other ancient symbols were contained in the text. One was a circle with a dot in the center. It represented the Sun and wealth, as well as gold. According to P. M. H. Atwater, an authority on very early Scandinavian runes, these glyphs were dedicated to the Scandinavian god, Njord, the father of Frey, or Freyja.

Another traditional rune seen frequently in the script was Wunjo, shaped like our modern letter "P." The Viking sense of Wunjo is joy and absence of suffering. There were other isolated rune glyphs occurring in the script, but the aforementioned symbols constituted about 50 percent of the script. Basically, they could be interpreted as: strength, the Sun, water, home, necessity, prosperity, and joy. It is possible that the Aztec script is an old runic manuscript that was mistakenly interpreted as alien.

After looking at the script sent to me by Dr. M, I had another look at the symbols sent to me by B's friend. Here I found similar symbols to the Aztec script: Laguz, or water; Uruz, or strength; and Sowelu, or the Sun.

I have heard that some individuals who have experienced abduction see certain glyphs and symbols during their experiences. Abduction researchers have been keeping records of these possibly to authenticate the abduction experience.

February 17, 1989

Several times this week I tried a visualization exercise to see if I could see (remember?) what the inside of a UFO looked like. What I was able to visualize was a huge semidomed space. It was as huge as an armory, but longer rather than wider. The floor was hard and very shiny, nearer to opaque glass or ice, but not as slippery. The light was greenish and seemed to filter up from the floor. The air had a static-electric feel to it and gave the occasional "pop" sound. There were no seats. I sat cross-legged (in my visualization) on the shiny floor. Overhead were girders supporting a huge, curved roof and, strangely, some sort of batlike creatures flying around the roof. The roof was too high to ascertain its height. There was a door near one end, but as I looked through it, it appeared to be a mortuary or operating room, so I quickly came out. I did not see any aliens or Visitors. Mariah likes to call them the Visiting Others. Why not just call them the Visitors?

February 25, 1989

I have been reading about and hearing stories of abductees who claim to have alien implants in their bodies. I have mixed feelings about these accounts. However, I decided to do a memory search and discovered a combination of sharp and vague memories associated with having my tonsils removed when I was a child.

When I was five years old, I went to the local hospital to have my tonsils removed. It was my first hospital stay, but I have the memories confused with another medical occasion. I asked my mother about these memories, and she says there was no examination like the one I remembered. Until I was older, I confused these memories and thought that a doctor had taken out my tonsils while I sat at the table. Maybe on that occasion I had an implant put in or taken out. Or the memories could have come from the overactive imagination of a scared five-year-old in hospital for the first time.

February 26, 1989

There is speculation from many cultures that our human race emerged from the intervention of extraterrestrials with the primitive people who lived at the beginning of time. Back in 1981 I was studying the *Wisdom of Solomon* from the books called Apocrypha contained in the *Oxford Annotated Bible*, and recorded the following in my journal:

> The *Wisdom of Solomon* 14:6: "For in the old time also when the proud giants perished,
> the hope of the world governed by Thy hand escaped in a weak vessel and left to all ages a seed of generation."
>
> *Genesis* 6:4 : "There were giants in the earth in those days and also after that when the sons of God came in unto the daughters of men and they bare children to them, the same became mighty men, which were of old, men of renown."

As part of my memory search, I found another dream in a journal dated December 3, 1983, a dream that takes on a new significance with my abduction research. I dreamed that I was taken to a seaside cabin. I was taken there by a man of my own age, tall, fair-haired and bearded. He was pleasant and kind. The cabin was large, furnished, and on one level. He left me at the cabin with a group of "children," and then he went out. The "children" were ugly, deformed, malnourished, and not at all attractive.

Several times this last weekend I have remembered hidden material and intended to write it down. However, I "forgot" each time. I am taking a few minutes before I go to sleep to see if anything surfaces, but nothing does.

February 27, 1989

I remembered that before the medical dream on January 25, I was lying in a bed (not my own) and summoned by another woman. It was a small narrow room and I was lying on a small narrow bed. There was a door to the left of the bed.

A while back in this journal I wrote that I felt I was immune from the phantom pregnancy syndrome as I had never been pregnant. This is not the case, however, as I was blocking out several very important events. I was married to my first husband in 1968 in England. During the year we were married, I missed several periods in a row and "felt" pregnant. Our family doctor felt that it was too early to jump to conclusions, but said that I was pregnant. I felt sure of it enough to buy baby clothes and a bassinet. Then I got a normal period, and with disappointment, gave the baby clothes to a colleague who was pregnant. It is strange that I should block out this event, as it caused such heartache at the time. Maybe I was meant to forget. If I had been pregnant, the child would now be about twenty years old.

The reason I remembered this was because a colleague and I had been talking about menstrual cycles and the differences between women who had given birth and women who had not. I had always classed myself as a woman who had "never been pregnant," but maybe I was?

There was another occasion, while I was at college in Oxford in 1972, when I missed several periods. I felt then that I was pregnant, and as the months went by, I called the fetus "little fish," then "little monkey," as it went through its developmental stages. Then I had a normal period and there was no baby. I had blocked out this memory, too.

There was also a time in January, 1979, when I may have been pregnant. I had a late period and morning sickness and thought I might be pregnant. I also had a week of bad headaches. Again, the "pregnancy" came to nothing. My Dad said he had seen UFOs over the city where we were living during the month of January.

February 24, 1989

Looking back through my old journals, I found entries that could be linked to my current search for abduction experiences. When I looked through the old journals the first time, I overlooked these entries as unimportant, but in light of what I have learned from other abductees, I now feel they could be important. I wrote in one journal, August 5, 1982:

> When I attempted to meditate I "blocked." I decided to look for my old dream diaries. However, I got distracted again and started sorting papers. It is as if my mind does not want to relive something. The word "terrible" comes to mind! But I feel—I believe—that whatever has happened, I should be aware of what has happened. I should be aware of it in this life.
>
> I am awakening to my whole self and this life is only a part of that self. I am a reasonably sane, calm, and mature individual, and I have the inner resources to handle whatever I discover. It may not be so terrible, seen in the light of time and experience.
>
> At the time that I wrote these words I felt these hidden memories were associated with a past lifetime. Now I feel that they might be associated with the abduction scenario.

Another entry from September 19, 1983:

> Lately I have been having vivid, vigorous dreams. Upon waking, I have been able to analyze these dreams, which are then forgotten. Even though I cannot later recall the dreams themselves, I remember the analyses and feel this is a valuable exercise. Most of the analyses have to do with continued healing of the psyche and self.

March 2, 1989

I found a profound quote I feel gives me strength to pursue my quest of the alien abduction phenomenon. "Have the courage to seek truth, the strength to stand alone, and the wisdom to be taught by all experience." I do not know the author.

March 3, 1989

I awoke in the night after having many dreams. I recognized that these related to my UFO abduction search, but I forgot the actual dreams, except one. In the dream, I was in my bed and someone was trying to pull me out of it. I was resisting vigorously, screaming and shouting, "Leave me alone, get off me, go away, leave me alone." I was struggling violently.

In a recent letter from Mariah Folger, she wrote that she decided to ask the Visitors for an artifact that she and X could share and recognize but that would not cause danger of recognition to the Visitors. I also decided to see what would happen if I asked the Visitors for an artifact. When I asked them, mentally, for an artifact, there was a shocked silence in my mind, then the response, "But you have never asked for anything before." When I asked if I could share the artifact with a few close friends, there was a sense of chaos, as if there were no protocols to cover such a request.

Today Mariah called and I asked her how I should proceed from here. She suggested asking for the return of some of the items that had disappeared, such as my amethyst pendant and my gold pyramid earrings. That request seemed to go down a little better. We will see if anything turns up. I have checked my jewelry box but nothing has shown up yet.

I had telephone calls and letters from Mariah and X regarding the Visitors. Mariah suggested that we get together for a meeting in May. There would be the three of us plus several others. There are many areas we could discuss, such as alien technology and medical concerns, but we will finalize these issues nearer the time. Mariah feels this would be a good time to meet and discuss many of these controversial topics. In her last letter, she put forward plans toward eventual and overt contact with the Visitors, but we both feel we are a long way from that point. My reactions are:

1. Mariah and X are taking this thing very seriously.
2. They do not think my ideas are crazy.
3. They both stress that the Visitors are like us in many ways, with good and bad points, but are not necessarily either evil or benefactors. We need cooperation between both them and us.
4. There would be a sharing of private information at any meeting that we held and many questions might be answered.
5. Things are moving, but maybe just a little too fast for me.

I found a poem I had written in 1983. I remember feeling almost guilty when writing it, as if I was betraying my human heritage by even thinking such thoughts. I hid the notebook, because I did not want anyone to see what I had written. I half suspected at the time that there might be some element of truth in what I had written but did not want to acknowledge it to myself or to anyone else.

Somewhere out there in the starry sky
Lies a land where I belong.
Past the planets, revolving slow,
Traveling alone on a song.
Such an empty feeling is here in my heart,
An ache, a craving, a need
To see this place from whence I came
When I was but a seed.
Such foolishness to have such thoughts
Why, I a mortal am,
Not an angel bright with flaming sword.
Just me: I am.

March 4, 1989

Over the past few days, I have continued to look back at old diaries and journals from 1976 and I have concluded that for a long time I have had a fascination with UFOs. I found lots of old clippings and notes about seeing UFO films such as *Close Encounters of the Third Kind* and finding it fascinating. There have been times of unexplained sadness and confusion and feelings of alienation. There was a growing awareness of my role as a catalyst in other people's lives.

In this month's *OMNI*, on the letters page was a communication from Ellen Crystal, who is the publisher of a magazine called *Contactee: The First Organization for Research of UFOs by Direct Observation*. Ellen Crystal's group has been trying to initiate overt contact with the Visitors. I have written to Ms. Crystal for more information.

March 5, 1989

I did some more free associating to look for suppressed memories. I rediscovered several memories that could have a missing time element and another of a possible UFO sighting.

When my ex-husband Randolph and I were on our honeymoon in the Dominican Republic, we were loaned a lovely beach house. We went snorkeling at the reef just off shore. One day, Randolph went out snorkeling and was gone for about eight hours. I was beside myself with worry and imagined myself becoming a widow on my honeymoon. Randolph eventually returned and said that he had only been snorkeling and couldn't have been away for eight hours. He was not that energetic a person.

When we returned from our honeymoon, we drove up to New York State to collect Randolph's young children, who had been staying with friends. It was the third week of March. We ran into a huge snowstorm, in which you could not see twelve inches beyond the windshield. Even though the snow slowed us down considerably, we should not have been five hours late. Maybe the Visitors were curious about my new husband and wanted to check him out too?

Last October, after attending the UFO conference in Connecticut, I thought I saw a UFO over Nassau Street in Princeton. It looked very much like the Gulf Breeze craft, like a lampshade, but without the lights, as it was daytime. It was gray in color but not shiny. There were heavy clouds and I saw it below the clouds. I became excited, because I thought I was going to see a real UFO. As I watched, it changed shape into a regular plane shape. I wonder how many UFOs seen by reputable observers are just misidentified terrestrial aircraft?

March 7, 1989

There were two major symbolic dreams last night, plus many others I could not remember. These reflect my anger and anxiety about the abduction phenomenon.

In my dream, Sydney, Emily's son, called to me that he wanted to use my computer. I said, "No, I am sleeping." He came into my room anyway, and I became angry with him. He was complaining to his mother because I said he could not use my computer. He said that we had come to an agreement, which we had not. Then Emily and I were fighting.

I feel that this dream is a release of anger and frustration I have felt about the Visitors coming during the night and at Emily because of her disinclination to discuss the alien abduction phenomenon. We don't usually fight, but I obviously felt some negative feelings toward her in the dream.

In the second dream, a film crew had come down to the parapsychology lab to do a surrealist Monty Python type of movie and we were chosen to take part as actors. I was saying to S how pleased I was to have been chosen, as actors are usually auditioned for the parts. One of my roles was to choose a "hidden man" character. In keeping with the surreal aspect of the movie, I chose a very tall man I met outside a diner. My choice was rejected, and a small woman was chosen instead. She flew from lamppost to lamppost, getting progressively larger. X was also involved somewhere in this dream, but I forgot his role when I awoke.

I feel that this dream signifies my impression that several of my colleagues have been involved in participation with the Visitors. Maybe it reflects my anxiety about the proposed May meeting with Mariah and X. Mariah has suggested that one day of the meeting be opened up generally to other colleagues and friends. I have not mentioned this to my colleagues yet.

I have also learned that the woman X wants me to share support with is Betty-Sue! Somehow I thought it might be her and I have very mixed feelings. Part of me says "No way!" after her theatrical outburst at the UFO meeting last August, when she said that Helen and X were messing with her mind. Yet, another part of me says I should put these feelings aside and proceed with caution, keeping my own counsel and giving her what support I can.

There was also another vague dream last night I remembered. In the dream I received a "death threat." If this came from the Visitors, they do not know me very well. Death threats hold no horror for me. I hope to live until I am an old lady, but when I do die, I feel it will be the "Next Great Adventure," another part of the bigger picture, of which this life is just one part.

March 8, 1989

Looking back at my life in a free-associative state, I remembered several occasions when there may have been missing time related to an abduction. There were times when I missed twenty-four-hour blocks of time, such as when I was in my twenties. This was during my nursing training days. I could not imagine how I could have slept through twenty-four hours and more. I would come off duty in the evening, go to bed, then wake up to answer the phone. It was the hospital asking why I had not reported for duty the previous day. This was very confusing, and I made excuses that I had been sick. There were times during my days off when I felt that I had lost a day. At the time, I dismissed these anomalies because I had no framework to explain them.

Mariah, X, and I have had some communications in which we have been comparing notes on communication with the Visitors. I have been giving this some thought and have come to the conclusion that selective attention may be a key. I have been playing around with different states of attention at the parapsychology lab. Maybe a focused attentional state might get the attention of a single Visitor, while a more diffuse attentional state might get a wider audience? Mariah says that the Visitors do things very much as a group and that direct attention throws them off balance.

B, my friend from Texas, recently sent me some writings from a friend of hers that contained recognizable runic glyphs. Today, B's friend, GS, called me. She was very anxious that I think of her as a sane, intelligent woman, which she is. She had experienced some overt UFO sightings. Recently, she had become fascinated with watching stars, and last night she saw one that shot away very fast. She had also experienced dream teachings and data downloads, which I have also experienced. I reassured her that she was not alone, that other people had experienced these things, and that there were support networks springing up all over the place. I warned her about people who might want to take advantage of her experiences and to keep them to herself at this time.

GS said she would send me some more of her writings and drawings to look at. She also told me she is an artist and usually thinks about or meditates on her pictures before she produces them. She sounds like a very interesting person, and I hope I can be of some support to her, as I unravel my own memories.

March 9, 1989

More free association brought up memories of dreams in which I am talking to someone and taking part in some actions but feeling extremely lethargic and trying very hard to wake up. My feelings in these types of dreams are that it is very important to wake up and see who I am talking to, and frustration at not being able to wake up.

There have also been dreams in which I felt it was very important to run and get away but my feet are stuck. When I was about seven or eight I developed a fear of going to bed, even though a hallway light was left on for me. This fear was so strong that as soon as I was put to bed, I became nauseous. I am not sure how long this went on.

March 10, 1989

I had a letter from Mariah with some suggestions for our proposed May meeting. She and X suggested the following topics for discussion at the meeting:

1. Physical Technology: With regard to what we would call physical technology, personally experienced and read about, how might one explain it? Grant the known perceptions in advance: round ships, tables that extend from the floor. We are looking for more unusual, less-known things.
2. Mental Technology: With regard to various forms of mental communication, what has been experienced or read about? How might we explain or describe it?
3. Participant Networking: Perceiving ourselves as "chosen" for some reason or other, how do we want to deal with this reality? How can we help one another?
4. Interplanetary Law: Most international law on Earth was begun as a set of mutually agreed upon customs or as a shared belief pattern. What customs would we like to emphasize and work for? What are the "human rights" in this circumstance? What about Visitor rights?

March 11, 1989

Last night I dreamed I visited a medical clinic, but I do not remember most of the dream except the emphasis that I was there voluntarily. Someone kept telling me in the dream that I was there "voluntarily."

Over the past few months, I have tried to imagine what the Visitors look like. If I have had contact with them, then I should be able to dredge up something from my memory store. What I have retrieved are glimpses of the Visitors—not fully three-dimensional, but split-second "looks" at what could be the Visitors. I see the occasional side view of a face, or head, or a body, never the full figure. They look quite real.

I thought about how we store memories of real people. For example, I had an undergraduate professor at the university. He was my mentor and encouraged my interest in neuropsychology. He died in 1980 from leukemia. When I try to visualize him, I get the same sort of glimpses: never the whole figure. I get his eyes or a certain coat he used to wear, or his smile. If my memory retrieval works this way for a real, remembered, person, maybe it works the same for memories of the Visitors?

I have been giving some thought to Mariah's idea that the Visitors seem to be more comfortable with women because of their ability to multitask, their generally nurturing personalities, their generally smaller size in relation to men, and their less aggressive personalities. I have also given some thought to my neuropsychology studies with relation to this idea.

Male brains, in general, are a great deal more lateralized than women's, and women seem to be able to use "whole brain" rather than strictly lateralized brain functions. The bridge between the hemispheres of the brain, called the corpus callosum, is much more developed in women. This allows for a greater flow of information between the hemispheres of the brain.

Unfortunately, the majority of research on the corpus callosum has been done with epileptics who have undergone split-brain surgery to relieve their seizures, or on acallosal (no corpus callosum) subjects. Very little research of the normally functioning corpus callosum has been done. The corpus callosum may act as a filter mechanism for psi information—individuals who are ambidextrous appear to have a greater psi ability. The Visitors are assumed to communicate via telepathy, and this may tie in with their larger brain. Maybe telepathy functions better between women and the Visitors. I realize I am pulling many unsubstantiated threads here but it is an intriguing set of questions.

An additional thought. There have been reports that individuals who have had Visitor contact claim to have developed greater psi abilities. It is possible that dormant psi abilities may be brought to the fore during or following Visitor contact. Perhaps contact with the Visitors activates callosal pathways that were dormant, leading to the manifestation of psi.

Maybe some callosal pathways can be blocked, thereby preventing contact experiences being remembered or verbalized. If the filter barrier could be breached, memories could be more easily retrieved. The process of hypnosis can aid this breach, as can free association. Hypnosis is a very little understood process. It creates various levels or states of consciousness. Some abduction researchers are using hypnosis as a tool to access hidden abduction memories. Hypnosis has an important place in accessing memories of the Visitors if offered by a trained professional in an investigative or therapeutic setting, and with the full consent of the participant. What about hypnosis that only activates the right or left hemispheres of the brain—would each tell a different story of Visitor contact?

March 12, 1989

There has been an unexpected and interesting turn of events. I worried that I might be putting the parapsychology lab's reputation at risk as a result of my interest in the abduction phenomenon. I thought that, perhaps, it would want me to keep my interests quiet. However, as it turns out, my senior colleagues have two propositions for me. One is that they would support me if I decided to keep my experiences private. Conversely, if I decided I wanted to explore the phenomenon further, they would encourage my interest, possibly with some research projects they had been unable to carry out because of lack of time and energy. It was quite a challenge. I was greatly surprised, as I had previously told my colleagues that, if my UFO interests potentially threatened their work, I would stop my overt search and keep it private. I feel excited by this turn of events and feel honored that they would give me their sanction and encouragement. I have decided to take up their challenge and see what they have to offer.

6

Skirting the Edge of UFO Research

"More than 10,000 sightings have been reported, the majority of which cannot be accounted for by any 'scientific' explanation. . . . I am convinced that these objects do exist and that they are not manufactured by any nation on Earth. I can therefore see no alternative to accepting the theory that they come from some extraterrestrial source."

—Air Chief Marshall Lord Dowding, commander-in-chief of the Royal Air Force Fighter Command during the Battle of Britain, printed in the *Sunday Dispatch*, London, July 11, 1954.

March 12, 1989

This has been an interesting year. 1989 marks another year of personal growth and development. My personal dream and memory search has brought me to the point where I can accept its validity but cannot yet accept its meaning. Initially, I networked with researchers and others in the abduction field but later realized that these folk could exploit experiencers. I have now grouped myself with some folk: Mariah Folger and X, whom I feel may have some intelligent answers to the abduction scenario. There has been a challenge by my superiors to take my personal search onto a more professional basis. Finally, perhaps, I can drop my facade. My personal and social lives have been full and active but I have not had a permanent male friend in my life since I finished the relationship with Dr. P a year ago. All in all, I feel happy, challenged, and fulfilled. Life is an ongoing adventure, and who knows where it might lead.

I was looking through some old photographs today and I came across some I had taken in September 1975. At that time, I was visiting the States from England, and my ex-brother-in-law had taken me to visit Washington, D.C., for the day. In several photos of the Washington Monument, unusual oval artifacts were flying in the air nearby. One photo, which I sent to my brother-in-law but which he never returned, clearly showed a domed top and bottom to the anomalous craft.

March 14, 1989

Individuals who feel they have experienced abduction often report scars, puncture marks, bruises, scabs, or blisters following the Interfaces. I have decided to keep a record of personal trauma that I cannot relate to any known injury. For example, upon awakening, I have often noticed bruises on my body in places there were no bruises the night before.

A few weeks ago I noticed a blister on my left inner upper arm, which has now healed to a small scar. A few days ago I noticed another blister on my left outer upper arm, and this is now drying up. There were no accidents or injuries that I know of that could have caused the blisters. This morning when I awoke I rubbed the top of my head and dislodged a small, crusty scab. It had a small amount of blood on it. It looked like the kind of scab you get if you bump your head. The spot does not hurt and I have not bumped my head recently.

March 20, 1989

Several strange things happened this week. One night I woke to find it light but decided not to get up until my radio alarm went off at seven in the morning. Then I awoke again a little later and it was dark again! So I went back to sleep again. Then I awoke to a real dawn and I got up. When I thought about it, I wondered: what had caused the first dawn? There is a phenomenon called False Awakening. Did I experience this?

In a different dream, someone is looking at the dried-up blister on my left arm and commenting about it.

I received a flyer from Linda Moulton Howe for her new book *An Alien Harvest*. She states that in 1979, while producing documentary films for a CBS station in Denver, Colorado, she began researching the worldwide animal mutilation mystery. In 1983 she began work on a film for HBO. That spring at Kirtland Air Force Base in Albuquerque, New Mexico, she was shown a "Briefing Paper for the President of the United States of America" about identified and unidentified alien craft and gray-skinned creatures retrieved both dead and alive from crashed disks. She reports that the briefing paper described U. S. government communication with gray "extraterrestrial biological entities" since the 1940s. That information, she states, implied centuries of alien intervention on Earth, including genetic manipulation of Earth life. Her book, *An Alien Harvest*, is her record of the mounting evidence she has collected, telling the story of animal mutilations, human abduction, and government knowledge about alien life forms.

March 27, 1989

Dream: I was at a large house at which a sale was going on. I was looking at some ceramic pins. They were modern and depicted tropical fish and marine life. X was there and wanted to give me one of the pins as a gift, but I could not decide which one I liked the most. As I was walking across the room, I heard X comment that he had a medical problem. I was worried that he would not be around for very long.

April 1, 1989

I have been wondering about the many dreams that I, and others, have about pools of water. The pools are often filled and emptied during the dream. They vary from small to very large. When my brother and I were younger, we had dreams of being able to breathe underwater.

The dreams could be related to the subconscious "memory and experience" pools I have been examining in my dreams. Or they could be pools to bathe or wash in before examination by the Visitors. It is an alternative answer I haven't thought of before. We must be very smelly to the Visitors and they want to sanitize us.

In early May, psychiatrist Dr. Z is planning a UFO abduction conference in New York. This meeting will be comprised mostly of health professionals and will confront the UFO/ contact/abduction scenario. More and more cases are being brought to the attention of the psychologists, psychiatrists, gynecologists, and obstetricians. There are radiologists who have found anomalous artifacts, such as BB-like formations attached to optic nerves. There are no guidelines for assessing and counseling these cases.

I will be attending the conference, primarily as an interested person with a medical background but also to update the lab, until we are able to get involved on a more substantial basis. There is also the need for a network of health professionals to refer people to. For example, one obstetrician is willing to examine on an emergency basis "missing fetus" cases. Another professional, a radiologist, is willing to examine "artifact" or "implant" cases. The conference promises to be exciting from many angles: meeting new people, learning new approaches to therapy and guidance, and possibly the beginnings of a supportive network for abductees.

April 3, 1989

I had a very vivid, symbolic dream in which my legs were heavily bandaged and in casts. I was with two women doctors who took off the casts. My legs looked white and somehow disjointed.

The message was clear: now that the bandages were off, I could make progress. The symbolism seems to be related to the metaphors of "taking steps," "stepping out," and "putting the best foot forward."

April 7, 1989

I dreamed I was at a conference, lining up to register. It was a medical conference but had a UFO theme. I saw several people I knew. There was a butterfly-shaped bruise on my left inner thigh this morning when I awoke.

April 9, 1989

I had a night of multiple dreams, but I remembered only one that was linked to the UFO theme.

I was at home in England, with several family members and friends. Every couple of seconds there would be an intense, vibrational buzzing, then it would stop for an equal length of time. Someone saw that the vibrations were being caused by a UFO, which was directly over the house. We timed the on/off vibrations, and they were exactly eight seconds apart. In the dream, someone wrote the numbers down and I saw them.

Then I dreamed that I awoke and I was here in Princeton. It was morning and Emily was asking me if I had heard the eight-second buzzing. But it was all a dream, as I really woke up later.

I have been wondering about the significance of eight seconds and also wondering if the vibrational speed of the buzz was also eight per second. Is there any meaning to the sequence "on eight seconds, off eight seconds?"

April 14, 1989

Sometimes I have dreams that seem more "real" than regular dreams. There is a quality about them that makes them very different from either sleeping or lucid dreams. In what I call "real" dreams, I feel as if I am actually experiencing the event. For example:

I was in a medical clinic setting, being examined for muscle strength. There was some concern that my right side was not as strong as my left. They were comparing the results with previous records. One of the tests involved holding a wooden bar with both hands, spaced about six inches apart, and squeezing it. The people testing me were human-looking women. There were also women in blue uniforms, and I was told they were from the air force. They were being tested as a separate group and left before I did.

In another dream last night, I may have dreamed about an event that took place in England, one that I may have repressed.

I was visiting my college friend. We were talking with another friend in the garden. From a distance came a squarish-looking UFO with a single beam of light emanating from it. I was excited yet fearful and I knew what it was. It came over the garden and circled around. The craft was about one hundred feet from the ground. I had to circle around to watch it.

A door opened and I was expecting a Communion-type entity (a "gray") to show at the windows or at the open door. I think the dream was lucid, because I was examining my emotional state and feelings about the situation. Finally, two entities came to the door and looked down. They were almost human-looking with sharp noses. It was difficult to tell their height. They wore very unusual headgear. Their hats looked like a kind of peaked hat with a neck flap, like the foreign legionnaires wear, except that the cloth flap came all the way around the neck.

I was intrigued by these two entities and watched them with amazement. I wondered how they could keep their balance in the open doorway while the craft circled around. Then, I was alone in the garden and it was nighttime. I was wandering around and looking for the craft, wondering where it went.

In preparation for building a database about the UFO field, I sent off a subscription to the Mutual UFO Network (MUFON), the Center for UFO Studies (CUFOS), and *Contact, a Contactee Newsletter. Contact* and MUFON responded promptly. There are several things about MUFON that concern me. These concerns include the test they give to field investigators. MUFON provides a manual and the "test" consists of an at-home questionnaire, in which you fill in the answers from the manual and other reference books. I also had to smile, because MUFON had given me the title of "research specialist." They don't know who I am and they are giving me honorary titles? It reminded me of the Dick Tracy Club. Will I get a secret symbol ring next? I might play dumb and go along with this and see how professional they really are.

Emily says the MUFON way of doing things reminds her of the Douglas Adams book *Dirk Gently's Holistic Detective Agency*. She suggested that I write a book about my experiences and call it "FUTON: Flying, Unidentified Truths and Other Nonsense!" I received the March MUFON Journal and was dismayed, because the issue contained backbiting, vindictiveness, and aggressiveness.

Psychiatrist Dr. Z is coordinating an abduction conference. The conference will define procedures for helping clients with "anomalous contact experiences." Dr. R asked the potential attendees of the conference for a few paragraphs and ideas toward the agenda. This is what I wrote:

> I notice from the list of participants that representatives from various UFO research groups will be present, as well as many private individuals. Over the past year, I have been skirting the edges of UFO research, watching, and listening carefully. What I have perceived is an honest attempt at cooperation and communication between these groups. However, I have also observed territoriality and elitism.
>
> At present, the UFO research field presents an extremely fragmented image, with its individual ideologies and presuppositions. The creation of an additional group could proceed in the same direction and become yet another fragment in the chaos. Or it could bring the existing groups closer together in

a mutually cooperative, working effort. Perhaps during the conference we can explore these issues and see how we can achieve this.

I suppose I should not be surprised (but I am) at the infighting, territoriality, and elitism between the various factions supposedly investigating the UFO and abduction phenomena. Researchers run each other down, and often to abductees. There are claims that rivals have failed to contact excellent cases and have bungled or completely mismanaged others.

Admittedly, with any collection of groups, there will be power struggles and infighting, and whenever funding is involved, there will be intense competition, envy, and denigration. I have made several resolutions for myself:

1. To stay on the fringes of all this negative activity
2. To act as a catalyst for resolve and reunion between the groups, on a very limited basis, if I get the opportunity
3. To learn as much as possible about the underlying conflicts, to avoid making the same mistakes myself

This week I called X to let him know that our proposed meeting could not take place because of the other participants' schedules. I have assured Mariah that I would still like to get together and would be willing to travel to her location, if necessary.

X mentioned again that Betty-Sue was still needing some support. It seems that she had contacted several of the abduction researchers and had been rejected by all of them. She claims that her conversations were recorded without her permission. She also claimed that the researchers told her that X was connected to the CIA. It seems that Betty-Sue is unemployed and without support of any kind. I tried to tell X that I am unable to be of direct support to Betty-Sue for the following reasons. First, she is talking about litigation. Second, if I became involved with her, I could open myself up to litigation. Third, and more important, if she knew of my association with the parapsychology lab, this would provide fuel for her "conspiracy theory." Although I feel very sorry for Betty-Sue and her problems, there is no way that I can be of much support to her at present.

April 15, 1989

I was watching clouds in my dream. I had read that clouds with dark spots contained UFOs, the black being from their exhaust. In the dream, I saw lots of these little clouds, which scooted here and there about the sky. I commented to another person that these were UFOs.

April 17, 1989

I dreamed that I found my mother lying on the floor in a room at home. Her hands and feet were bound with heavy wire. She was in shock and could hardly speak, which was why she could not call me. I undid the wires with difficulty and noticed that some of her fingernails were turning black where the circulation had been cut off. I rubbed her hands and put her hands and feet into warm water to improve her circulation.

I feel that this dream relates to the fact that my mother's life has been "bound" with rules and regulations, imposed on her by her father, my father, and herself. By going about my life, taking chances and opportunities, I have shown my mother that it is okay to undo the knots and get free.

April 21, 1989

This week I tried two visualization exercises to see if I could uncover any more hidden memories. I got some vivid material, but it is hard to know where imagination ends and memory begins.

In the first visualization, I remembered a local river bank where my brother and I went to play. In the exercise, I was about nine and my brother was six. We approached what we saw as a small round "hut." There was an open door and we went inside. There was a circular bench around the walls, and the "hut" could hold maybe six people. I felt a strong sense of familiarity. We moved upward as if in an elevator. There were no entities in the small room.

Next we were in a huge space like an airplane hangar. Again, the strong sense of familiarity. We went through doors and my brother and I were separated. I was concerned about him but was told that he was "sleeping." I sat in something like a dentist's chair, which tilted backward and into other positions. Several times I was crying and said "I want to go home." There was constant reassurance. I have no real recollection of what was done to me, but there was some pain in my abdomen and head. Eventually, we returned by the same route we had arrived. I remember the Sun being very strong and bright when we returned to the river bank.

The second visualization took place at a beauty spot near where I grew up as a child. Dingle Dell is a hilltop, once a hill fort used by an Iron Age culture. It is reached by climbing a path through bluebell woods. It is a very pretty walk. My mother had taken me and my brother for a picnic on a sunny afternoon to Dingle Dell. My brother rode in a stroller: he was maybe two years old. I must have been about five years old.

As we were playing and eating jam sandwiches, the sky darkened. My mother thought it was going to rain. Suddenly, she realized that it was not clouds darkening the sky but something large and metallic. She scooped up the cloth with all the picnic stuff and put it into a basket, put that and my brother into the stroller, and me into her arms. She ran with us to the gate to get down into the woods. My mother was crying and so were we because she was. It was a terrible journey through the woods. It did not seem beautiful any more. Somewhere I lost a new shoe, but we did not go back to look for it. Several times, when we were older and walked through the bluebell woods, we would wonder if we would find the missing shoe.

I had a lone stray thought while thinking about the Visitors, "The thing I don't like about the Visitors is the gag!" What gag?

Received the April issue of *Psychology Today* and read an article by Elizabeth Bird entitled "Invasion of the Mind Snatchers." The article is basically a skeptical piece about UFO abductions. She quotes psychologist Robert Baker's opinion that abductees who recall their experiences under hypnosis might be recalling something they have previously read about abductions. Basically, that this is "wishful thinking" on the part of want-to-be abductees. When they contact a UFO researcher, he makes them feel important and special, and the abductee is impelled to come up with better stories. Even though these individuals can pass polygraph tests regarding their experience, Baker believes this is because, with the retelling, the abductees come to fully believe in their confabulated story.

Robert Baker also attributes many of the abduction experiences—finding ourselves wide awake but unable to move, being confronted with a bizarre entity or apparition—to a condition called sleep paralysis. He reports that fantasy-prone people report these experiences more often than others.

Psychologist Milton Rosenberg of the University of Chicago, writes Bird, suggests that UFO abduction tales represent a "pervasive modern myth that has been much propagandized, circulated, and diffused through the telling and the retelling." This might be the explanation for a few cases, but Baker's and Rosenberg's explanations do not cover the whole story. They do not consider mass abductions that involve more than one individual, or the physical trauma that results from these experiences.

May 1, 1989

I received a Time-Life book today entitled *The UFO Phenomena*. Reading it brought back memories of a recent dream and an evasion game I played as a kid. If I was walking along the road and a car was coming, I would try and reach the street corner, turn, and get out of sight, up a side street, before the car came by. There were many variations of this game, but they all involved hurrying and hiding before a car or a person could reach me. This game was accompanied by feelings of anxiety, increased heart rate, rapid breathing, and shaky knees. The frequency of the game diminished as I got older. I wonder now if the game had anything to do with possible abductions?

May 4, 1989

On Tuesday night, I awoke in the night after having a fantastic dream. I thought about it and traced the dream back to its beginning. I commented to myself how important this dream was. It involved all of the parapsychology lab members plus many mystical happenings from the past. Unfortunately, when I awoke in the morning, I had forgotten the dream.

Last night I had another important dream that sort of explained the lost dream. I was at a conference and we were talking about information overload. I quoted the St. Ives poem: "As I was going to St. Ives, I met a man with seven wives, each wife had seven sacks, each sack had seven cats, each cat had seven kits: kits, cats, sacks, and wives, how many were there going to St. Ives?"

Of course, it is only one, but because of interfering, information overload, we were forgetting original, important information and we were unable to answer the question correctly. I will bear this in mind for the upcoming abduction conference. It is so easy to get loaded down with irrelevant material when, very often, the simplest answer is the best: look beyond the irrelevant material for the truth.

May 18, 1989

Life has been running on "fast forward." This last weekend at the abduction conference, I linked up with a man with whom I have felt a mystical connection for many months: X. He appeared in my dreams before I actually met him, which could be precognitive or maybe evidence of a karmic link—who knows. There was a lot of unspoken communication. Even though I don't consciously know when we will meet again, I know that we will.

May 19, 1989

The following are my impressions of the abduction conference that took place this past weekend. It was an enthusiastic, intense weekend meeting of a multidisciplinary group of people who were willing to set aside personal belief systems and explanation of the Visitor phenomenon in order to examine the available evidence (mostly soft and anecdotal, some hard evidence).

I networked with about forty-five individuals, professionals with varying degrees of involvement in, and experience with, the abduction scenario, sharing thoughts, ideas, anecdotes, research, and plans. I examined my own dreams and memories in this context to see if they fit any particular pattern of abduction. My conclusion is that some do and some do not. I plan to remain involved, at a minimal level, with the groups studying abductions.

May 12, 1989

I dreamed I was talking to an old school friend. We were talking about UFOs and abductions. It seems we shared some experiences. She suggested I talk to another school friend, who now lives in Canada. Maybe subconsciously I recognize that all three of us share possible abduction experiences. Maybe I should contact my school friend in Canada? What would I say to her?

May 23, 1989

I remembered that when I lived in Manchester between 1979 and 1981, I shared a house with a younger woman. At that time, I was having lots of abduction-type dreams of entities invading the house. One morning, my housemate awoke to find her arms and legs covered with bruises, and she was sick with a fever for several days afterward.

June 3, 1989

There was a terrific storm in the night. It was right over the house at one point with a flash and crash of thunder and lightning. Before I fell asleep, I was having hypnogogic images flash in front of my eyes, and they were of gray aliens. When I awoke this morning, I had several very small bruises on my right inner thigh. I showed them to Emily, but I had no explanation for them. They had appeared in the night. There were three bruises in a triangular pattern, each bruise being about one quarter inch in diameter. Near the bruises was a circle of five red dots.

This afternoon I remembered that I awoke in the night and the inside of my right thigh was sore. I got up and put some baby powder on it. Later today a friend noticed a large bruise below and behind my right knee that I had not noticed. It is about one and a half inches square, but does not hurt.

June 4, 1989

The bruises are rapidly fading and the circle of red spots is gone already.

June 19, 1989

I returned last night from a week-long scientific conference held in Boulder, Colorado. I need to record some events that seem strange and may include some missing time on a field trip up to Rocky Mountain State Park and Estes Park. X and Mariah were with me on this trip.

According to time estimates, our group left the hotel at 1:30 p.m. to make the one hour drive to Estes Park. We had several ten-minute photo stops, but it was four p.m. before we got to the town, where we took a short break to get sodas. It took another two hours to get up to the Rock Cut at 13,000 feet in the Rockies. Our host commented that by car the trip should have taken half an hour, or forty-five minutes by bus. We were out on the mountain for about an hour and eventually reached the Lazy B Ranch for dinner about 7:30 p.m. They were waiting anxiously to serve us dinner and get on with the evening's entertainment. At the dinner, I was concerned whether we had all made it safely back from the trip. I kept looking around to make sure that we were all there. When I got back on the bus after the stop on the mountain, I noticed a bruised area on the inside of my right ankle. It has been sore for a few days.

I talked with a few people after the trip, and the general feeling was that the trip seemed to last for a very long time. According to Mariah, who seems to retain some hidden memory of these events, we may have had two Interfaces with the Visitors on the trip: first between the hotel and the town, and then second on the way up the mountain. Mariah remembers that she was first off the bus and trod on my ankle as she climbed over me to get off. She reports that the bus was surrounded by mist and that two Visitors were standing at the entrance to the bus. She checked that X was okay, then she got off. Her memories stop there.

The night after the trip some of the group said that there was a terrific thunderstorm, with a flash of lightning and clap of thunder overhead. I did not hear a thing, which is unusual. Several others said they did not hear the thunderstorm, including Mariah and X. Were we there?

I made an affirmation to remember something about the event, through my dreams. Last night I had several dreams with a medical theme; they might reflect what happened to us when we got off the bus.

The first event in the dream was that I was in a medical setting on a small table, being given some IV fluids and blood. This was supposedly in preparation for an "operation." It seems that I was supposed to have had this "operation" a long time back but it never got done. What concerned me was that the "doctors" kept getting people's identities wrong. They would call another person in the group "Angela," and I would say, "I am here." This happened several times, and I suggested to them that they say, "Which one of you is Angela?" so as to avoid confusion.

I was in a small waiting room, and then I was walking out to a larger area where a lot of people were waiting. I recognized many people from the bus who were looking sort of dazed. I was given a large, soft teddy bear and I hugged it to lessen my anxiety about the forthcoming "operation."

I did not see Mariah or X during these events. The locations in the dreams were unknown to me and the fact that the "doctors" kept mixing up identities makes me feel that these were a different group of Visitors than the ones I usually interact with.

July 7, 1989

I dreamed a real dream in a medical setting that may be linked to the missing time episodes in Colorado:

A long complicated dream of which most was forgotten. The two main memories that are left are: a procedure in which a push-pin-type device was pushed into my temples, one at a time. It hurt and I was concerned that they were pushing the pins in too far. After they had done one side, I was anxiously waiting for the pain when they did the other side. The pain was like a hypodermic sting followed by a deeper pain. The second dream memory involved a device that looked like kitchen tongs. This device went into my mouth and throat. It may have been used to hold my tongue for some procedure.

July 11, 1989

Basically, the UFO research field presents a fragmented ego-based face to the public. Composed of various subgroups, such as MUFON, CUFOS, and FUFOR, the field is divided by petty, territorial jealousies and ego wars. Each group is striving to understand the phenomenon but lacks a cooperative interdisciplinary stance that would enable the groups to work together as a cohesive whole.

Currently, the major battle in the UFO field seems to be between the therapists and the investigators. For many years, the investigators have held the abduction field, valiantly assisting abduction experiencers with hypnosis recall and support groups. Now the licensed therapists, psychologists, and psychiatrists are claiming the field and denouncing the work of the investigators. However, what seems to be at the core of all this is money.

Abductees seem to be getting exploited on several levels: first by the aliens themselves; second, by the investigators, eager to cash in on the experiencers' stories for commercial benefit; and third, by the therapists, who see the claimants as a potential client source. It is a sad state of affairs.

July 22, 1989

I have just finished reading an interesting three-part article in the *New Yorker*. The article concerned the dangers of extremely low frequency (ELF) radio waves. ELF is used by various industries and the military and is thought to cause childhood cancers, miscarriages, and birth defects. However, according to the article, although the dangers of ELF seem to be apparent, the military continues to build ELF-producing towers all around the coastline as an "early warning system." They plan to increase the number of these over the years. A thought comes to mind: Why are the towers planned or even needed when *glasnost* is gearing up to produce disarmament on both sides?

Anecdotal evidence also exists from David Jacobs that the aliens do not tolerate ELF well. Jacobs notes that abductees experience relief when they keep a ceiling fan or other electrical device going all the time. These produce electrical fields. If the alien abduction hypothesis is true and we are being visited by other life forms (who cannot tolerate ELF), and supposing that the "government" knows about this, then it might make sense for the military to erect these ELF-producing towers.

July 23, 1989

Lots of dreams last night. I kept waking and commenting to myself that these dreams were connected to my UFO research. Most of the dreams were forgotten, but two small incidents remain. During the night, I heard a car screech to a halt outside our house (I was awakened by this). It blew its horn several times, as if to scare something out of the road, then drove on. It could have been deer crossing the road. Another time during the night, I awoke when I heard eight very closely spaced electronic beeps, then nothing. I have heard these beeps before, and I dreamed about them recently.

Last evening I watched a TV show about children with a condition called progeria. The children only live to their middle teens and in those few years they age eighty or ninety years. In appearance, they look like the representations of the aliens. People with progeria are usually about three feet tall, have large, bald heads, very large eyes, and thin body and limbs. I looked up progeria but could not find it in my medical textbooks. I wonder if it is a new condition? There are some theories that the Visitors are us from the future, coming back to correct genetic damage that we have inflicted on our descendants. One of the mothers of the progeria children commented, "Maybe they are from another planet. Whatever, we still love them!"

I wrote to my doctor colleague, John, to find out about progeria, and he sent me a page of information. Progeria is also called Werner's Syndrome and Hutchinson-Gilford Disease and is classified as an autosomal, recessive illness. Symptoms include premature aging of all body organs, atrophy of the skin, cataracts, early osteoporosis, diabetes, and early cancers. The individual affected by progeria, which usually develops after the first year of life, shows a gross retardation of growth, a senile appearance, and has dry, wrinkled skin, total alopecia (no hair), and birdlike facial features.

Last weekend I updated the parapsychology lab on what was happening in the UFO field and the various groups working with abductees. They were as discouraged as I was with the infighting and personal differences between the various groups. The lab asked who was doing sound research in the area. I thought about this. There is Dr. Richard Haines, who is developing a systematic regression tool; Dr. Kenneth Ring, who has completed a survey of abductions versus near-death experiences (NDEs); Drs. Don Johnson and Ron Westrum, who are proposing a survey to assess the degree and range of abductions; and Mariah Folger's group, which is assessing medical interventions in abduction experiences. I plan to write to the various groups to find out the status of their research. The lab has decided to stay out of the UFO and abduction field of research for now.

I had a call from Mariah. She is going to visit another researcher in Los Alamos, New Mexico. She asked if she could share some of my experiences with him. Mariah still feels that an Interface happened at Boulder and that the Los Alamos researcher might have been included, because he was on the bus. She wanted to find out if he had remembered anything.

July 25, 1989

I had several long and complicated real dreams last night centered around a swimming pool. Pool dreams seem to be connected to my Visitor research. This pool was oblong and looked like a regular swimming pool, except the water was much warmer. There was a three-foot barrier around the pool, and the swimmer entered the pool through a series of oblong openings in the barrier.

At several points in the dream, I was floating on my back in the pool, and with very little effort. The water seemed to be supersaturated and more buoyant than regular water. I looked into a doorway at the side of the pool and observed a khaki army backpack and a chaos of old newspapers. I looked through a barrier opening at the far end of the pool and found comic books featuring war stories.

July 27, 1989

We got a call at the parapsychology lab from the director of the psychophysics lab to let people know that it was finally closing down. The "writing has been on the wall" for a long time, with only several part-timers running that lab. Helen has already moved on, and I have lost contact with her. I mentioned to colleagues that it almost seemed orchestrated—all the major psi labs closing down within a year. I wonder what will happen to the critical community when there are no more psi studies to comment on? I imagine they will have enough fodder with the New Age fads.

July 29, 1989

I had a long, complicated dream in which I was part of an important family that had recently taken on the responsibility of a new school or institution. I was driving with the wife of the important family. I looked into the sky and saw four very large, saucer-shaped UFOs. I drew the woman's attention to them, but I had to explain their appearance to her: four large round circles, reflecting light, covered with symbols. Then she saw them.

Then I was at a house, feeling very tired, and was given a hard, narrow pull-out bed to sleep on. I remember my body being manipulated and being turned over, but I could not wake up. At another point, I was still sleepy and someone was trying to paint my face with some cold liquid. I resisted this and covered my face with my arms and hands. I was torn between wanting to sleep and objecting to these things being done to me.

August 5, 1989

I have decided to take next week off from work, as a time of semi-retreat and replenishment. I have arranged several appointments but nothing major. I plan to carry out some more intensive work on my abduction research and catch up on my dreams research, and correspondence.

August 7, 1989

I recently received a lengthy draft of a talk to be given by Bill Moore at the Las Vegas MUFON conference. He is a writer and UFO investigator. In reviewing the twenty-three legal-size pages of single-spaced text, I felt the whole thing to be verbose and superficial. I reread it, underlining points that seemed to have some relevance. Moore could have written this paper in ten pages or less, including his position points and questions.

He leads the reader along with teasing statements such as: "I have something interesting to say"; "I have information that will add to your knowledge of the UFO phenomenon"; and "I believe we are getting very near to those answers we all claim we want." He courts the reader with revelations to come: "I will have considerably more to say at a later date," and "The rest of the story will ultimately be told as well." Unfortunately, when you strip away the "fluff" (one of Moore's own words), there seems to be very little substance left for the interested reader that has not already been documented elsewhere.

However, there are several topics from Moore's paper that I would like to explore further, including his involvement with an unfortunate young man, Paul Bennewitz, and with Bennewitz's research. It seems that Moore, under the guise of friendship, ostensibly investigated Bennewitz for the government, and Bennewitz, the poor man, ended up in a mental hospital.

It is possible that Moore felt that the ends justified the means, but at the destruction of the sanity of another man? Moore admits that he was acting voluntarily and knew precisely what he was doing. He writes that his actions secured him a seat in the "right theater" and allowed him to be in a privileged position. A position, he admits, many ufologists would have viewed as negative and would have backed away from, either in anger or disgust, as soon as they discovered what they were dealing with. He says that he acted in self-interest, and he was aware of the negative effect it had on Bennewitz. Moore even counseled Bennewitz to get him to drop the "UFO thing before his health is completely destroyed," but Bennewitz ultimately ended up hospitalized under psychiatric care.

If Moore was so concerned for Bennewitz, as he defensively protests, he could have done more to alleviate the stress this young man was under. Moore admits he signed no security oath and could have informed Bennewitz of any danger without compromising his own privileged position. In my opinion, Moore acted unethically.

Bennewitz was supposedly picking up electronic signals which he interpreted as coming from UFOs. He described these signals as "electromagnetic, or low-frequency, signals." They could have had a terrestrial source. A recent article in *OMNI* reported on GWEN (Ground Wave Emergency Network; Sherry Baker, August 1989). GWEN is the air force's private Doomsday radio station, reserved for the transmission of top-level military messages following a nuclear attack. GWEN uses low-frequency (150-175 megahertz) radio waves that "hug the ground." The article stated that radio towers are planned that will be spaced two hundred miles apart from coast to coast and that so far fifty-three towers linking thirty-eight terminals have been built. GWEN towers are already broadcasting test messages, according to *OMNI*. Was Bennewitz picking up these signals with his equipment?

August 11, 1989

I took a long, refreshing nap today and did a lot of dreaming, most of which I forgot. There was one dream that remained:

I was walking down a street toward a building where a UFO Research Club meeting was about to take place. Outside, two colleagues (a researcher and a medical doctor) were engaged in a mock battle to raise funds for the group. Inside, I was informed that I had been selected to take over the group. However, there was a woman already in charge, and she resembled Dr. Z. She was complaining bitterly that the group had not raised enough funds. She pointed to some bare windows that had holes drilled over them. She was shrilly complaining that she had bought all the materials for hanging curtains, but there was no money to hang them. I wondered why she was worrying about curtains when there were other, more important, issues to worry about.

I sat in the audience next to two young men who were working with a colonel who has been implicated in the "shadow government." The time came to give a speech, and I confidently voiced my opinion that we should concentrate on the real issues, not on raising funds. There was no need for the antics of colleagues or to be fighting to attract attention.

I feel that this dream reveals my frustration at the infighting in the UFO community and their pleas for more money.

August 12, 1989

I dreamed I was given a type of watch-chronometer to wear. It was very thin and appeared to be made of a dull brasslike material. It was unlike any watch I have ever seen. There were dials and symbols inscribed on the face. The partial brass cover was able to rotate around the circumference of the face. Its face was partially covered with a curved, tapered, brass piece, and the watch was only about an eighth of an inch thick and about one and a half inches in diameter.

I have the feeling I've seen this device before, but I cannot recall the symbols on the face of the dial. I would guess it to be a triangle and a cross with two bars. What impressed me most was the lightness and thinness of the device. I had it on my right wrist, but it was only "on loan." I realized I could not wear it as a dress watch. It would have been interesting if I could have brought it back with me.

August 13, 1989

After last night's dream of the alien chronometer, I conducted an autohypnosis exercise to see if I could access any further hidden memories. After about three quarters of an hour of free association and memory search, I came up with the image of myself lying on an examination table with my feet placed against two metal plates. My feet were bare and the metal plates felt cold. I do not remember the purpose of these plates but would guess them to be some measuring device.

August 20, 1989

Half awake this morning, I was thinking about several dreams I had in the past in which I was exploring a beach at very low tide. In these dreams the tide has gone out a long, long way and has exposed a sandy beach littered with large rocks and shells. There is an air of mystery as I turn over rocks, looking for treasure. This was a symbolic dream and referred to the uncovering of new information.

While I was thinking about these dreams, I remembered a strange incident when I was vacationing on the island of Iona in Scotland. In 1970 I spent two weeks of my vacation on Iona. One day we took a boat trip over to the Island of Seals. We saw lots of seals on the boat trip over and saw seals diving and swimming in the crystal clear water, down to the sandy bottom. The trip over to the island took about half an hour.

The group of us (between eight and twelve people) spent the day at the island, watching seals and fish, eating a picnic lunch, and searching for semiprecious green gems at the water's edge. We left the Island of Seals late in the afternoon to boat back to Iona. While we were on our way back, a heavy sea mist came down and the boatman could not navigate. He had to turn off his engine and we sat in silence in the mist. At one time, we saw one light, then several lights circled around us. There was no sound. The boatman, thinking it was another boat, shone his flashlight in that direction. I think the light in the mist was red, but it soon went away. We sat there for a long time until the mist started to lift and we could navigate back to Iona. While we were becalmed, I was worried that we would drift out to open sea. When we saw the light, I started thinking about Scottish myths and legends of sea creatures. We got back very late to Iona and were late for dinner. I had forgotten this incident until it resurfaced today. This memory was submerged for almost twenty years.

August 26, 1989

A couple of months ago, I sent a copy of my personal dream and memory search to the psychiatrist Dr. Z. She has been developing a research and treatment training group of medical and other professionals who are interested in the abduction phenomenon. I sent this material to her for several reasons: first, to ask her to assess the contents for any signs that I needed professional help. But Dr. Z felt that my own feelings of good mental health and vigor were correct and found nothing to indicate mental ill health. I found this reassuring.

Second, many people with similar experiences feel they have suffered great trauma. Some of them exhibit signs of post-traumatic stress disorder syndrome. I do not feel my experiences have left me grossly traumatized. I think I function very well within society. However, I worry that I might be denying or repressing something. According to Dr. Z, it seems I am not. This has been reassuring to hear from a psychiatrist. The third reason I sent her these materials was that I felt my experiences might be helpful to others.

August 31, 1989

I had lots of dreams during the past few weeks, but most of them were forgotten as soon as I woke up. However, the realization remains with me that some of these dreams are important. They are linked to my UFO research and contain characters from my recent interactions with folks from the UFO investigation field, including X. I do not have the feeling that these dreams are traumatic but that they involve a sorting out of information relating to the abduction phenomenon.

September 8, 1989

Dr. Z had asked several of us for suggestions for the upcoming conference. She had sent us an outline of suggested talks. My comments centered around the need for more "down time" during the weekend so that the participants could meet and discuss the talks in smaller groups. I felt that the scope of the conference was too broad and that there was a need to screen the participants. The guest list included many "flakes" from the parapsychology field as well as some debunkers of the UFO field.

September 24, 1989

A dream that involved a medical procedure: putting a device like a telephone jack (but much smaller) into my ear canal. The "jack" had two tiny protrusions at the intersection surface.

Someone had threaded this device into my right ear but had met some obstruction. The "operator" kept double clicking the device but nothing happened. I guess the double-notched device had to latch onto and push the obstacle ahead of it. I had the impression that I could also see what was happening on a video screen. Fiberoptics within the device? The obstacle appeared ball-like. It produced no pain, only a pressure. Eventually the double clicks worked, and the ball and notched device moved smoothly. There was anxiety regarding this among the "operators" and much conferring.

This dream may explain another physical anomaly. Midweek, I discovered a patch of white "crud," a couple of inches across on my scalp behind my right ear. I managed to pick it off in pieces and comb it out. It looked like plaster of paris dried in a thin layer. It took some scraping to get it off, and my scalp was sore afterward. I sent a sample of this to X.

September 30, 1989

There have been many dreams that seem to contain Visitor themes, and the rooms where these interactions occur deserve some description, because they seem similar. It may be that the Visitors want us to feel "at home." The rooms are laid out as if by a person without any idea of aesthetics, design, or color. The furniture consists of many old, wooden pieces, arranged as they would be for a garage sale: tables next to cupboards next to wardrobes next to dressers and chests of drawers. The furniture looks like it was picked up off the street. The rooms are medium in size and the beds are covered in gray. The walls are bare. Many abductees have mentioned these starkly furnished gray rooms.

This week we had a visit from a Russian scientist who is the head of one of the major research institutes of learning in Moscow. He gave us a talk on his learning theories and how they apply to *perestroika*. He seemed positive that the changes would be for the good of the Soviets but had to be handled carefully as to "timing and acceptance." The last day we took him out to dinner and gave him great bear hugs at the end of the evening. He seemed very appreciative. I have a feeling that we have been instrumental in some way to help heal the rift between the two great countries.

7

Study It in Its Fearless State

"The evidence that there are objects which have been seen in our atmosphere, and even on terra firma, that cannot be accounted for either as man-made objects or as any physical force or effect known to our scientists seems to me to be overwhelming. . . . A very large number of sightings have been vouched for by persons whose credentials seem to me unimpeachable. It is striking that so many have been trained observers, such as police officers and airline and military pilots. Their observations have in many instances . . . been supported either by technical means such as radar or, even more convincingly by . . . interference with electrical apparatus of one sort or another."

—Lord Hill-Norton, chief of Defense Staff, Ministry of Defense, Great Britain, 1973, and chairman, Military Committee of NATO, 1974–77, quoted from his foreword to *Above Top Secret,* by Timothy Good (Morrow & Co./Quill Books, New York, 1988).

October 9, 1989

Disharmony within the UFO and abduction research communities is increasing as a result of ego and personality clashes. Recently, I replied to correspondence from a key investigator in which I supported one of the therapists trying to encourage cooperation and goodwill. In response, the investigator sent a four-page reply in which he poured out his complaints and, in effect, asked me to act as a mediator and to help heal the rift within the group. The investigator also sent a copy of this correspondence to one of the financial sponsors, who became alarmed at the discord within the field. The sponsor called other key members, who agreed on some compromises and resolutions of the conflicts. The main therapist was not able to agree to the compromises, and key players have dropped from the game. Unfortunately, they plan to form a countergroup. The therapist may go ahead with the splinter group despite the loss of some key players. It will be very interesting to watch the game proceed.

For the past six months or more I have been corresponding with Mariah Folger, who has an extensive range of experiences with the Visitors. She is able to access memories of visits with the "small grays." Actually, she is able to remember a variety of Visitors, ranging from tall and slender entities to short and slender, through colors ranging from gold to pale, white, to dark gray and light gray. They take various roles, such as "information gatherer," "technician," "friend," and Mariah appears to learn as much from them as they learn from her.

I seem able to access Visitor memories through my dreams, while Mariah seems to have delayed, actual memories. One of Mariah's main aims is to encourage overt contact with the Visitors with full memory retention of the Interface. She also wants to gather a small group of people who seem cognizant of Visitor contact. Whether this small group will ever experience overt full conscious contact is uncertain. What is certain is that the group could provide mutual support and reassurance. If the Visitors are a reality, then overt contact could be a fascinating, instructive, and rewarding experience.

October 10, 1989

Over the past two weeks, an escalating state of chaos has existed, not only at the parapsychology lab, but everywhere. Everyone I have talked to recently has commented on the current state of chaos. During this time, there seems to be a catabolic process going on, a breaking down of the state that was. Now we seem to be in the anabolic state, a rebuilding and restructuring, a repatterning. Some of my colleagues think the chaos is linked to some unusual sunspot activity. I feel it is linked to a larger universal pattern of periodic ebb and flow, catabolism and anabolism, that affects the

Sun's cycles and ours. I feel that there are peaks and troughs in this activity and that, as we explore space, we will find evidence of this cyclic pattern in and around our own solar system—maybe even further afield. It is a cyclic process, so pervasive it affects systems as diverse as the Sun's, and down to the human cellular level.

From November 7 through December 7, I will be in England and Africa. My trip to Africa is a dream come true. I took up a friend's offer to visit her in Nairobi and I am on my way. Somehow I feel that visiting Africa at this time is important and timely. It is said that humankind has its roots in Africa, and maybe we need to get back to the source to find some answers . . . and maybe to understand the questions?

October 10, 1989

Headline in the *New York Times* today: "Tass reports the Landing of Aliens from Outer Space." The official Tass report stated: "Scientists have confirmed that an unidentified flying object recently landed in a park in the Russian city of Voronezh. They have also identified the landing site and found traces of aliens who made a short promenade around the park." Tass also reported that the people in Voronezh who saw the aliens "were overwhelmed with a fear, which lasted several days."

October 11, 1989

Two dreams that could be linked to an abduction event.

I was at a furnished location. In this dream an effort was made to make me comfortable with my environment. There was a bed, chair, and TV monitor. In the second dream, I was visiting an army location to see someone. I found myself being recruited into the army. I was with a group of people who were asked to give a blood and urine sample and to have a vaccination. I saw a person getting a shot, and about 5 cc of clear liquid was injected. I protested that I had just received a tetanus shot in getting ready for my trip to Africa, and I showed them my sore arm. I was excused from having the shot but had to give the blood and urine samples. The vial used to store the blood sample was a rounded flask with a narrow neck. There was an angry altercation when an "assistant" made a mistake and added a chemical to the blood too soon. Guess they make mistakes too. The collections were made in a long plain room that contained several armchairs. I cannot remember the appearance of the people involved, but a senior officer was friendly and seemed pleased with me.

October 17, 1989

A supermarket tabloid has an article about an insurance company in Altamonte Springs, Florida, that is offering UFO abduction insurance. A Florida insurance man named Mike St. Laurent is offering a ten-million-dollar policy for $7.95—if you can prove that you have been abducted by aliens. Mike admits, "We don't expect to ever pay off on a policy, but if push comes to shove, we might agree to pay off the claim at the rate of $1 a year for 10 million years!"

October 18, 1989

I awoke in the early hours when it was still dark. An electrical malfunction had occurred and my electric clock was flashing 4:25 a.m. It was not a power failure, because other electrical devices had not reset. The malfunction occurred following an interesting dream.

In the dream I was asked to visit a movie theater in which we discussed the differences between the Russian UFO landing and the entities that were seen by the people of Voronezh and the small grays.

I heard from Mariah Folger, who commented that she had been encouraged by the Visitors to be extra careful with her personal hygiene. I wonder if I had a similar directive as I have recently begun to shower at night instead of in the morning, but I do not remember any explicit instructions.

October 20, 1989

I dreamed that I had a fairly good view of half a dozen "Visitors"—grays! I knew that they were adults of various ages. All seemed about the same short height, but the degree of wrinkling of their skins depended on their age. The gray skin tone also seemed darker in the older entities. Four or five of them were behind a counter and a couple were in front. Their lack of noses gave them a piglike appearance.

Following these dreams, I have a vague memory from sometime during the past week that I looked out of the bathroom window during the night to see a thick mist outside. This memory had a different feel than a dream.

October 23, 1989

This last month has been terribly significant in terms of personal contact. I am writing this from an intuitive level. I do not have any factual evidence, just a "gut" feeling. My dreams have taken on a different theme too. Rather than reliving or remembering medical or instruction sessions, I have been able to remember actually seeing the small wrinkled grays. I look back at this dream (memory?) with a feeling of excitement and awe. Several times before going off to sleep I have had "profound insights," which I intend to remember, but I have forgotten them when I awake. This is very frustrating, because I feel these insights are important to my quest.

Female abductees claim that medical procedures such as laparoscopy, egg harvesting, and other abdominal procedures are performed while they are detained in a UFO. Recently, I have been looking at my own experiences to see if there are any strange occurrences that may have connections with an abduction experience.

For example, during my teens and twenties I frequently had a "leaking navel." I told my mother about this condition, but her advice was to make sure I cleaned my belly button. She did not take me to the doctor. I have since talked to other abductees who have also noticed the "leaking navel" condition. These experiencers have reported laparoscopy-type procedures during their abductions. Laparoscopy is a surgical procedure to view the inside of the abdomen and is usually done through the navel.

In 1978 I had a lower GI series of barium tests for an irritable bowel syndrome. The radiologist seemed puzzled and asked me if I had ever had abdominal surgery, which I had not. There seemed to be something odd about my appendix. The radiologist asked if I had received surgery to remove my appendix, which I had not. He could have seen that I did not have a scar.

During my twenties and thirties, I had a strange condition in which my pupils were unequal. The ophthalmologist said it was not serious, but I think he did not know why I had this condition. Also, I do not seem to have any plantar reflexes. I read in a medical textbook that there is a neurological condition that occurs in young women that is manifested by unequal pupils and lack of deep reflexes, including the plantar reflex. It does not seem to be a serious condition, and the textbook said it was temporary. I have been wondering if other women have suffered from these conditions. I wonder now if it has anything to do with abductions, or whether these were totally unrelated conditions. The presence of correlations does not presume causation.

October 26, 1989

I have been thinking about the timing of possible Interfaces with the Visitors. When I dream about the Visitors or an Interface, it is difficult to know if the event is (a) real-time, occurring on the night of the dream; (b) a recent event, within a week or so of the Interface; (c) a long-term memory dream from months or even years ago; or (d) just a dream.

On the night of October 18, when my electric clock malfunctioned, I feel that an actual real-time event occurred. The dream of seeing the Visitors on the night of the 20th may have been a delayed-memory dream, from October 18.

Real-time events appear to be linked with electronic malfunctions and physical trauma such as bruising, scars, needle marks, or scratches that are discovered the morning after the dream. Recent trauma, discovered after real-time Interfaces, has included a triangular-shaped trauma to my left arm. Long-term memory dreams of Interfaces are not linked to any recent physical trauma.

November 4, 1989

A long, complicated dream that took place in a school or institution. I forgot most of the dream when I awoke but knew it was an Interface dream. The main characters were myself, a younger woman, and lots of small children dressed in gray. Part of the dream took place in a medical setting, and I was horrified to see medical equipment lying around on shelves and not in proper sterile containers.

November 22, 1989

I have been in Kenya one week and am having a great time sightseeing. There have been several interesting events regarding the Visitors. Last Wednesday night at Nygasha Game Park, I think there was an Interface, and possibly another at Samburu Game Park on Saturday night. Sunday, I dreamed of a large round submarine sitting on top of the lake; I was talking to the occupants. On Monday I was comparing insect bites with my friend Jean and noticed a strange bruise on my left inner leg. I said to Jean, "Oh, I know how I got that." But actually I do not know where it came from. Why did I say that to Jean? The bruise was an intense purple, triangular in shape, about a quarter of an inch darker bruise surrounded by a lighter bruise. The bruise was painless. This triangular bruise is similar to others I have noticed after an Interface.

December 2, 1989

Just returned from Kenya, Africa, and am back in England for a week. Following the triangular bruise episode, I had further medical dreams.

Today, my niece, who is twelve years old, asked me if our house was haunted, because she had heard steps on the stairs at night. She also complained of blood in her left ear. We thought it might be from her pierced ears. When I tested her ear with a cotton tip, there was a little fresh blood in her left ear canal. I reassured her that it was okay. I did not mention the grays to her, and she has not read any abduction literature, although she knows about my UFO interest.

I wish I could have visited the Dogon people while I was in Africa. They live in a region south of the Sahara Desert and consist of four related tribes that call themselves the Dogon. The Dogon apparently have knowledge about the universe, which they represent through patterns and symbols they draw in the dusty ground. As astronomical discoveries were developed in the Western world, it was found that the Dogon already had knowledge of these celestial events and bodies.

The focus of the Dogon's knowledge is the star Sirius (a binary star system). The first person to see Sirius by telescope was Alvan Clark, an American, in 1862. However, the Dogon already had knowledge of the system's size, color, length of orbit, the elliptical shape of its orbit, and the fact that is was a "heavy" star because of its density.

The Dogon also had other astronomical knowledge. They knew about the halo that surrounds Saturn, about the four main moons of Jupiter, that the planets revolved around the moon, that the Earth was round, that the Earth spins on its own axis, and that the Milky Way is a spiral galaxy. Another major belief is that all of this knowledge was given to them by extraterrestrial Visitors.

December 5, 1989

While I was in Africa, I noticed that my friend Jean had numerous small scoop marks on her shins, but I did not ask her about these. Similar scoop marks have been seen on the fronts of the shins of individuals who claim to have been abducted. Maybe I will send her some of the abduction literature. At a family gathering in England, one of my cousins mentioned three scoop marks on her buttocks "like three finger holes in a bowling ball." Again, I was reluctant to mention the abduction scenario.

I thought of a name for our group of people interested in UFOs and abductions: Interface. I will share it with them when I return to America. Mariah Folger is in Argentina. I wonder if she has had any Visitor contact there?

In *Smithsonian* (November 1989, vol. 20, no. 8), I came across a book review by Bill Gerbert entitled "The American Crow and the Common Raven." The article is about wildlife researcher Kilham and his wife, Jane, who studied a group of wild crows. The comments in the article could apply equally well to the ongoing Visitor research. I have quoted from this article: It is the Kilhams' belief that hands-on research, no matter how carefully conducted, often results in physical and psychic injury, and invariably distorts the behavior of birds and mammals. "If one wishes to understand any animal that is intelligent, sensitive, and capable of conscious thought, it is imperative, I think, to study it in its fearless state."

December 21, 1989

Long dream last night, set at a location in England, with people I met during my visit there. In the first part of the dream, I was relaying documents to and from a scientific group in Bristol. Then the dream changed slightly and I was having trouble with my clothes. I kept finding myself undressed, and I was trying to explain to people why this was so. Then I found myself paralyzed from the neck down and felt a device attached to the back of my neck. I could move my face but nothing else. Someone was talking to me. Gradually, I was able to gain control of one arm, which surprised the person with me. It was not supposed to happen. I gained more and more control until, to the consternation of the people monitoring me, I was able to walk. I went to a bathroom, but I was embarrassed when they came with me.

December 27, 1989

During this past year, I have been hearing and reading much about the abduction phenomenon and theories that have been put forward to explain it. These theories have ranged from a mythological origin (as fairies, elves, and gnomes); a purely psychological phenomenon (as altered states and imagination); government intervention; and the extraterrestrial (ET) hypothesis. All have been equally interesting and puzzling, but none seems to account for the whole picture.

Last night I had a symbolic dream in which I fought back against my abductors. I feel this is a healthy move. During the dream, I felt physically weak but was determined not to be a victim. This gave me the strength to fight. The dream took place in the basement of the house (my subconscious?) and the abductor came through a broken cellar door (lowered defenses?). I attacked him with a piece of wood, and he defended himself with a chair. I was yelling and calling for help. I was successful and the man gave up the fight.

As far as I remember, the attacker was small and dark and surprisingly strong. We were grappling for some time. There were also other people upstairs (other areas of my consciousness) who heard me and who came to my aid, but I overcame my attacker before they arrived. The rest of the dream took place in and around the house (my psyche), checking for broken windows (vulnerability) and making sure the house was secure.

December 30, 1989

A few weeks ago, after I returned from Africa and England, I received a thirty-four-page rebuttal by one of the therapists in the abduction field. A document criticizing the therapists' ethical standards had been sent around by one of the researchers. A short copy had also been sent out by a sponsor to all the recent conference attendees, outlining his reasons for withdrawing financial support. Both the researcher's and the sponsor's papers sounded rational and clear. The therapist's paper was long and rambling. The therapist mentioned my letters of support several times and also stated that because the researcher had distributed copies of my letters, she felt no hesitation in also doing so. All this was done without my consent or approval. Shortly afterward I received a short note from the researcher, assuring me that he had never copied or distributed my letter to him, as it was a personal letter.

These further developments have convinced me, more than ever, to disassociate myself from this wrangle and to let them fight it out among themselves. It may even come to litigation between the therapists and the researchers. If only all the time and energy could have been put to the use for which it was primarily intended—trying to solve the abduction enigma!

December 31, 1989

On Friday I received correspondence from my colleague Mariah Folger regarding her recent Interfaces with the Visitors. She seems to be increasingly angry about her experiences. This may be because her son has recently undergone hypnotic regression and recounted episodes of abduction since childhood, some of which include Mariah and the rest of the family. I think she is beginning to realize that the Interfaces are not as benign as she has portrayed. I will continue to be supportive but will not share my experiences for a time while she is sorting out her own emotional reactions.

In Budd Hopkins' book *Intruders* and at various UFO conferences, he has shown photos and slides of a garden in which a UFO was supposed to have landed. The grass stopped growing in this area and snow would not settle there. This last summer I noticed a wide circle of dead grass in our next-door neighbor's garden and wondered if this could be a similar phenomenon. I took a photo of the yard for my records. It seemed particularly interesting, because our neighbor is rather obsessive about his lawn: mulching, raking, and mowing. If there was a fungal or parasitic infection of the lawn, he would have dealt with it. Also, it was a wet summer, so drought did not play a part in its formation. Today, I noticed that the area surrounding the circle was snow covered, but the circle was clear.

8

More Interesting Than Science Fiction

"I must say that if listeners could see for themselves the mass of reports coming in from the airborne gendarmerie, the mobile gendarmerie and from the gendarmerie charged with the job of conducting investigations, all of which reports are forwarded by us to the National Center for Space Studies, then they would see that it is all pretty disturbing."

—M. Robert Galley, French minister of defense, interviewed on radio by Jean-Claude Bourret, February 21, 1974.

January 1, 1990

1989 was a good year with lots of interesting new things happening—some good, some bad. The researchers-versus-therapists fiasco revealed the fragile egos and emotive subject matter of abduction research. The verbal duels between the therapists and the researchers were shameful, and the field lost many good people. I have decided not to attend an upcoming abduction conference but to monitor the field from a distance. The lab has seen a constant stream of fascinating visitors from all walks of life and from all over the world. But I feel an obligation to defend the parapsychology lab from the vicious infighting in the UFO field.

Some interesting developments in regard to X. When I got

back from vacation, I found some information in the lab files dealing with X's history and stressing his multiple security and government agency connections. It made interesting but uneasy reading. There was another paper that had been sent to the lab by a local writer that implicated X and others in a paranoia-inducing account of government activity using the UFO story as a cover. Part of the paper accused X and the original psychophysics lab of being part of a cover-up story for clandestine research. Again, it was uneasy reading.

I have decided to store this information, along with the other theories regarding the UFO and abduction scenario, and to try and sift out the "signal from the noise." At the moment there is still a lot of random noise, but a common thread that seems to run through all of this is X. If I do continue to meet with him, it will be with my eyes wide open and aware.

January 5, 1990

I dreamed that I was doing some experiments in eye tracking. A doctor was concerned that my right eye had a slight tremor. He was going to examine my eyes, but I told him I had been a forceps delivery. It was agreed that there might have been slight nerve damage to my eye when I was born.

Emily told me this morning that she had dreamed that she awoke and in her dream found the front door open. She then found an intruder in the basement. In her dream, she found herself shouting and leaning against the basement door. Emily felt that this dream had been precipitated by her hearing one of the cats out on the porch, which caused her to worry about an intruder.

Another dream from last night involved a possible "hybrid" baby. The baby was small for her age and about a year old. I was holding her on my lap for most of the dream, while I was talking to some people. At one point, I was looking for X. Then I saw the baby in a clear plastic baby seat. A small person was feeding the baby. But it was all wrong. The baby was lying down, the nipple had been taken off the bottle, and the baby was choking from too much milk. I told the small person to put the nipple back on the bottle and to put a larger hole in the nipple. I sat the baby up to stop her choking. I noticed how pale her skin was. I complained that she was not being looked after properly and she did not have enough clothes on. When the small person came back with the bottle, I noticed that indeed the hole had been made bigger, and the whole top of the nipple had been cut off. It seems as if they have no idea of child care and nurturing.

When I instructed the small person to put a larger hole in the nipple, I thought she might be offended, but she went to another person and asked for this to be done. I do not remember actually talking to her; there were lots of mental impressions and I did hear her talking to someone in the other room.

The baby's seat was made of a clear plastic material with a hood over it. I have the impression that this was to provide oxygen. The baby was small and pale but quite vigorous. Although she was about a year old, she had not reached the one-year human developmental milestones, such as walking and talking. She seemed quite alert and bright.

I remembered that when I was holding the baby in the dream, I became "conscious." The people with me recognized my change of consciousness state and were concerned about the baby. I convinced them that she was okay and kept her sitting on my lap. They seemed to accept this.

January 9, 1990

Before Christmas, Emily, John (a doctor friend), and I had been jesting about writing a spoof on *Men in Black* by writing a funny tale about "Ladies in Black." This would be about little old ladies dressed in black who ride bicycles. I actually saw such a lady on a bicycle dressed in black last year. Yesterday, while Emily was giving me a ride to work, we saw another elderly lady, dressed all in black, with an old-fashioned hat and bicycle. She did not look quite real, cycling along the sidewalk. She may have been a ghost, although she looked real. However, everything about her was anachronous, out of place and time—her clothes; her bicycle; her upright, stiff manner; her lack of expression. Also, it was bitterly cold, yet she did not wear a coat or gloves.

This morning, Emily asked me to look at some long multidirectional scratches on her back. Most were on her left side. She cannot remember getting these scratches. They happened overnight. They do not look deep, but they are definite scratches.

January 16, 1990

Lots of dreams these last couple of nights, which I have forgotten as soon as I awaken. The only thing to remain with me from last night's dreams was the word "metamorphosis." This could reflect the culmination of the last two years of personal growth and change.

January 17, 1990

A very disturbed night: nightmares that may indicate encounters and Interfaces during the last few nights. I awoke in the night following a disturbing, surreal dream involving the woman from SAIC with whom I shared a room at a UFO conference.

The dream included very real images of small grays, face to face with me. As I was seeing these images, I had terrible feelings of fear and panic. The woman from SAIC was talking in my right ear. I was calling out, "No," and, "There is too much noise." There was a lot of background noise. It was very disturbing and may have been the end result of my reluctance to go to sleep last night—very unusual for me.

Later, in another dream, I was watching two small identical beings with large eyes talking about genetics. They talked in turns and seemed to share the information. As one talked, the other mouthed the words. At one point, I was surprised to see small facial movements around the eyes of the beings. Until then, their upper faces had seemed fairly static. This morning I had a small round raw area on my right index finger. Whatever it is must have happened during the night.

January 21, 1990

On Saturday, making my way to Penn Station to catch the train back to New Jersey, I saw another "Lady in Black." This time she appeared much younger and was dressed in a 1920s outfit with small hat and gloves. She was very pale and wore old-fashioned spectacles. She walked around, looking nervous, and stood with her back to the announcement board, which seemed odd. Was she a ghost of Penn Station?

January 22, 1990

"Curiouser and curiouser," as Alice in Wonderland once said. Earlier this month, I wrote about a paper I had received from a researcher named Martin Cannon. He forwarded his paper to us via an airline pilot named Chuck. Cannon's paper, entitled "The Controllers: A New Hypothesis of Alien Abduction," outlined a strange theory that the government is actually creating the UFO story as a cover for clandestine experiments involving brain implants, hypnosis, subliminal instruction, and behavior control. The paper mentioned a woman (whom I assume is Betty-Sue) who, like me, had participated at the psychophysics lab, who had undergone hypnotic regression, and who felt that more had happened to her there than was consciously remembered. The paper implicated X and other government affiliates in this scenario.

Out of the blue this morning, Chuck called wanting to take me to lunch. I felt I had to make it clear to him that the parapsychology lab does not do any UFO research, apart from our own general interest, but he was still interested in meeting me.

I discussed this proposed visit with Emily. We decided that all of these dynamics had the making for a great novel. Maybe one day these journals will form the basis for such a book. It could be a lot of fun. A project for my old age! Before Christmas, I was looking in a Barnes & Noble for something interesting to read, something with a science fiction basis involving time, space, consciousness, parapsychology, UFO, and intrigue. It suddenly struck me that my current life reflected all these themes, and I was actually living as interesting a life as I was looking for in the bookstore. I had to stop and have a little chuckle.

January 30, 1990

What wonder! I think I touched one of the Visitors last night and discovered that they are as nervous of us as we are of them. During the night, I became aware that I was awake. I felt some bedding being pulled off the bed to my left. The right side of my bed faces the wall, the left is open to the room. I thought, as I woke, "Oh, my goodness, this is real." However, I was not brave enough to open my eyes. Curious, I reached out my left arm and felt the solid body of a small Visitor. I feel strange writing this, a sort of awe. I put my hand around what would have been the waist, but there was no indentation for a waist. I touched its left arm, pressing the solid arm. My impressions were that the body I was touching was real, tough, and muscled, but I felt no rounded muscles.

The being I was touching was standing very still and straight. However, its companion was making a whistle-piping sound with anxiety, and I sensed their nervousness that I was touching them. I decided to send them reassurance and loving thoughts and withdrew my arm. I think I had been pinching the arm too hard. I received the same thoughts reflected back to me, and I remembered no more until I awoke in the morning.

I have been wondering why the Visitors allowed me to touch one of them, and I have come up with two possible explanations. First, it could be that there was some concern over my recent combative attitude during Interfaces. During these, I have fought physically, assuring myself that I would not be a victim of the Interfaces. Maybe the physical encounter was planned to assure me that no harm was meant and that there were anxieties and insecurities on both sides. During the Interface last night, I was thinking about their sharp nails, but I did not feel them. Looking back now, I feel that I initiated the touching and the loving, calming thoughts, although these were reciprocal. I felt relief from them when I removed my hand.

Another reason for the physical Interface might be the upcoming meeting with Mariah Folger's group in August and our quest for a fully remembered, full-consciousness Interface with the Visitors. I must let Mariah Folger and X know soon about this new and amazing occurrence.

9

Requesting an Interface

"I don't laugh at people any more when they say they've seen UFOs. I've seen one myself."

—President Jimmy Carter, remarking on his sighting in January 1969, on *ABC News*, January 1999.

February 1, 1990

A few nights ago, I had a real and lucid experience, which I am still going over in my mind. During the experience, I did not say, "I am now dreaming," but "This is real." The experience involved putting out my hand and feeling the solid small body of one of the Visitors. I have been thinking about this Interface. First, the small body of the Visitor was clothed in a smooth, almost shiny fabric like spandex, although I could not see the color, because I kept my eyes closed. Second, I do not recall any respiratory movements from the body. It stood absolutely still. Third, there was a definite substance to the body, a solidness, and I was surprised that the thorax, or chest, was rounder than is depicted in illustrations of the Visitors.

When I first put out my arm, I encountered the Visitor's right side and I think he was turned, communicating with another Visitor to his left. I could feel his back. He must have turned toward me, as I was then touching his right arm, squeezing it in an inquiring way. I continued touching until the companion Visitor became anxious. That was when I withdrew my hand and tried to send loving, reassuring thoughts to them. I think we both surprised each other and then tried to generate feelings of nonthreat and reassurance. I distinctly remember the whistle-piping sound made by the anxious companion.

My involvement with the Interface group started by Mariah Folger has continued for the past year, and I have shared my recorded dreams with Mariah and X. The dreams recently took a healthy turn from a combative effort against seeing myself as a victim to experiencing and actually touching the night Visitors. Mariah is coming for a visit on the 10th, and the group will be meeting at her house in August.

On a personal level, I have continued to record instances of synchronicity on a daily basis, interesting Interfaces and encounters, spontaneous psi and other anomalies. Unfortunately, my recent interest in the UFO abduction phenomenon has had to be put on a back burner because of the bitter animosity among the key players. I am not attending the upcoming abduction conference, but Mariah and X said they would update me when they returned.

Various odd explanations have been put forward for the UFO and abduction scenarios. The most recent one, proposed by Cannon, is that the whole scenario is a government mind game, using the UFO story as a cover. This and alternative explanations have been stored in my "mental data sorter," where I will do a sort of signal-processing looking for patterns and similarities between various theories. Dennis Stillings is strongly advocating the imaginal explanation, and Kenneth Ring is advocating the strong associations between abduction and childhood abuse. Ring's study found a high reported incidence of childhood abuse among abductees. However, as I have mentioned before, correlation does not always indicate causation.

February 2, 1990

We have a total of five cats in the house, including "Shade," a young black short hair, which has a very trusting, affectionate nature. Over the last six months, he has progressively lost a lot of fur and looks like a chemotherapy patient. The thought has crossed my mind that if the Visitors are a reality, Shade might have been included in their contacts. He likes to follow me when I leave the house. There have been anecdotal tales of cats being included in abductions, such as the tales related by Whitley Strieber. It is possible that the Visitors could control the movements of a human abductee but a cat could get into all sorts of strange places, could encounter possible noxious materials and perhaps suffer the consequences.

February 3, 1990

I woke in the night, anxious and gasping for breath. I felt myself gasp several times. I think I was having a nightmare but could not remember what. Later, I dreamed that I was at the abduction conference. I was witnessing a young boy who was able to levitate. I was looking for Dr. Z to show her the boy's amazing feats, but I could not find her. The dream involved a lot of physical effort and stress.

February 5, 1990

When I awoke on Sunday, I discovered a half-inch cut above the bridge of my nose, between my eyes, but a little bit more to my left side. The cut was not sore. It was there Sunday and still there Monday morning. I had some bad headaches both days.

February 6, 1990

I remembered a medical dream in which I was asked to "huff" breath into a chilled flask. The breath condensed on the cold glass, and the fluid was collected as a specimen. I have never heard of this kind of test before.

February 8, 1990

My friend B called on Wednesday, and we talked about the abduction conference, which she had attended. She seemed to think that it went very well and enjoyed the talks. She asked me about the Cannon paper, whether I had received a copy of it and what I thought about it. I told her that it was well researched but that if the paper were true, it was horrifying and would involve the interaction of personnel on the scale of the Holocaust. B mentioned that she had asked X if the paper was true and his cryptic remark was "Some if it." I have sent copies to Mariah Folger and X for their comments.

February 13, 1990

Mariah was here visiting for three days, and we had some good discussions regarding child care, nurturing, bonding, and how these ideas could be interpreted in the light of Interface experiences. Mariah felt that there was an Interface on the second night of her visit. In fact, she had made a mental request of the Visitors to come in the middle night of her stay. However, I felt that if anything had happened, it had happened on the final night of her stay, because in the morning I discovered a bruised shin and had a real dream related to the Interface.

I first dreamed that I found myself in a room about as big as my bathroom but completely bare. Thinking that I was in the bathroom, I wondered where the tiles and shower curtain were. The walls were bare gray plaster, very roughly manufactured. I was alone in the room for some time. In the dream, there was also a physical examination, with an instrument that I could not see but that hurt me. I believe that the examination took place in the bare room. I watched a TV monitor on which I viewed a person wearing aviator goggles.

February 14, 1990

I found dried blood in my right ear canal twice during the day. During the morning, several large bits of dried blood were on the cotton swab with which I dried my ears. Also this evening my right ear was itchy, and I discovered several more bits of blood. My ear does not hurt, and I do not remember any obvious trauma to the ear.

Last night I had numerous dreams but all the details were forgotten when I awoke. However, I was left with the feeling that a lot of issues had been resolved, that a lot of explanations had been given and many answers found. No idea of what, though. There were also vague memories of waking between the dreams and commenting to myself that the dreams were important and significant.

February 15, 1990

Last night I had an interesting and instructive dream. I was at a large house that had a wide staircase. I was attending some kind of meeting. I found that I was able to levitate and float down the staircase, catching myself as I reached the bottom by holding onto the bottom post. During the dream, I was reveling in the free feeling that this was giving me. In the dream, I was being very cautious because there were people around, including a chief of security services of the United States and a full colonel, whom I had met at the parapsychology lab. I was torn between spontaneous expression and caution that I would be seen and my abilities put to a negative use by these people.

I feel that this dream illustrates my natural caution and tendency not to draw attention to myself and not to expose my abilities. However, in the dream, even though they could see me float, the military folk ignored me. I felt relieved and carried on floating down the stairs and into the lower meeting rooms. Perhaps the dream means that, despite my feelings of caution, my abilities will not be recognized and misused, and that, in reality, these negative sources are not really interested. Which means I can continue to be who I am. This does not mean that I should stop being cautious but that I should feel free to express my abilities.

February 16, 1990

I found an interesting article about pet implants in a copy of *OMNI*. The implant is a microchip, as small as a grain of rice, that is surgically placed in the muscle between the pet's shoulder blades. The device is marketed by Infopets, a company in Agoura Hills, California. An electronic scanner reads the identification chip. The scanner emits a beep and a ten-digit ID number is produced on the scanning wand. The article says that the system already has been used to catalogue about ten thousand pets in cities around the United States, such as San Francisco; Boston; St. Louis; Eugene, Oregon; and Yuma, Arizona. An Infopet spokesperson reported that the device could work equally well on rabbits, horses, cows, and llamas.

This article caught my interest, because I have heard about abductees who report that they have had implants inserted in their bodies. The scientific community has ridiculed these claims by saying that the technology is not available. In fact, it is available and has been for some time. There is now talk about implanting children with this technology with the rationale given of being able to track the children if they are physically abducted.

Late last year I sent for a copy of a publication put out by the Fund for UFO Research (FUFOR). It contained the final results of a UFO abduction questionnaire that was posted in *OMNI* in 1987. Based on the questionnaire responses, *OMNI* reported some interesting results:

The number of people with missing time was 42 percent.
The number of people who reported seeing strange figures as a child was 48 percent.
The number of females who reported an odd pregnancy or baby dreams was 48 percent.
The number of people who reported observing a UFO was 75 percent.
The number of people hearing their name called "in head" was 59 percent.
That UFOs are real, maybe ET, 65 percent.
That some abduction reports were genuine, 67 percent.

Taking into consideration that the readership of *OMNI* includes many people who have read UFO books and articles, which may have biased their responses, these percentages are still high enough to warrant further investigation.

February 18, 1990

Last night I slept twelve hours, and it felt wonderful and healing. I slept for another two hours this afternoon. I had lots of dreams, but I forgot most of them.

One dream involved a strange situation. In the dream, I was challenged by a small woman who looked like the psychiatrist Dr. Z. It seemed that someone had emptied a whole bottle of some toxic substance into a lake and killed all the fish. I was devastated at this terrible waste of life and grieved for the fish. I hid my face in my hands. The small woman waved an empty chlorine bottle in the air and accused me of killing the fish. I protested my innocence, claiming that I would never do such a thing. I felt helpless that no one believed me. I felt a great sadness for the lake and the fish. However, there was an underlying suspicion that my emotional reaction was being tested. The dream situation had an unreal feel to it. In the dream I never saw the lake or the dead fish, just the bottle and the woman.

I was going to write this dream down earlier but I forgot, which is a sure sign that it is an important dream, psychologically, and that maybe I was blocking it.

February 20, 1990

Mariah Folger contacted me and sent me her account of the Interface that happened when she was visiting here. My first reaction, on reading her account, was to laugh uproariously. I do not know if this was from a release of tension or what? Her account was not particularly funny, but my reaction was laughter. I nearly fell off the bed laughing. Mariah reported that the Visitors expressed surprise at finding her, saying, "It is her, look, it is her." Mariah remembered there being several small Visitors around her bed saying, "Honored, honored, honored that you chose us." Mariah has always requested the Visitors to "knock first" and respect her privacy as much as possible. Mariah experienced headaches and nosebleeds following the Interface, and I had headaches and found dried blood in my ear. Mariah reported that she hit her elbow on a bookcase as she was led back to bed.

Mariah also felt that this group of Visitors did not know her. When our group visited Boulder, Colorado, a few years ago, and experienced an Interface there, the Visitors did not appear to know us as a group. This sheds some light on the Visitors' functioning. There seems to be a degree of intergroup sharing but not at a person-specific level, unless very specifically requested. Each Visitor group seems to have both an own-group database and a shared intergroup database.

Another interesting thing noted by Mariah was that the Visitors exited through the bathroom door. In many of my remembered Interfaces, the Visitors have come up the stairs and into my room through the doorway. There have been no instances of them floating through windows or walls, like some abductees report.

February 23, 1990

I awoke at about 4:25 A.M. following a dream in which I was supposed to do something at four A.M. There was emphasis on some message or communication. However, I forgot the actual content of the dream.

February 24, 1990

I awoke again at 4:14 A.M. The cats were crying to go out. I let them out and went back to sleep.

I dreamed that I was taking pills and capsules but they seemed unusual. Some were clear gelatin capsules with clear centers, others were clear capsules containing a yellow substance. I was not given any water to drink to wash them down. I found a yellow capsule that was not completely filled and I was squeezing it and playing with it, changing its shape and having fun. The "person" with me (who looked like X) seemed amused at what I was doing.

I have come to the conclusion that my Interfaces typically seem to occur between approximately two and four A.M. I will try several strategies to wake up during this time period and see if anything unusual is happening.

I recently came across an article on gnomes. I was struck by the attributes given to gnomes and those given to the Visitors. For example, that they are not seen by everyone, only by those capable of perceiving them. Gnomes are supposedly concerned about the management of our planet, as are the Visitors. Both are reported to have underground homes or bases. Ellen Crystal, a New Jersey writer and musician, is said to have found areas in New York State, around Pinebush, where underground noises are heard and warm updrafts of air are felt, from apparently isolated areas. Both gnomes and Visitors seem to generate an emotional reaction in people in general.

The second-century B.C. pseudepigraphal Book of Enoch speaks of an entity named Azazel, who taught humans to make swords, knives, shields, and breastplates, also jewelry and the use of metals in cosmetics and medicine. Azazel also taught humans about the various metals of the Earth and the art of working these metals. According to records contained in Enoch 9, Azazel also gave humans knowledge about the heavens. Were Azazel and the gnomes of early Earth what we now know as the grays?

Throughout Celtic mythology, there exists a realm inhabited by nonhuman creatures consisting of elves, fairies, devas, elementals, gnomes, leprechauns, dwarfs, spirits, sylphs, undines, and sprites. Stories of these "wee folk" may or may not be connected to Visitor contact.

However, there are similarities in the appearance and behavior of these beings that allows for the possibility that the early stories might be related to modern contact experiences. For example, the elves were a legendary small people with the following characteristics:

1. They lived underground in mounds;
2. They were said to lure humans to their lands for a variety of different reasons; and
3. They were rumored to be either extremely tall (seven feet and over) or extremely small (three feet or less).

Several individuals have written on the possible mythological origins of the Visitors, including Peter Rojcewicz, who has noted the similarities between gnomes, fairies, and Visitor behavior. These ideas seem to have quite a following. There is a popular notion that gnomes may have developed technologically, just as we have. Our knowledge of gnomes seems to be stuck back in the 1600s, when we ourselves were just coming out of the Dark Ages. Folks who postulate a link between the Visitors and gnomes bolster their argument with the following:

In the four hundred intervening years, it would not be surprising that gnomes and other small folk had developed along similar lines to us, or even more so. Gnomes have always been known for their skills in metalworking, their wise ways, and their anomalous means of communication. They are also reported to be less bounded by time and space than we mortals are. It is possible they have made discoveries and found ways to interact anomalously with us that far exceed our present knowledge. Like the Visitors, they can risk being seen occasionally because the perceiver not only will be disbelieved but may also be ridiculed.

February 25, 1990

As an act of personal verification and exploration, I decided to carry out a daily meditation requesting a mental interface with the Visitors, with several aims in mind. First, to see if I could access any information about the Visitors, to exchange information; second, to see if we could understand each other's goals; third, perhaps there could be some degree of cooperation between us and the Visitors. Initially, I did not plan to include other people in my meditations, but there is the possibility of other people participating in some way.

At first, I mentally signaled "request information" and "request Interface" following a meditative period. I realized that "request" put us on an unequal standing. "Demand Interface" would also do the same thing. I changed my mental statement to "Interface open" to indicate an openness to dialogue. I visualized myself behind an open window through which an Interface dialogue could take place. I sensed interest and curiosity but nothing happened.

Then, I found myself in an English woodland scene. It was summer, and sunlight could be seen through tall trees. I did not understand at once, then I realized that we were meeting on neutral territory, neither theirs nor mine. A sort of virtual scene had been created. I walked through the woods and sat on a stone seat and waited. I want to point out here that I am not a channeler. I do not channel disembodied spirits or convey information from departed souls. This exercise was carried out for my own information and curiosity.

From out of the woods came "the Wise One," one of their seniors, very wrinkled and slightly stooped. We exchanged looks and each of us held out a hand. I decided to be honest and told the Wise One that his hand reminded me of a chicken claw and was repulsive to me. He replied that, to him, my hand was just as repulsive! This got us off to a good start. The Wise One appeared to want to understand our world as much as we want to understand his.

He—I assumed he was of a male-like gender—asked who I represented. I said that I only represented myself, but that I indirectly represented many people, both in close circles and wider groups. However, the decision to Interface was mine. His reply was that he represented all of his kind, not that he was above or better than others, just chosen as a representative. We agreed that there should be a sharing of information and a statement of goals but that we would have to decide what information and what goals. This was easier for him, because a consensus already existed at his end as to what could be represented. I was at a disadvantage, because I spoke directly for myself but indirectly for others, a different process than his.

We decided that there should be mutual cooperation and that we should return to discuss other topics. I decided to "close the window," because it was taking a great deal of energy to maintain the Interface. However, it was decided that the open window would be a signal to indicate openness to Interface together, and that we would meet again in a neutral mental setting. Some information would be given and translated by means of their technology. The Wise One and I would Interface again when the next opportunity arose.

February 26, 1990

At ten P.M. I entered a meditative state and visualized "Open Interface" as an open window. I had random thoughts regarding the phrase "Open Interface" sounding like "Open Sesame." My mind wandered onto mundane work thoughts, but my attention was brought back to the Wise One standing on his side of the window. I asked him to come to my side of the window, and we entered a virtual room. He stood and I sat. I asked if he wanted to sit, and he told me that sitting or lying down were human actions. He asked me why we had not adapted to gravity over the centuries, and why we still had to counter its force by sitting and lying down.

We agreed on the first of several ground rules:

1. We would each do what was normal for us. He would continue to stand, and I would sit. We would not expect one to conform to the other's idea of normalcy.
2. We would be honest with each other, even to the point of offending the other. This way we could learn from each other without false pretense.
3. The Wise One said that my opening the dialogue was one-sided and that he should also have the opportunity to initiate an Open Interface. At first I commented that this might not be convenient but realized how unilateral this was, so I agreed that we should both have the opportunity to initiate dialogue, if necessary. It was agreed that communication could be telepathic; sometimes in the form of back-and-forth dialogue, sometimes in shared visual form. I realized, at one point, how unstructured I was being and I commented, "Where shall we begin?" To which the Wise One replied, "We have already begun."

After about five or ten minutes I said that I was tired and wished to end the Interface. The Wise One commented that I was being unreasonable, by calling him to dialogue for such a short time, which took such an effort for him. I explained that it was very tiring for me, too. Also, I was trying to multitask: being in a meditative state to achieve the Interface but also maintaining some vigilant faculties to dialogue, and to remember the Interface in order to record it correctly. This was energy draining. We agreed to close the Interface and to try again another time.

Perhaps it will get easier with time and practice. However, I feel comfortable that we were able to lay down some ground rules that are mutually agreeable. Although it seems as if nothing major has been accomplished, I still feel that these two Interfaces have been successful preliminary stages.

February 27, 1990

In a long dream, I found myself in an assembly of people in a church or college auditorium. There was a feeling of it being very old-fashioned. I was at the front of the church and was supposed to be learning a new language. The sounds were like Amharic, the Ethiopian language my friend in Africa is learning. We were given very old books and were chanting the sounds from the books. I looked back and saw X in the congregation. There was a flurry of activity and I recognized an elder senator and a famous business financier entering the congregation, as well as other men of power and influence. There was an expectation in the air, an excitement and feeling that things were about to happen.

I had decided not to Interface today but perceived the Wise One requesting an Interface around 10:35 P.M. So I meditated and Interfaced. We found ourselves in a lighted globe. The Wise One had a companion and requested that I bring another person to Interface. I explained that this was not going to be easy. Telepathy was not a strong characteristic of humans, and I would have to arrange an Interface through physical means, such as the telephone. However, I tried to mentally contact Mariah, whom I requested to Interface with us. I felt Mariah to be present and visualized her wearing a purple warm-up suit. However, the contact was not maintained. The companion to the Wise One remained quiet. The Wise One and I talked about our different concepts of time, theirs communal, ours individual.

The Wise One said that time was something that someone else measured and they received moment-by-moment instructions regarding what they should do. There was no planning ahead; for them, time was only related to *now*.

I explained our concept of time as objective or linear, as well as time being subjective or holistic. The Wise One could accept a nonmechanistic version of time. He asked me to describe clocks. I began by saying that clocks were devices for measuring time and took many forms. The earliest, simplest ones were just a stick in the ground measuring the shadow of the Sun as it passed overhead. The Wise One queried, "But you are measuring the passage of the Sun only, not time." I tried to explain the idea that when the Sun passed from point A to point B, that interval was accepted as a measurement of a unit of time.

There was a similar dialogue regarding clocks. I used the same argument that the interval between tick A and tock B was agreed upon as a unit of time. The response was that we were "only measuring sound." There was little acceptance of the concept of linear time—I almost said that the concept was alien to him!

This Interface presented two new issues:

1. The acceptance by them that more than one person could Interface but the realization that it was easier for them than for us; and

2. The dialogue regarding our concepts of time and its measurement showed the differences in our acceptance of those concepts. I think we both realized we only covered the surface of our queries. I started thinking personal thoughts toward the end of the dialogue, and the Wise One abruptly terminated the session by stating "Interface closed." There was no reproach or anger, just a decision to end the dialogue until the next time.

March 5, 1990

For a couple of days I have been experiencing "what if" dreams of a nightmare quality, accompanied by realistic scenarios such as "What if you drowned your kitten and cooked her for breakfast?" This was accompanied by a visual image of a sink of warm water and a struggling cat. I compromised in the dream by giving the cat a bath in the warm water. No way was I going to harm her. Then there was "What if we drill your teeth." I felt the novocaine being injected, tasted the stuff and my mouth went numb, just as I woke up.

Possibly these nightmares are a result of stress in getting my Ph.D. application together and fighting a cold, or it could be a continuation of the information-exchange initiated with the Wise One.

March 11, 1990

There is much anecdotal material written about the reasons for the abduction experience. One is that it is to provide genetic stock for the Visitors. In the literature there are accounts of gynecological procedures, ova and sperm collection, and missing pregnancies. Over the past few years I have been recording dreams relating to these types of procedures and noting the similarities of these dreams to the experiences of others. The dream recollections span eleven years and for brevity I will write about two that felt like real dreams:

April 2, 1979: I dreamed that I walked into a drug store and behind the counter was a sickly baby lying on cotton. It was shielded by a glass case. It had a long scar with stitches down its back. I spoke to the pharmacist, who explained why he was looking after the baby—all the hospitals were on strike. I was worried, because the people in the drug store were not being very gentle with the baby and it was being exposed to infection.

October 25, 1987: I dreamed that I was breast-feeding a tiny baby at my left breast. I was surprised at the suck of such a tiny infant. When I awoke in the morning my breasts were sore.

March 27, 1990

For the last couple of weeks I have lacked energy because of an infected hand that turned septic. I have been feeling wretched. However, now that my left hand is on the mend, I will update my journal and include the following dream: Sometime last week I dreamed I awoke in a strange room, like a hotel room with good furniture. There were two beds and I was in one of them. I wondered who would be coming to sleep in the other one and I returned to sleep. This dream felt very real.

Mariah Folger has suggested that the abductees involved in Interfaces may have compromised immune systems as a result of their physical interaction with the Visitors and that any infection will take longer to heal, be more severe, and involve more medication. I question this immune system involvement because there would be additional manifestations. However, abductees' systems may be altered in some way that delays healing but does not affect the general energy level or functioning of the individual on a healthy day-to-day basis.

I had a terrifying dream last night involving energies generated by the Visitors. I was at a house talking to a psi researcher (who looks alien). I was looking out of a side window and someone encouraged me to go outside, where I was bombarded with blue lasers. I was terrified, because I felt these would harm me. I constantly dodged these blue beams. A male colleague was also outside, but the beams did not seem to bother him as much. I woke in a panic.

March 28, 1990

Mariah Folger sent me a letter asking questions about the presence of energy, water, houses, furniture, and large picture windows in her Interfaces and her dreams. I responded with the following:

There may be some symbolic role of water particular to you. For me, water in my dreams has a healing quality. For example, water running through a dream house symbolizes a cleansing action.

Houses in my dreams are myself and usually involve several floors or levels connected by a staircase. The top floor or attic represents my mystical self and is usually represented by a large ceremonial room, richly decorated. Sometimes there are a series of attic rooms filled with memorabilia (memory symbols). You should ask what your room and house symbolize and how the Visitors would use this data in their interactions.

Large picture windows have figured in several of my Interface experiences, to view either an outside scene or a staged tableau. These tableaus look real but are incongruous to the scene within the room. Upon closer inspection, they are revealed to be staged scenarios.

Interestingly, the furniture in my dream Interfaces has improved over time. You may remember that I commented several times that the furniture looked as if it were off the streets, old-fashioned, old, and colorless. Lately, the dream Interfaces involving rooms full of furniture have been different. Either actual Interface rooms have been furnished with new stuff or my interpretation of the rooms has altered in some way. The furniture is also more appropriately placed compared to earlier Interfaces. Before, all the old furniture was pushed against the walls, as if in a store room.

Now, the various rooms have furniture placed in their appropriate places. There has been some effort to normalize the environment. However, the furniture is not my style, being French provincial, ornate, lavish, and large. I think that if I were furnishing these rooms, they would reflect my own style, which is more modern, colorful, and lighter in effect, more airy and spacious. I have one earlier dream memory in which I was asked to participate in moving the furniture and found it to be very heavy and cumbersome. It seemed like someone had seen the ads in the newspapers for room lots of furniture and decided that was what most people preferred. That would be logical for a Visitor mind. Anyway, I must not complain; the real dreams are a lot more comfortable than they used to be.

Regarding columns of water: The cylindrical tube of water, light, and energy you mentioned could be described as "white noise" or "white light"—a chaotic, random flow of energy. Lab experiments have shown that some individuals can produce order out of chaotic patterns like these. Practical applications of this effect could be the transfer of information and modification of matter. These are just my random thoughts. Maybe the Visitors already know about these things.

March 29, 1990

I went to sleep early but had a disturbed night with an unusual real dream. I dreamed that I woke up to put the phone receiver back on its hook. Emily came upstairs to ask me why the phone was off the hook and I answered that one of the cats must have knocked it off. Someone else also came up the stairs and into Sydney's room.

In the morning, I asked Emily if she had come upstairs during the night and she said "No." She also said that she had not asked me about the phone. The quality of the dream interactions seemed to be of a real dream rather than a "dream state." I feel sure that I was awake when I heard someone come up the stairs.

March 30, 1990

I awoke in the night around three A.M. and experienced a piercing pain in my back. Incongruously, I did not get up to take a pain pill. (I had been in the habit of getting up in the night to take a pain pill for my infected hand.) Instead, I lay still, somehow knowing that the pain would gradually fade away, which it did.

April 14, 1990

I awoke about 7:30 and had some tea and fruit, then decided to go back to bed. I spent several hours in a half-sleep state. At times, my mind was awake and I was in a state of total physical relaxation. I tried to move my body but without success. During this state, I experienced a tremendous input of "information" flowing through me. I could visualize this "information" as streams of symbols flowing from left to right across my visual field, a little like a continuous strip of film. The symbols were scrolling very fast. I made an effort to slow down the scrolling to see what was written on the film, but there was no writing as such. The film contained randomly placed, randomly oriented, alphabet letters such as A, C, G, and symbols I did not understand. I have no idea what this was but speculate that it had something to do with the DNA chain of elements. I then let the film scroll at its fast speed. After viewing this scroll of symbols, I experienced a high-pitched sound in both ears, like a high-frequency vibration. It got so intense that I started shaking. At that point it switched off abruptly.

April 18, 1990

I dreamed that I was given a shot in the thigh by a small foreign woman. The dream location looked like the pavilion in Philadelphia that houses the Liberty Bell, with its glass windows, a small enclosure. I recall looking at the woman and saying "No." This morning I noticed a small, round, red, raised, puncture mark on my right, upper thigh. I then remembered my dream.

Yesterday we smelled the resin-like smell that we had in the house when we found the oil resinous substance in the house. We looked but could not find any physical evidence of the substance.

April 21, 1990

Next week some of the senior parapsychology lab staff members are off to Albuquerque to meet with a group of professionals to discuss the current UFO field and its investigations. This is a follow-up of a meeting two years ago at Cornell. I feel disappointed that I was not able to go.

April 29, 1990

I slept about twelve hours, catching up after a busy work week. I had several real dreams suggestive of an Interface plus a large one-and-a-half-inch bruise on my right thigh that had not been there last evening. I have also been ignoring a sore place on my left upper foot that has been there for some time. Every time I decide to do something about it, I forget about it. It looks like a strip of skin was lost, about half an inch by quarter of an inch.

In one of my Interface dreams, I was asked to levitate bottle caps and, to my amazement, I could. Later someone was asking me if I could open my eyes. I tried several times but I couldn't and said "No."

May 3, 1990

Yesterday, I rented copy of Whitley Strieber's movie *Communion,* which is based on his book of the same name. I felt conflicted watching this movie. There was a sense of excitement but I was also very anxious. However, the movie turned out to be mild and the aliens looked like Muppet characters. The only really scary part was when the "Tin Man" flew through the room toward the main character. I suppose the movie was made for an audience that wants to be entertained. The movie itself is good low-key propaganda for the phenomenon and may act as a catalyst for abductees to "come out of the closet."

May 5, 1990

Coincidentally, my friends Heather and John said they had also rented *Communion.* They too found the characters Muppet-like but felt the subject matter was intriguing. We talked at length about the phenomenon and I lent them Budd Hopkins's *Intruders.*

May 9, 1990

Emily woke up this morning with her legs covered with what she called "insect bites." They had not been there the night before and we have not had a problem with biting insects.

May 25, 1990

Mariah Folger called and I shared some ideas with her. Lately there has been a spate of dreams that seem to occur around the time I am ovulating. I mentioned to Mariah that if the Visitors were manipulating the abduction scenario, this would be an ideal time for them to visit. There have been some theories put forward that the Visitors are here because they want to breed humans to repair their defective genetic stock.

From time to time, I have experienced a missed period, which is unusual for me, followed by an extra-heavy period. The abduction community feels that these "late or missed" periods indicate a possible insemination by the Visitors. Mariah suggested that if this happened I should consider a home-testing pregnancy kit. If it turns out positive, I should contact a doctor to confirm it. I had very mixed feelings about her suggestion.

I had already considered the possibility of getting a pregnancy kit, but my ambivalence about the whole deal has prevented me from carrying out my intentions. I ask myself if alien abduction is the only reason for the missed periods. There are physiological conditions that cause missed periods, such as hormonal imbalance. But the fact that I am usually so regular rules this out.

If a home pregnancy test were positive, what would I say to the doctor—"I'm pregnant by an alien intervention." They would refer me to a psychiatrist! Most doctors will not diagnose pregnancy before two missed periods, and I usually only miss one. Also, my health-care group has a waiting list for appointments, so by the time I got to see a doctor, the event would have passed. But what if I am pregnant by alien means and it is tested and documented—what do I do then? Are there gynecologists who are sensitive to this situation? Is there a list somewhere? The whole deal scares me to death.

May 31, 1990

I awoke about one A.M. feeling very anxious from a nightmare in which I was encountering invisible monsters in my closet. I decided to throw hot tea at them to scare them away. I had a cup of hot tea in my hand. I approached the closet saying, "Here I come," and I threw the tea under the closet door. I had the impression that they left. I never saw them but heard a grunting like small pigs. I went back to sleep after reassuring myself that all was well.

I think this was a coping dream, my trying to make some sense of the events that have lately occurred. I can usually rationalize these events in my waking hours, but they emerge during my sleeping consciousness.

June 1, 1990

Judging from some usual physical signs, I have been ovulating these past few days. According to Mariah's suggestion, I went to a local drugstore to buy a home-testing pregnancy kit. What a fiasco! It was funny and embarrassing at the same time. I could not find the kits on the drugstore shelves, so I asked a saleswoman, who yelled across the floor of the store, "Where are the pregnancy kits?" I felt like ducking and hiding. Then when I got to the checkout, another saleswoman smiled and asked me if I was hoping for a boy or a girl? I said that I was not sure but I thanked her for her concern. I purchased a kit that gives a permanent reading if it is positive. Then I will have a record. But the literature that came with the kit says that "false positives" sometimes occur.

June 2, 1990

I woke this morning with bruises on my upper left thigh and on my left calf. They had not been there last night.

June 3, 1990

Dr. Z, the psychiatrist, called me. Mariah had suggested that I be in contact with her. She is an interesting woman who has set up a research center to investigate the abduction and Interface phenomenon. Her organization has been operating for several years. I told her about the bruises and suspicions about my being pregnant. She laughed at my story of buying the pregnancy kit. She did not think I was crazy but was supportive and constructive. I told her that I would do the pregnancy test next weekend and would call her with the result. Dr. Z advised me to date the test. I had thought about confiding in Emily, but she has been critical and negative about the phenomenon and has her own problems to sort out.

June 9, 1990

I did a pregnancy test this morning and I am not pregnant. It is good to know for sure. I will call Dr. Z later and let her know the results. I said I would call either way, if it was positive or negative.

When I walk to work, I use this time to meditate on feelings, memories, ideas, whatever pops up. Today, I remembered an occasion around 1965 in which there might have been some missing time. I was training to be a nurse at Poole General Hospital and working on a medical ward. I was asked to accompany a patient who was being transferred to a hospital a hundred miles away. We would travel by ambulance and return the same day. The ambulance driver and his wife were neighbors of mine and old friends from Red Cross classes. The patient was not too sick and it looked like it would be a pleasant trip. Our destination was Bristol, the town where I was born, and where I lived until I was sixteen years old. We left Poole a little after nine A.M. and got to the Bristol Infirmary about lunchtime: the journey took several hours. We settled the patient, had lunch in the hospital cafeteria, and left the hospital around one P.M.

The journey back seemed uneventful. It was summer and we stopped and bought wonderful Cheddar strawberries at a roadside stand. I rode up front in the ambulance as my duties were over. I was expected back at the hospital to complete my late afternoon shift, but we did not arrive back until around seven P.M. The senior nurse was furious and demanded to know where we had been. All I could say was that we had been to Bristol and back. She made me work the two hours before the night shift came on duty at nine P.M.

I felt very confused and could not account for the time difference. I had blocked out this memory until today.

There was considerable blockage surrounding this memory. After I remembered it in the morning I decided to write it down in the evening but forgot. I knew that I had to write something down but I could not recall the event at all. I had to meditate and "retrace" my thoughts to recall the event. Thinking about the ambulance trip, several things came to mind. We were traveling through remote country areas where we would have been isolated. There was about a two-hour time loss. There are no memories of an Interface taking place, just a good feeling about buying and eating those delicious strawberries, somewhere around Cheddar in the Cotswold Hills.

I would like to record here another puzzling recollection from my childhood. Whether this has anything to do with the Interface experiences, I am not sure. At the moment I am just trying to make sense of all these experiences.

When my brother and I were little, there was a man who regularly visited our house to collect insurance payments. He called about once a month. In postwar England it was customary for insurance agents, bill collectors, and salesmen to make regular house calls to collect their payments. I learned that he had been a member of the underground during the Second World War. He had remained in England and worked clandestinely. About once a year, he would insist on taking a picture of Alan and me, together and singly. It seemed important for him to do this. In fact, when I was five and Alan was three, my mother had to stuff my brother's mouth full of chocolate to distract him from crying so that this man could take our picture. My mother was very anxious and said something like, "Well, that's over for another year." Sadly, a few years later we learned that the man had committed suicide.

On examination, the photographic paper used for the one remaining picture I have bears a crown watermark. I have been told that this type of paper was used by the military and government for their photographic work. I am puzzled by many questions. Was the insurance agent still working clandestinely? Why did he insist on taking our picture every year? As far as I know, we only have one of these pictures. Why did he commit suicide? I have asked my mother about him, but she says that she does not remember. Does this have anything to do with the Abduction scenario? Probably not, but there are lots of unanswered questions.

July 5, 1990

All last week I had dreams related to escaping from perilous situations: I was caught in a tornado; I was running from lava that was pouring from a volcano; and I was attacked by someone wielding a fork, which he stuck in me several times. I believe that these symbolic dreams are related to my recollections of strange events and circumstances that might be related to the abduction phenomenon. On Monday night I had a real dream.

I "awoke" in the night to find myself in a medical setting. I was lying on my left side, and the whole right side of my face, head, and neck felt numb and swollen. There were people around me, but I did not want to move or look around. I thought, "Maybe I have been in some sort of accident." However, I went back to sleep and have felt a reluctance to record this dream until today.

This evening I was touching a sore spot behind my right ear and again found some plasterlike material stuck to my skull, matted into the hair. I scraped off some of the material and put it into a plastic bag. The place where I pulled off the material is quite sore.

July 16, 1990

Last week I received a copy of Robert Monroe's book *Journeys Out of the Body*. I first heard of Robert Monroe ten years ago when I was exploring my own out-of-body experiences. At the time, I could not find a copy of his book in England. In the beginning of his book, Monroe details his discoveries and explorations. Later chapters go into details of experiences very similar to Interface events. He records missing time; a sense of communication with nonhuman type entities; paralysis; and access of information. He does not say he had communication with the Visitors but alludes to such. After reading Monroe's book, I attempted to Interface with the Wise One and asked about Monroe. I was told that Monroe was given "information that he has chosen not to share with others."

I awoke about six this morning remembering a real dream conversation. In the dream I was commenting to someone that both Emily and I had experienced a Visitor Interface that night. I have no recollection of an actual dream or an Interface. However, yesterday Emily complained of a red itchy "handprint" on her left shoulder blade. She showed it to me. It had disappeared by the evening.

July 19, 1990

A medical dream in which I was waiting for some sort of medical treatment. I sat in a chair and leaned against a bed, at the end of a hallway. The area was busy, and I was waiting for my turn to be seen. Why was I there? Where was I?

July 22, 1990

I had a strange real dream with a definite Visitor theme. In the dream, there were several of us who were abducted by tall, whitish beings and taken into an aerial device like a rotary blade of a helicopter, but it was noiseless. We saw it in the sky and thought it was a helicopter. Then we realized that it was alien. We were in a large room with panels around the walls. We managed to open the panels to find our clothes and escape.

The most important element in the dream was a nonhuman hand I was drying with a small cloth. The hand was gray and long and had five fingers of unequal length. The middle finger was longer than the others, and the last two on the right looked as if they had been damaged. They were shorter. The act of drying the hand was an act of recognition, of respect, and felt highly symbolic. The drying of the hand was done very carefully over a long time.

July 27, 1990

A long dream during the night, which had a decidedly medical setting. I saw beds and IV equipment, tubing and bags of liquid, but have no dream memory of any procedures. There was a lot of waiting around and feeling bored. There were other "patients" present but no clear details. Maybe more will surface as I think about it during the day.

Earlier this month I received a letter from Dr. Z asking for research suggestions for her group. I decided that I would share two ideas with her:

1. One of these I called an Interface components database, which could collect and compare Interface events to look for patterns within the experiences.
2. Another idea would be the biophysical monitoring of anomalous events. This would entail an ongoing correlation of recorded Interfaces, by measuring physical samples over a long-term period.

July 28, 1990

A continuation of the dreams in a medical setting. There was a feeling in the dream of a recognition of the situation but no recall of the content of the dream. The only recall is of people, large and small, being present in a definite medical context.

July 31, 1990

Another strange real dream, most of which took place in a cubicle-sized room. I was being questioned about what I would do if someone wanted to force me to have sex. I gave several answers, including active resistance, passive resistance, and avoidance. There was one main person who was questioning me, but the bulk of the dream got lost when I awoke.

10

Threats and Promises

"The phenomenon reported is something real and not visionary or fictitious."

—General Nathan Twining, chairman, Joint Chiefs of Staff, 1955–58, on September 23, 1947.

August 1, 1990

The last six months have seen a great many changes and the next six promise to be even more exciting. Over the past two years, Mariah Folger and I have been adding ongoing records to an Interface database. We have been looking for similarities between our experiences. Over the past few years, I have been coming across more and more professionals who have experienced Interfaces. It seems, too, that the Interface experience is tied in with psychic ability and spiritual values.

August 7, 1990

I awoke at two A.M. following a very vivid dream. I dreamed that I was walking down a road carrying books or papers. I saw a large car, a station wagon type. I recognized with pleasant surprise that X was driving. He had on a short-sleeved, white shirt and looked good. He smiled and asked if I wanted to go for a ride with him. I accepted and got in. This dream may have reflected my anticipation of meeting X and Mariah later in August.

August 12, 1990

This weekend, three of us, Mariah Folger, X, and I, met in California to discuss the abduction phenomenon. The main conclusion I came to after the weekend meeting was that we share many similar experiences that are colored by our individual worldview. We were able to cover a great deal of ground, such as our attitudes and feelings toward the Interfaces. Unfortunately, we did not cover the physical trauma that often results from the Interfaces, such as bruises and scars. Neither did we cover reproductive issues or coping mechanisms. Maybe we can get together at a later date to meet and talk again.

On the night of August 8, 1990, we decided to spend the night at Mariah's with the intention of eliciting an Interface. All day August 9 my eyes were sore and I felt very tired, as if I had not slept well. In fact, Mariah and I moved over to our conference motel the following day and were in bed and asleep by 8:30 P.M. I dreamed of "eyes," but there was no contact. The night of August 10 at the conference motel, I awoke shortly after I went to sleep to experience static, like music and voices, in my right ear. The static cleared when I paid attention to it. I dreamed of a medical examination. Someone had some concerns about my heart, but I did not remember much about the night. Mariah reported that she woke and saw a tall male at the foot of my bed, plus a small female bending over me. Mariah was told by these two that all was okay.

After the conference, I went to stay with Andy in San Francisco. He has a small apartment in the city. While we were there, I had a strange real dream:

I found myself on an island that I heard called Angel Island, in a building with many people. I recognized an older engineer colleague who works for a major aerospace company. I sat in a room with several other people, and the engineer appeared to be in charge of the gathering. He stated that I had been selected to be part of a secret research project, known to very few. The dream was like something out of a fantasy novel. I was then introduced to several other people in the room, one of whom was a psychologist whose face looked familiar. He looked like an older version of my cousin Richard. I was asked if I knew this psychologist, but although his face was familiar, he was unknown to me. We talked, but I forget what we talked about. I was told that if I related any of the details of this group to anyone, I would die. I don't consider writing this down to be relating. It was a strange experience.

August 15, 1990

I asked Andy if he knew of an island called Angel Island, up or down the coast. He said that Angel Island stands right in the middle of San Francisco Bay and can be seen from his apartment. It is a large island, owned by the Parks Commission but partially federally owned. Part of the island used to be a military hospital. I may have remembered Angel Island from a previous visit to San Francisco, but I do not have any conscious memory of it. The death threat troubles me. Not that I give it much credence, but I am troubled that such a threat should emerge from this experience. I have been reading some conspiracy theories recently that the abduction phenomenon is not real but is a front for government mind-control research, which could have colored my dream. I also recently read *Journey into Madness,* which documents government mind-control experiments during the 1960s and 1970s.

August 17, 1990

I napped during the day to get over jet lag, because I had traveled overnight from San Francisco. I had a real dream I feel is related to the recent dream in San Francisco.

I was in a medical and psychological setting with two men. We were at an apartment by the water's edge, where boats were tied up. After talking with these men for some time, the first man mentioned a contract. I wanted to see it. The man said that he and his partner had drawn up a contract and he began to read it to me. I demanded to be able to read it myself. They wanted me to sign it. I replied that I didn't sign anything I hadn't read. The wording of the document conveyed that I had hired two "hypnotists" to enable me to "recall details." I protested the wording of the contract, because I had not hired them and they were acting on their own. However, I do not recall reading any more and I do not recall adding my signature. Throughout the dream, four people were there, as well as myself—three men and a woman.

August 27, 1990

A long night of dreams, most of which I forgot. However, I remembered one dream in which I was shown various ancient texts containing runic material, some of which I knew, some of it new. I was asked to interpret the texts. I believe the people who were asking me to do the translation were humans.

Surprisingly, since my last trip to California, there have been no dreams containing small grays or other Visitors.

September 24, 1990

We have had an increasing number of people calling the lab and a good portion of them express an interest in UFOs, crop circles, and abductions. A professor of physics who visited the lab told us that he had witnessed a group of grays around his bed when he awoke following a nightmare about his daughter. They ran away through the bathroom when they realized he was awake. He was curious to know if we had heard any stories like that. We assured him that we had and that he was not alone in his experiences. He seemed relieved.

While I was out in California, I told Andy about the abduction phenomenon, but his attitude was that abductees must lead incredibly boring lives. He thought they must invent or fantasize the phenomenon to make their lives more interesting. I did not tell him about my experiences.

A while ago I was sleeping in Emily's spare room while my room was being painted, and I had a real dream with medical content. I was lying on the sofa bed, which is low, near the floor, and two "medics" were discussing a common surgical routine in which a suture is inserted into the cervix to retain a problem pregnancy. One "medic" was using my right fist to represent the cervix and was demonstrating how the suture would be inserted (without using any sutures, of course).

There has been some current interest by the public in crop circles, which have been occurring in England, mainly around Stonehenge in Wiltshire. For many years these have taken the form of circles and concentric circles within each. Now, according to a *20/20* television program, the circles have become more elaborate. They appear to resemble geometric figures. Having studied the ancient runes, I can see runic symbols within the designs, especially an F-looking one, which is the messenger rune.

Last Thursday John, a medical colleague from California, was visiting and we discussed dreams. I mentioned my "death threat" dream, and he said he had a similar type of dream at about the same time. However, his dream occurred when he was on the East Coast, while mine occurred on the West Coast. Some similarities existed between parts of our experiences. For example, there was the element of being "selected" to take part in something important; there were people in the experiences we recognized from our personal lives; there was an element of ritual and task-solving involved; and there was a threat made, overt in mine, assumed in my colleague's, that would be acted on if the content of the experience was told to anyone or the instructions disclosed. In both his and my dreams there were no Visitors, no small grays, just regular people. My real dream seemed to take place on two levels: on one level I was actively participating, and on another level, I was overhearing conversations in which I was not taking part. The nonparticipatory part was where I heard the reference to Angel Island and remember that someone had said that they had "finally been able to purchase it."

October 8, 1990

Several interesting real dreams with a Visitor theme.

In the first dream, I awoke to feel a great deal of pain in my left ear and was alarmed that someone was pulling on my pierced ear or pulling an earring out. In another dream, I visited a cellarlike area. I went down a short flight of steps into a gray stone room. The room has a low ceiling and there are boxes lying around. Over in the right-hand corner is another cubicle-like room with a taller ceiling and a low bed. I have visited this room before many times. Each time the room has been laid out slightly differently, as if to add some human comfort to the bleak cubicle and bed. There are no windows and the light is low.

October 9, 1990

In my meditations, I remembered a dream that I had while I was visiting Mariah Folger's house in August. I had repressed it until now. I dreamed that I went outside Mariah's house and said that I could see UFOs. Outside in the sky we saw hundreds of small discs in the sky, which seemed to come up over the hilly horizon. We were very excited and watched the discs hover in the sky.

We were not afraid, and there was a general feeling of excitement. The discs were reflective and made of a light-colored material.

October 10, 1990

I dreamed that my doctor colleague John and I were attending a ceremony, which I interpreted as an adult baptism. We sat in a large hall on hard chairs. I somehow recognized the hall from other dreams. I was feeling embarrassed as I was only wearing a flimsy covering, which had a plastic feel to it. John sat next to me. We talked, but I do not remember what we talked about. There were figures in authority, including a doctor with a stethoscope around his neck. The rest of the dream involved watching a video of John talking to other people. The film had been made some time ago, because he appeared chubby in the video, whereas he had recently lost weight.

October 20, 1990

Very busy week with visitors to the parapsychology lab, so I did not get time to write down several interesting dreams.

Last week I dreamed I was taking an IQ test. At first I was not sure what I was supposed to be doing. Then I realized I was trying to solve a written puzzle. It had rounded shaded symbols and went something like this: "If this shape is related to this shape, what does this other shape relate to?" But it was longer and much more complicated. Once I realized what I was doing, I progressed easily through the test. I remember dropping my pencil several times and noting that it was only a stub of pencil. I was told that my IQ was 170, which is more than 20 points above what I usually test in the awake state.

Last weekend X came to visit Princeton. He had been entertaining some guests from Russia in Washington, D.C., and drove them over on Friday night.

X has just returned from a trip to China. While he was there, he asked about UFO research and he heard about a crashed UFO the Chinese had recovered. The craft had been dismantled for evidence, and he had been given some metallic filings from the craft for analysis in the United States. He told me he had given some of these filings to our Russian colleagues to get an independent analysis.

I became curious about the Chinese and whether they had any history of the Visitors and found some interesting information on the Internet. Unfortunately, I could not find a source for the information, which goes as follows:

On the border between China and Tibet, in the high mountains of Bayan-Kara-Ula, is a series of interlinked caves that were excavated in 1938 by Chinese archaeologists. The researchers, headed by Professor Chi Pu Tei, found neat lines of graves that contained the skeletons of beings with unusually thin bodies and large, overdeveloped heads.

Further exploration of the caves unearthed a large, round stone disk. The stone had a hole in the center and grooves running from the center to the rim. The groove was, in fact, a continuous spiral of carved symbols or glyphs.

The stone was taken to Beijing and remained undeciphered until 1963. Then, Professor Tsum Um Nui translated the characters. The information found on the stone was so disturbing that, according to records, the Beijing Academy of Prehistory "forbade him to publish his findings." A further 716 grooved disks were said to have later been discovered.

It was not until 1965 that the professor and four colleagues received permission to disclose their findings. A Chinese article was reportedly written. The translation of the discs related the crash of an extraterrestrial craft in the Baian-Kara-Ula mountain range. The occupants of the craft survived and, according to the script, were of peaceful intent. When they tried to interact with the local inhabitants, the Visitors were misunderstood. The Visitors were hunted and killed by the Han tribe, which lived in the local caves. The Han referred to the Visitors as the Dropas.

In the intervening years, since the discovery of the graves and the discs, corroboration of the story has come from local legends of the region. Local legends relate that small, thin, yellow-faced men came from the clouds. The Visitors had oversized heads and thin, spindly bodies. They were thought to be so ugly and repellent that they were hunted down by the local tribesmen. The description of the Visitors in the legends tallies with the description of the small bodies found in the graves in the caves.

According to records from the 1930s, the caves were still inhabited by two fairly primitive tribes, known locally as the Han and the Dropas. Both tribes were frail and stunted, averaging only five feet in height. They looked neither typically Chinese nor Tibetan. Perhaps not all of the Visitors were killed during the hunts, and some interbreeding occurred.

October 23, 1990

Long complicated dreams during the night. Two dream segments remain in my mind this morning:

I found myself sitting on a medical examining table as a doctor was trying to elicit a response from my right knee with a handheld electrical device. He resembled a local doctor who visits the parapsychology lab. The device did not hurt but made a "pop" sound as it discharged. He tried various places around the knee, and I commented that maybe he should use a regular patella hammer to get a response. He told me to relax and put my legs out in front of me. He kept trying to get a response. The device was tubular and silver.

The same doctor appeared in another dream, in which he held a video camera. He was showing it to me. He started to film me, and I was embarrassed, because I did not know what to do. I think I made some silly faces. There was another sensation of sitting down in a padded seat and it tipping backward suddenly, surprising me. Then I relaxed and it was quite comfortable.

October 28, 1990

I awoke and realized that my clock radio had been reset back an hour. It was due to be set back, because of the end of daylight savings, but I had not done it. There had not been a power failure; the light diode was not flashing. It was reset to the exact minute. It is a difficult clock to reset and would have needed a light to be on. My recollection is that I slept through the night, so who reset my clock?

November 22, 1990

Over the past month there have been several medical-type real dreams, mostly involving humans but not the Visitors. These medical dreams have included the insertion of an airway into my mouth. I also felt a sting like a needle in my left foot. There was also a dream about a device for collecting blood. It was made of aluminum and curved over my arm at various points. There was no pain involved.

Last Wednesday I had dinner with Chuck, an airline pilot for a major airline. Chuck is also a UFO investigator. He has an ongoing interest in Cannon's hypothesis that abductions are being carried out not by aliens but by our own government. Cannon claims that the alien impression is left behind as a screen memory by the abductors. X has been working with a woman named Betty-Sue, who feels that she has experienced unexplained abductions, which started when she visited the psychophysics lab where Helen worked. She had also met X and felt that he was involved in the ongoing abduction scenario. However, Betty-Sue is rather theatrical, and I wonder how much of her experience is real and how much is fantasy.

Chuck shared some of her material with me for my comments, which I will review over the holidays. I feel very ambivalent about sharing my material with Chuck because of his connection with Betty-Sue. I will write out some of my experiences for Chuck, in the third-person format, under a pseudonym, and trust that he will keep my confidence. I wrote to Chuck after our dinner appointment and compared some of my experiences with Betty-Sue's recollections:

1. Betty-Sue had responded to an invitation to visit the psycho physics lab through an article in an A.R.E. (Edgar Cayce) pub lication. Subjects were also solicited through a story in *OMNI*. Helen used one name at the lab but used her married name at home on her answering machine.
2. Betty-Sue felt that she had been hypnotized, but Helen denied the fact. However, the setting at the psychophysics lab was ideally suited for a hypnotic induction. I heard Helen comment several times to subjects that they had been in a hypnotic trance during their experimental sessions. Helen used hypnotic regression techniques on at least three people outside of the lab. She has a master's degree in counseling and has trained in hypnotic techniques.Helen once claimed that hypnotic induction was so easy for her that she could do it "at the drop of a hat."
3. Betty-Sue was directed to attend the UFO club in New Jersey, where she shared her story. Helen also urged me to attend the UFO club, where I heard Betty-Sue tell her story. There was a young man at the club who had also attended the psi lab. He had been told by the director that the lab received "black"government funds.
4. Like Betty-Sue, I have wondered if someone has been coming into my apartment when I am not around.
5. Helen became a close personal friend both to Betty-Sue and myself, but Betty-Sue and I never met while we were visiting the psychophysics lab.

6. Like Betty-Sue, Helen was also asking me about possible UFO dreams, baby dreams, and unusual experiences.
7. I remember Helen telling me about her break with Betty-Sue. Helen did not give me any details but asked me what she should do. I could not give her an answer as I did not know the circumstances.
8. I have since met Betty-Sue's Destiny Man—I call him X. I have asked him several times and he has denied ever having anything to do with the psychophysics lab or its research. He did admit to having an ongoing telephone friendship with Betty-Sue. X suggested that I contact Betty-Sue and be supportive of her, but I declined.

Chuck shared one of his own weird experiences with me. Every six months airline pilots are required to undergo a medical examination that includes vision and hearing tests. Usually he has to schedule these examinations weeks in advance because of his busy flying schedule. Chuck received a postcard in the mail offering examinations at a fast, walk-in, no-appointment-needed clinic that specialized in airline physicals. He found the clinic and experienced several disorienting events such as the power going out and finding himself with a triangular trauma to his thigh, which consisted of three bleeding puncture wounds. The doctor was more concerned with Chuck's slacks and rinsing out the bloodstains than with attending to the injury. Following the visit, Chuck experienced a strong compulsion to return to the clinic, even though the staff had acted very unprofessionally.

While we were at dinner, Chuck said something interesting. He said that he knew a lot of people who had abduction experiences. He commented that every one of these people had someone "attached" to them who was either currently employed in the military or government, or had just resigned, or was with one of the intelligence services or the medical field connected to the military. I thought about the people who were "attached" to me and realized that what he said was true for me. Starting with Dr. P, who was employed in the Federal Mediation and Conciliation Service, and who had worked for the Office of Special Intelligence (OSI) and the CIA. Lately, there has been Andy, who was an army medic. Then there was the young lawyer who dated me in West Orange, a retired army major, who had worked at the Pentagon before becoming a civilian lawyer—the list goes on and on! And of course there is X.

I felt sad this week, because I received a letter from Andy in San Francisco telling me that he was seeing a woman from his tennis club and would like to make this relationship with her permanent. However, he said that he would like me to continue to use his San Francisco apartment when I visit California. It seems he still wants to be friends. However, I will write to him and say that, under the circumstances, I will decline his invitation, as it would not be fair to his new relationship or to me. It would be hard for me to be there, knowing he would be in the city with another woman. And there also is Chuck's observation regarding the "attaching" of military and intelligence watchers to abductees to consider.

A few weeks ago, before the first week in November, I felt an increased sense of foreboding over the Middle East crisis. I had felt a similar tension over Tienanmen Square in China. Even though I wanted the students to prevail, there was an overwhelming feeling that translated into the single word "bloodshed." That was the word that came to mind again when I thought about the Middle East. I felt it as strongly as with the Chinese situation. I mentioned my sense of foreboding about the Middle East to my colleagues and to X. In the past week or so, hostile talks have increased, and President Bush is considering an all-out attack on Iraq's Saddam Hussein. There is the possibility that the Iraqis have the atomic bomb and there are the cream of American young men and women, sitting in the desert. I hope I am wrong.

I watched a fascinating video called "UFO Special—The Best Evidence," which was about Robert Lazar and was hosted by George Knapp. The video documented the fascinating story of Lazar's experiences in Nevada at a top secret desert establishment called Area 51. Supposedly, alien technology is stored and tested at this location. After Lazar "blew the whistle" on this project, he found that records of his education and employment were "lost" and he was rapidly becoming a nonperson. He decided to go to the media to reveal what he knew. I'm keeping an open mind on this one until I learn more.

November 25, 1990

I slept about ten hours last night and had lots of dreams but forgot most of them as usual. However, I remember one lucid dream. I was in the kitchen of a big house where I had been taking part in a metaphysical conference. There was a telephone call for me and, although I did not answer the phone, I knew it was X. The woman who answered the phone said to X, "No, she does not know yet." I asked the woman what the phone call was about and she replied, "Nothing." The phone rang several times after and each time it was X. I wonder if he has been trying to get in touch with me. He is due back from Moscow around the first of December.

Since the Angel Island real dreams this past fall and Chuck's observations at dinner the other evening, I have been having some concerns about my friend Andy's involvement with the government. Chuck had commented that many abductees had someone "attached" to them, who was either military or government. I do not want to appear paranoid. I have been assured by some very good friends, who are psychiatrists, that I am mentally healthy and the fact that I have been considering these matters worries me greatly. My concerns regarding Andy have remained unwritten until now. I feel a need to record them to make some sense of my worries. These events are probably a series of unconnected happenings, but a thread seems to run through them. This is what I want to write down.

My meeting with Andy was odd. Seven years ago my father died in England. I met Andy when I was returning to the States after my father's funeral. Several of us were "bumped" from a flight and we had to spend the night in London. Andy and I stayed together for the day and had lunch at a pub. When we talked we discovered that Andy had visited many of the same places I had visited when I was home. He also told me that during his trip to England he had been visiting government offices in London and had dined at the Houses of Parliament. He told me that he had been a medic in the army, and he was wearing his army T-shirt when I first met him. As my father had just died, I was emotionally vulnerable. Andy wined and dined me and took me to the theater. Although we spent the day together, we did not really know each other at that time.

Andy and I have met up quite a few times over the years and have spent hours on the phone. There has been a strong romantic theme running through our relationship. Back in August, while I was visiting with Andy at his San Francisco apartment, a strange thing happened. We had attended a conference banquet, then went for drinks at a local bar. We slept late the next morning. Andy made me a breakfast of melon and tea and I started to write in my journal, relating details of the conference. Andy and I had a full night's sleep and had woken refreshed. However, following breakfast, we both became extremely tired and returned to bed. We spent the rest of the day sleeping until 5:30 P.M., when we finally dragged ourselves out of bed to get some food. Throughout the day, I drifted in and out of consciousness. At one time I found myself in a sort of limbo land between sleep and waking. I could not move my arms or legs and I commented to myself, "This is what it must feel like to be drugged." I remember lying unmoving, with my eyes open, just gazing. Andrew appeared to be asleep. It was during this strange state that the Angel Island real dream happened. I blocked out a lot of these events until today.

The next day, Andy and I took a trip down the coast to Monterey, where we met up with some German friends. Driving to Monterey, we passed the vast expanse of the Monterey Army station, mile upon mile of coastline establishment. We also passed the Defense Language Institute outside of Monterey. Andy said that he had been stationed there during the early days of his army experience and knew the place very well. Recently, I came across a reference in a parapsychology book to some Sensory Deprivation (SD) experiments that had been conducted at Monterey during the time Andy might have been stationed there. I sent him a copy of the article but he never commented. Quoting from this reference I noted that:

> The generic title under which this research has come to be known is Sensory Deprivation. This research area, which from initial reports appeared to be highly exciting and promising, was soon overshadowed by negative valuations and the non-repeatability and idiosyncratic character of results. A great variety of aberrations, including hallucinations, long-term disorientation, and perceptual distortion, cognitive disintegration, and negatively valued subjective states were reported.
>
> More recently it has come to light that the SD work was highly instigated and covertly funded by national security agencies of the U .S. government, as were the bulk of experiments with LSD and other psychotropics during the same period. Work sponsored by the CIA and army intelligence and chemical warfare branches generally violated both ethical canons and the standards of sound scientific research. It was concerned with applications in indoctrination, interrogation, coercion, and degradation.

I was able to interview one person who was a victim of this

> quasi-research. As an army enlisted man he had been required to spend up to six days in an SD chamber covertly operated at the Defense Language Institute in Monterey, California. His report of his experiences, and subsequent psychiatric history, suggests to me that he had been dosed with drugs (perhaps LSD) without his knowledge or consent, while in SD under military orders.

Whether or not Andy was involved in this research, I do not know, but I plan to write to him and see if he has any knowledge of these early experiments.

November 29, 1990

I dreamed I was on board a plane and saw a UFO. I realized, however, that it was a mock-up and only made of aluminum wrapped over a frame. I was disappointed. Then I saw a real UFO and was awed. It was elaborate and very large. At some point I found myself aboard the UFO. There was a woman who looked like Dr. J talking to me. There was another smaller woman with her. I do not remember much of the dream except that I was in awe of the size of the craft.

In a later dream I was telling Emily about my first dream and about seeing the UFO. I described the inside of the UFO. I said that it was like being inside a large hotel, with lots of polished surfaces, that it was very clean and very large. Later in this dream I was walking up a plywood ramp and feeling anxious because it was so springy underfoot. In the dream I recognized the fact that my mother had once carried me up such a ramp and that my anxiety sprang from this event. There was writing on the ramp but I do not remember what it said. The dream then deteriorated to a childhood memory of when my younger brother was pestering me. I eventually locked my bedroom door to be alone. People kept knocking at the door but I ignored them, enjoying the solitude.

Emily mentioned this morning that she, too, had a dream about being on a plane.

November 30, 1990

A strange medical real dream that involved a doctor with a sense of humor. In the early part of the dream, I was being taken to a medical venue and I feel that this might be a continuation of the dream from the other night. It was understood that I needed some adjustments to my ears and eyes. This would involve putting needles into these organs. There seemed to be Hispanic people around me at the medical facility.

I sat on a hard stool and had to lean my head back so that it rested on a table. It was not comfortable at all and I hoped that I would not have to sit long. An IV was set up, and I hoped the medics would give me some sort of analgesic before they started probing my ears and eyes. The doctor, a tall, older Hispanic male with graying hair took my blood pressure and commented that it was a little high but okay. I thought to myself, "If you were going to have needles stuck into your eyes and ears, your blood pressure would be up too!"

The doctor showed me something like a shower cap and put it under my left arm. I sat there with the shower cap under my arm. He stood there looking at me and laughed. Then he took the shower cap and said, "No silly, you put it on your head." He then proceeded to put the shower cap on my head. I think that when I put my head back, someone put a blanket over me and I remembered no more. All day following this dream I felt incredibly tired but my eyes and ears seem fine.

December 9, 1990

Last night I dreamed I was given a blood transfusion of two packs of blood. In the dream I remember that I was walking around, not confined to a bed, and that my arm was not splinted. I was told to be careful not to move my arm too much.

This morning, to my consternation, I found a large puncture trauma on my right forearm, a hole, like a puncture scar that is left after an IV. For a while I ignored it, as it did not hurt and had a good scab on it. This seems to be the usual reaction to these bizarre traumas. The fact of acknowledging that something physical may have happened to me during the night fills me with conflict and I enter a state of denial. Eventually, I will have to acknowledge that something real is happening. However, I certainly felt great this morning. I walked in to the lab, a distance of about two miles, did three hours of psi experiments with great results, and then walked home.

December 14, 1990

Visiting with my friend B in Charlottesville, Virginia; we were up until two A.M., watching the Geminid meteor shower. A spectacular display of shooting stars. Strange as it may seem, until two years ago I had never seen a shooting star. After I arrived today in Charlottesville, B's husband, Jack, called from Texas to tell us about the meteor shower. We took blankets and quilts out onto her lawn and watched meteors for nearly an hour. We must have seen fifteen to twenty, until we got too cold. It was the greatest gift anybody could have given me.

The next evening Dr. Z and X came to Charlottesville from Washington, D.C., to host a UFO meeting at B's house. The meeting went well, and the people there seemed very interested in the abduction phenomenon. A strange thing happened at the meeting. Dr. Z asked if people minded having their pictures taken. Most people said okay. Then X got up and systematically began taking individual pictures of everybody in the room. We had assumed that Dr. Z wanted a group picture. After X had taken three or four individual photographs, his camera jammed. After the meeting, several participants commented that they felt very uncomfortable with their pictures being taken in that manner.

B told me about an interesting New Age group that lived nearby in Schuyler, Virginia. This group lived in a communal arrangement at an old hospital that had been converted into a lovely home. They are a group of friends that originally lived together in New York City. They are doctors, nurses, and business people, who are all self-supporting and all contribute to a communal lifestyle. They share personal belief systems that incorporate Christianity and Judaism, as well as New Age beliefs and a strong interest in UFOs. The folks saw the old hospital when they were visiting Virginia and decided that this was where they wanted to live.

The hospital was built to serve the population of Schuyler and the soapstone quarry employees there. Eventually, as the soapstone quarry and factory closed down, so did the hospital, which was left abandoned and decaying. The group bought it very cheaply and in ten years had renovated it completely. They refurbished the house with elaborate woods and fabrics, brought in antique furniture and rugs and decorated each room in a different style. For example, one room might be French Provincial, another Moroccan with antique wall hangings. About fifteen people are now there and many of the group have adopted new names upon entering. B and I went over to visit on Friday night and helped the group get ready for their Saturday Christmas party, to which they invite the whole community. They have decorated the garden with twenty-six thousand Christmas lights and it looked like fairyland. On Saturday, fifteen hundred guests turned up. It was the largest party that I have ever attended. I learned that the leader channels alien entities that give him information regarding future events. They were a very interesting group.

December 17, 1990

Definite Visitor contact last night, which I remembered through a real dream.

The experience involved seeing two small grays. Someone put a metal tube in my mouth to look at my throat. I saw the Visitors in a group of human people. The oral exam was unusual in that I did not have to open my mouth wide and the metal instrument only went as far as the back of my throat. It did not go down my throat as I have often experienced in these states. It was not painful, just uncomfortable.

December 22, 1990

I dreamed that I was with a group of people who were encouraging me to do some psychokinesis (psychic metal bending) experiments using round pieces of metal that looked like tin can ends. I realized that I could do this easily and acknowledged in the dream that I was in an altered state of consciousness. I twisted one round piece of metal in half, then into quarter folds. The metal became very soft and easy to manipulate.

In waking life, I have not been able to bend metal, although I have tried many times by myself. Maybe the dream is telling me to expand my expectations and abilities. At the parapsychology lab I have been having some great success with the micro PK experiments, so maybe the dream is also a celebration of my achievements?

December 24, 1990

Early last month I gave a talk to a local adoption group. I talked about a group of orphans I cared for in Colombia in the early 1970s, and how I have been following their development. At the meeting, I encountered two "little people" who came to the meeting. Before I gave my talk, lots of people were milling around and I went to get a cup of coffee and a cookie. Next to me in line was a diminutive man, about four feet, six inches, whose age was unclear. He was dressed normally in slacks and a jacket. However, his face was tiny and wrinkled and had the look of a little "apple-person." He looked like those toy characters whose faces are carved from dried apples—they have a very distinctive look. He asked if I was the speaker for the night and we shook hands. He pointed out his tiny wife sitting in the audience. Her feet did not touch the floor she was so tiny. She waved at us and smiled. She looked identical to her husband and also looked like a little "apple person." The man walked very stiffly, as if his head, neck, and back were fused, and he was slightly stooped. He said, "See that little lady there, that's my wife. I'm very proud of her. You would not believe it to look at her but she has advanced degrees in music." I took him to be religious, because he talked about God leading our activities. They both listened attentively to my talk. They must have left the meeting early as I did not see them after the talk.

Later, I asked the leader of the group about the little couple. She commented that she had never seen them before, they had not been invited, she did not know their names, and they never inquired about adoption. If they came specifically to hear my talk, I feel honored—whoever they were.

December 31, 1990

Last night I had another real dream in which I felt a metal tube being inserted into my mouth. This is the second time this has happened in a real dream. Both times I have been in a state of paralysis, awake but unable to move. The first time the tube did not enter my throat, and only went as far as the back of my mouth. Last night I experienced the sensation again and realized that I was consciously awake. The tube seemed to rotate as it entered my mouth and I realized that it was being inserted further back in my throat. I gagged. Whoever was inserting the tube tried again. I kept gagging and the tube was removed.

My reaction to all the information I have been collecting is bewilderment. The methods I put in place to collect personal memories and dream recall of abduction events have worked far better than I had hoped. However, I vacillate between absolute rejection of all of these retrieved memories and real dreams and amazement at the richness and realness of the information that is being uncovered.

11

I Will Not Be Enslaved

"The number of thoughtful, intelligent, educated people in full possession of their faculties, who have 'seen something' and described it, grows every day. . . . We can say categorically that mysterious objects have indeed appeared and continue to appear in the sky that surrounds us."

—General Lionel M. Chassin, commanding general of the French Air Forces, and the general air defense coordinator of the Allied Air Forces of NATO, in his foreword to Aime Michels's *Flying Saucers and the Straight-Line Mystery* (Criterion Books, New York, 1958).

January 10, 1991

Since my visit to Charlottesville, I have heard that Dr. Z and X have visited the New Age group that B and I visited over Christmas. The group may give Dr. Z some financial assistance for her abduction conferences. X and Dr. Z are going down again this weekend to discuss funding with the group. I hope that Dr. Z does not alienate the folks there, as she has done with other benefactors. Unfortunately, if the pattern is repeated, she will antagonize them.

January 19, 1991

I am dismayed at the continued infighting within the abduction groups. One of the researchers has written an article about his work with abductees. In it he refers to one of the therapists as incompetent and goes on to describe her in other uncomplimentary terms. To this, the therapist responded with a twenty-page rebuttal, followed by another twenty pages of updated rebuttal! These were mailed not only to the researcher but also to practically everybody in the abduction field. It is such a waste of energy and resources. If only they could ignore the criticisms and not air their grievances in public.

February 1, 1991

I had two real dreams last night. In the first dream, I was being helped to take off my sweater. I felt cool hands touching my back. The hands stayed a while on my warm skin, and I had the impression that whoever was touching me was enjoying the experience.

In the second dream, thoughts about the Gulf war were going through my mind, and I was overcome with intense emotion and sobbed. I cried and cried to the very depths of my soul. I woke this morning with sore eyes.

For several days I have had a large bruise on the back of my left hand but cannot remember any real dreams that could account for it. At first I was in denial about the bruise, saying to myself, "I know where I got that bruise. Don't worry about it." But I do not consciously remember injuring the hand.

February 25, 1991

A few weeks ago, I dreamed of being in a large building and traveling horizontally, as well as vertically, in an elevator. There were no pulleys or chains; instead it worked on vacuum and gravity. There were little seats near the elevator floor, and a traveler sat rather than stood for the trip.

Last night I dreamed I was at the parapsychology lab. In the dream, I became hysterical and lay on the floor. Then I was up and moving around. I noticed that "something" was protruding from my left nostril. I pulled at it but it was stuck. My colleagues were in the room so I got a tissue and went into the next room to work on it. I blew my nose and I pulled on the protrusion. I heard an audible, internal crunching from my left nostril. I pulled slowly and a string of small, silver balls and shapes came slowly out. I held it in the tissue. It was about four to six inches in length.

I have had a sore place in my left nostril for the past week, which has bled occasionally. I have mostly ignored it. I think an Interface occurred last week, causing the trauma. The dream perhaps revealed some of the details. But who can say for sure. Maybe the sore place in the nose triggered the dream. This is the proverbial chicken and egg dilemma.

February 27, 1991

A real dream during which I heard the front doorbell ring. When I went to answer it, our neighbor, a psychologist, came into the house accompanied by a stranger. I asked them to leave, because I had not invited them in. The stranger was in his thirties, black, tall, and elegantly dressed. He had on an overcoat and good shoes. He did not speak.

March 3, 1991

Real dream with a medical theme during which I resisted being examined. At first I had difficulty moving. Finally, I got free and a group of people were trying to persuade me to relax and get back up on the table. One person held a silvery device that looked like a nail file and was about six inches long. I managed to lock myself in a bathroom and called out for a colleague to help me. However, he could not or would not come. I finally came out of the bathroom and subjected myself to the "procedure." I am blocking out the nature of this procedure.

I decided to feign difficulty in breathing, so that the medics would stop the procedure. I slowed my breathing so that it appeared irregular and apneic. I was given oxygen and the procedure continued. At one time I felt something on my head and rounded devices in my ears. It seemed that a new mold had to be made from some rubbery material. This was placed in my right ear and the excess scraped away until the mold was set. The rubbery molds were hollow and fit inside my ear canals during the various procedures. It seemed that the right mold had deteriorated and a new one was needed. I felt someone's finger sticking in my right ear several times, as the substance was shaped and hardened. The ear molds looked a little like rounded diaphragms. These ear molds were made specifically for each person and stored until needed.

New ones were made as the old ones wore out. I can only guess at their function.

March 6, 1991

One of the suggested reasons for the Visitors' interacting with us is that they are breeding hybrids that are a genetic cross between us and them. Many abductees share dreams that involve tiny infants who do not have the vigor and size of normal human infants. This morning I remembered part of a longer dream that included such a hybrid infant.

I was with a tall man and his teenage daughter. We were looking at a tiny baby. She was very small and fragile. I put my little finger into her mouth and she suckled on it. Then I held her tiny hands. She grasped my little fingers with her tiny hands. I was explaining to the man and his daughter the importance of touch and how vital it was to maintain contact with the infant. I felt a bond with this infant, who responded to my touch with soft cooing and purring sounds.

March 9, 1991

A worrying real dream last night in which I was waiting in a large hall with others. Rows of chairs were set out in straight lines. Many people were waiting. Then I was being interrogated by a group of people that was trying to convince me that I should tell what I knew. I said, "No, they would kill me." The interrogators were assuring me that this would not happen. I again repeated that I would be "searched for and killed."

March 10, 1991

Over the past two years I have been friendly with a young black woman named Heather Jones and her husband, John. They have a toddler, James, who is a delight and is my "adopted godson." During the past six months, both Heather and John have been channeling entities. These entities appear to be benevolent and give advice that seems to be fairly focused. Heather has become interested in the Visitors and feels she may have had some Interfaces.

Recently, Heather experienced some strange and disturbing events. She was on the way to visit a friend and was stopped by a man who was standing by his car. He was a well-dressed black man, and there were other people in the car. He asked her for some directions and then asked if he could take her photograph. She agreed and thought no more about it. Later that week, she had to go to the college library and went into a side room to look for the specific book that she needed. There on the bookshelf was the photograph of her that the man had taken. She was quite shaken by this experience.

Yesterday, Heather and I were talking about "walk-ins," (cases in which one personality departs a body and a new one, even an alien soul, enters in its place) and I lent her a book from my library. When she was reading it, she came across a reference to two young men she knew in her freshman year of college. These two young men were involved in a "walk-in" case. These two men were also channelers and accessed much the same information as Heather and John did. The name of the entity was the same, too: Rama. Heather feels sure that she never discussed "walk-ins" or channeling with these two young men.

April 11, 1991

For the past two days we have had a lady visitor to the lab who works as a biofeedback therapist. She comes to the parapsychology lab from time to time to participate in the PK experiments. I have never discussed my Visitor experiences with her and, as far as I know, she had not experienced anything like this herself. This visit she stayed at Emily's house, and last night I gave her the bedroom where I usually slept, while I slept in the other room on the futon.

This morning she asked what kind of a night I had. I remarked that I had woken at 4:14 A.M. and saw that the downstairs lights were still on, that I heard voices and thought that she and Emily were up all night talking. However, it seems that they had gone to bed at two A.M. She had woken up later, heard voices and assumed that Emily and I were up talking, so she went back to sleep.

She woke up again later to go to the bathroom. She found herself standing on the rug with two small Visitors. One was looking sideways out of the bedroom door, looking toward the room where I was sleeping. The other one was looking toward the back window. She said they had faces like "gargoyles" and had an air of bad intention about them. She asked them, "What do you want?" At that point, they fled. I had been sleeping in that room; perhaps the Visitors were confused to find someone else sleeping there.

Emily's reaction was interesting. She was very angry that this had happened and decided to sleep in the room herself to discourage the Visitors. I can understand her concern. Up to this point I could keep the Visitors within the realm of myth and imagination, I could keep them nicely segmented in the world of dreams, and did not have to ascribe a reality to them. Now that someone else has seen them I have to face the fact that they have an existence independent of my own consciousness. I was still very much in denial up to this point, even though I had heard reports, read books, gone to conferences, and heard all the evidence. Now it was all very real.

April 13, 1991

The night after the Visitors were seen by our guest, I dreamed that I was living in a large house and the house was being attacked by men with guns. I was going around the house locking all the windows and doors to keep the invaders out. Last night I dreamed that someone was holding my left hand and taking my pulse. I think these dreams are reflecting my state of anxiety and conflict regarding the reality of the Visitors.

April 25, 1991

I dreamed that I was being taught new words. They were short words that did not have many vowels in them. They contained a lot of triangular letters. It was almost as if I was in school again. I also dreamed that someone who looked like my doctor colleague was examining my abdomen. I felt embarrassed. There were other people around. He continued his examination and seemed satisfied with his conclusion, saying, "okay."

I slept late this morning despite setting my alarm clock for an earlier time. Waking late and feeling tired during the day usually indicates to me that an Interface has occurred.

April 28, 1991

I had a long series of dreams all night, but the only part that I could remember was meeting with a group of men who represented American power, wealth, prestige, and politics. It was as if everyone was assembling before some sort of ceremony to see how things were going.

May 6, 1991

Last night I met with half a dozen people, including Heather and John, who had all experienced Interfaces. The group also had experiences with UFO sightings, had encountered "Men in Black," had anomalous medical procedures, or had pregnancies that disappeared. One young lady had grown up in Roswell, New Mexico, where a purported UFO had landed in the late 1940s. We went around the group sharing our experiences, assuring each other and comparing notes. It was reassuring to hear other people voicing my own concerns.

May 12, 1991

Early Sunday morning I had a real dream. I was walking down the stairs and encountered a gray on the stairs. I perceived it as male, although the stairs were dark. I remember grabbing the back of the entity's neck and holding him away from me. I was saying to him, "What do you want? What do you want?" I said this over and over but got no reply. He was trying to reach up and gaze into my eyes and I did not want him to do that. In my panic I bit him on the head! It felt like biting into a rubber eraser, yielding but hard.

All day I have had "flashbacks" to the biting dream.

June 5, 1991

While I was at a conference in Charlottesville, I talked with a psychiatrist friend about the Visitor experience and the dreams in which I fight back. He said that he would be happy to talk to me about these experiences, and he commented that his wife was also encountering the grays! He reassured me that biting the gray was a normal panic reaction and that I should not feel bad about it.

June 25, 1991

I am in California for school and came early on the weekend to visit with Mariah Folger. It was a good time to relax and catch up on sleep. We took some time to talk about the Visitors. Mariah refers to the Visitors as the "Folks" and us as the "ffolks." We discussed the problem that "Womenffolks" have with Interfaces, such as missing pregnancies, weight gain, and sexual and social dysfunction. "Menffolks" have similar problems specific to their gender.

Both sets of "ffolks" have such problems as reduced immunity following contact. Mariah feels that the "Folks" suffer a cumulative degree of physical damage from contact with us and never fully recover. I told her about the time I bit one of the grays. She was reassuring in her estimation that the grays may have fewer peripheral nerve endings than we have. Mariah and I decided that sometime in the fall we would have another meeting to which various interested people would be invited. At the meeting we would share experiences, strategies, and ideas toward the goal of fully conscious interaction with the Visitors.

While I was in California visiting with Mariah, I believe that there were Interfaces with the Visitors. The first night I went to bed around 8:30 P.M. and slept through until 6:30 A.M. the next day. However, after I had gotten up and had breakfast I was still tired and went back to bed until 10:30 A.M.

During the first night, I dreamed that I was explaining many things to "someone" and, when I briefly awoke, I repeated things to myself that I had clarified in my dream, During my morning nap the next day, I dreamed I was watching a computer screen, which was scrolling information about fractals. When I awoke and lay with my eyes closed, I experienced images and symbols scrolling across my visual field. This was something I had experienced before. However, this time I could not slow the information down to view the content in greater detail.

I asked Mariah her impressions of the Cannon paper and its idea that many abduction experiences were government generated. She did not feel that this was the case, but I reminded her that Cannon had included a great deal of well-researched documentation about past government intervention and experimentation. I feel that if clandestine interaction is occurring, it is highly unethical. I feel that if the government is going to such lengths to access information about the Visitors, why not just ask the experiencers in full waking consciousness. However, I realize that this probably would not happen, because then they would have to admit to the reality of the Visitors' existence.

June 26, 1991

I dreamed that I was in a medical setting and my ears were being inspected. I dreamed that small tubes were inserted in my eardrums and I was able to see the procedure on a video screen. Then a doctor made stars on a record sheet as well as cryptic notes.

I asked the doctor if this indicated I had implants in my ears and was told, "Yes."

This morning I discovered a sore place on right side of the roof of my mouth and later I felt a small hole where the soreness was. It felt increasingly sore during the day. I took a look with the aid of a flashlight and discovered a red, inflamed area with several small holes. This may have occurred last night or it may have been residual trauma from an Interface at Mariah's over the weekend. The dreams may be delayed memory traces.

July 19, 1991

I received a letter from a high-ranking government employee, X, with whom I had been corresponding and meeting for several years. We had talked at length about the abduction phenomenon, and he intimated that he might have had several Interfaces during his lifetime. Today, I received a two-page emotional letter from him. In his concern to maintain his privacy he did not sign his name, just initialed it to me and Mariah. To maintain his privacy, I will never reveal his identity. I feel that his plight is an indication that Interfaces are happening in every level of society, government, military, and all age groups. The abduction phenomenon is no respecter of persons. His letter, in full, reads as follows:

> A few months ago, following several years of introspection on and about what may be going on in my life about which I only have shadowy reflections, I reached a decision to regain something precious that I feel I have lost: control over major decisions about myself. As a friend in spirit once said (approximately)—as I will not enslave anyone, neither will I be enslaved.
>
> Formal notice was given that I want all implants removed and not replaced. Without waiting for them to do this and recognizable action taken to implement it, I have undertaken a series of steps to do it myself. Frankly, it is impossible for me to determine on my own what success I am having, but the will could not be more determined on this issue.
>
> I am ready at any point to reconsider my action, but only under the condition of direct communication with walk-away memories.
>
> I acknowledge that my action may be at variance with a prior thoughtful and solemn agreement. If that is the case, I deliberately vacate that agreement at least as long as it is consciously unknown to me. If and when there is a willingness to openly reveal that agreement I will consider renegotiating it.

At this point I am disappointed at myself and irritated at them, I am beginning to feel better toward myself as a result of the decisions I have made and the action I am taking. I will wait a few more weeks before I decide whether to transform my "irritation" into a more active category.

If I am important to whatever process is going on, the cost of keeping me on the team is to trust me as a full team player.

I have no delusions about my ability to derail the train, but it is well within my capability to decide whether I am going to be part of the train crew, a passenger on the train, an observer, or an attempted saboteur of the train.

When I asked for help on this, dolphin and whale energy came in and has been most supporting. I am not asking either of you to intervene on this issue but will not object if you do so for your own reasons. This is my battle, but as an ancient warrior I know the value of allies. I also know that in a larger sense it may be more important for a potential ally to stay in camp because of timing and other factors such as the war being more important than a particular battle. I don't think I am confused about who the enemy is. At this point I do not perceive the short grays or any other group as the enemy. At some point I believe that we are all engaged in a war against those factors that deny that we are all one family and hence keep us enslaved to fear and dangerous pockets of spiritual and tangible poverty.

In his letter he writes: "I am not asking either of you to intervene on this issue but will not object if you do so for your own reasons." In the spirit of this understanding, I am sharing his letter with whoever reads this, in an effort to inform *those factions* that I too am with my friend 100 percent.

July 20, 1991

I just got back from a two-week trip to Moscow. There I attended a humanistic psychology conference and stayed the rest of the time with Russian colleagues who had previously visited the parapsychology lab. During my stay in Moscow, there were several occasions when Interfaces could have occurred. One morning I awoke to find a line of bruises around the upper part of my right arm and several reddish needle marks on my right arm. There were also dreams of tall, white "wavy" forms different from the usual Visitors encountered in the United States. The second time that this happened I was worried because they took away my "housemate," a Russian woman who was sleeping at the apartment.

July 22, 1991

After getting the letter from my colleague in Washington, D.C., I also made a conscious decision to resist the Interfaces and to ask for the removal of any possible implants. While I am not sure if I even have implants, it would not hurt to take an active role in this phenomenon. After I had voiced my decision not to allow any further implants, I had the following dream, which might be related to the implant decision, or the decision could have prompted the dream. I dreamed that someone was placing a grid against the roof of my mouth. It was some kind of diagnostic device for detecting implants. It was understood that any implants would be removed at a later date.

July 28, 1991

Very busy night dreaming about UFOs. I dreamed that I was looking out through a window and saw several people looking up into the sky. As I was watching, the lights came closer and I saw a UFO with a large letter A on it. I became scared and tried to climb up on some high furniture to hide, but I was not very successful. I "awoke" in the dream to find myself in a medical situation and someone was taking my pulse at my wrist. I was breathing fast but calmed down as I become more conscious. I consciously noted that I was feeling agitated but that I was getting calmer. In a later dream, someone was questioning me about my UFO experiences.

July 30, 1991

I dreamed I was in a situation in which I was talking with President George Bush and other politicians. One of these men in suits told me his name and spelled it out for me. It was "Scherr." I seemed to know that I had met him before. I said to him, "Nice to see you again." There were other people there, representatives of the Strategic Air Command, but not in uniform. I was told who they were and was introduced to them.

August 29, 1991

Earlier this week I dreamed that I was meeting with the Visitors and they gave me gifts: a red silk scarf that was as soft and light as a cobweb, and a round ceramic brooch. The brooch was large, about six inches across, and was made of some sort of white, pearl-like ceramic material. There was a smaller circle cut out from the middle that went behind the material to fasten the brooch. I was disappointed when I woke that there were no physical gifts. But the dream was pleasant.

September 14, 1991

I had a real dream in which I "awoke" in the night to experience bony fingers with long nails that had a grip on the hair at the back of my neck. The fingers were probing my skull. I tried to get the hands out of my hair but was unsuccessful. Then I found myself crying in terror, but part of me was observing myself doing this. My wish for a fully conscious Interface with the Visitors might be more traumatic than I imagined. The hands had quite a strong grip, and the Visitors did not mind my touching them.

September 15, 1991

I have realized that over the last couple of months my Interface dreams have taken on a new slant and moved to a different level. It seems like the Interfaces have taken on an interrogatory or questioning form, instead of the traumatic, medical experiences of the past five years. For instance, last night and the night before I was being questioned about my Interface experiences. Some of the questioning has involved some very traumatic material, and I have wept and wailed in fear. Last night I was being questioned again, and I was drawing diagrams on a backboard. I think that this new turn of events signals a new phase. It is as if I am going through therapy, in which a therapist asks questions and elicits emotions. But I seem to be doing it in my dreams. During these dream experiences, "I" seem to stand apart from myself as I am being questioned.

September 19, 1991

Twice this week I have stubbed my foot and the middle toe on the left foot is very bruised. I dreamed that a doctor was examining my toe. He asked if it hurt and wiggled it—it hurt! I sat up and tried to stop him from touching my toe.

September 24, 1991

Another real dream in which I awoke to find a mask over my

face. I was breathing some sort of gas mixture. I tried to remove the mask, but it was secured. I had to breathe the gas, and I felt light-headed but did not lose consciousness. I do not think it was an anesthetic.

Thinking about the dream this morning and what the gas mask could have been, made me think of PET scans, where the patient breathes a gas mixture containing a radioactive tagged isotope. The PET scan maps the brain and its functions. This ties in with the new stage that the Interfaces have reached. Although I initially panicked when I felt the mask on my face, I was able to relax and breathe the gas. Another person was with me, but I could not open my eyes to see who it was. In later dreams last night I recognized two doctor colleagues from my waking life.

October 5, 1991

Yesterday, Dr. D, a psychiatrist friend of the parapsychology lab, was visiting and we got into some great group discussions about matter and energy, myth and mythology. I told Dr. D about how my Interface experiences had entered a new phase, where I was expressing a good deal of emotion in response to intense questioning. He said that he would be willing to work with me. Dr. D would take me through some breathing and visualization exercises. We set up an appointment for the afternoon at his office. I was very nervous about the visit, but I felt that this could unlock some emotional doors. However, the encounter turned out to be quite disappointing. I am sure his therapy works with some Americans, with their "let it all hang loose" attitude—remember that I am British-born and quite reserved. I am quite capable of expressing emotion when the situation arises and it is appropriate. But I feel blocked when asked to produce emotion on demand. I have to have the emotion inside in order to express it physically.

So, during the session, I banged the couch and shouted at Dr. D's instructions but did not feel that it was genuine emotion that I expressed. I said over and over again, "I hate them. I hate them for what they have done to me." But I do not really hate the Visitors. (This ambivalence reflects the swings of belief that I have in what is happening to me. It is typical of the victim who simultaneously loves and hates her abuser.) The emotions I express in my dreams are intense and overwhelming. I also feel reluctant to get into an emotional catharsis when Dr. D will not be around to continue the sessions. He will be returning next week to his practice in California.

October 6, 1991

Following the psychiatry appointment this past week, I had the following dream: I had jumped or dived into very deep water and realized that I could not breathe underwater. I decided to raise my arms so that I could float back to the surface. I did this and rose through the water to the surface. However, as I then realized that I could breathe underwater, the need to reach the surface was not urgent.

I think that this dream relates directly to my session with Dr. D. At the end of the appointment with him, I had the impression that I was looking down into a very deep well and hesitated to jump into the water. Dr. D reminded me that water represents emotions.

Emily told me that a few nights ago she woke up to hear noises upstairs. There were scraping sounds that sounded like furniture being moved. I assured her I was not up at night moving furniture.

October 12, 1991

Following my session with Dr. D, I decided that it was time to do some regression work with a qualified psychologist. I want to understand the Interface experiences of the past few years. I also want to uncover earlier experiences. I asked a few people for a referral to a local psychologist but could not find anyone suitable. I therefore decided to look for one myself. I found Dr. V, a local psychologist, who was trained in an alternative to the classical, conservative school, and who might be open to the phenomena I was experiencing. Dr. V has a Ph.D. in psychology and she practices locally. We talked last week, and we knew several people in common. I also discovered that Heather, a student friend, had gone to her for dream work a few years ago. I set up an appointment for later this week.

The session took place at Dr. V's office, in her home in the countryside. She explained that she encourages her clients to work on all seven layers of the "person." Most of the first session was taken up with Dr. V outlining the seven chakras, or levels, and me listening to find examples of each for myself. Then she asked me to choose a time period to work on. I wanted to go back to the earliest time that I had had an Interface.

I visualized an outdoor playgroup where I stayed when my mother took my brother to the local child development clinic. I was about three years old. There was a sandbox and nurses to look after us. A blanket was rigged up to a tree for shade, and there were lots of toys. It was a hot sunny day. I talked (to Dr. V) about my feeling of anxiety at being separated from my mother and her recent grief over the death of my toddler brother from pneumonia.

During the session, I realized that I had experienced my mother's grief in great detail and that this had helped develop my empathic nature. In trying to nurture and protect my mother from her grief, I became her nurturer and have spent most of my life nurturing others. However, now I am nurturing myself. I also confirmed my feeling that I had been chosen to go through this lifetime childless, so that I could nurture and love without the ties or distractions of my own family. We did not really touch on the Interface experiences. Dr. V views the aliens as creatures from another dimension, rather than being extraterrestrial or from the future. I have decided to have several sessions with Dr. V to see if we can work together on these issues.

I dreamed that I was on a train with an Asian family. I recognized the fact that in my dreams, Asians often symbolize the grays. As I approached my station, I got into a conversation with the Asians/grays, and realized that the train was already leaving my stop. I needed to get off. I was quickly gathering up my luggage and realized that I would not be able to get it all together in time. I decided to wait until the next stop and get off there.

I feel that this dream relates to the first regression session with Dr. V, which did not cover any material about the Interfaces or the grays. It reflects the anxiety that I feel about the whole process and my decision to continue the regression. I got off the train too soon, ended the session prematurely, and need to go to the next stop, the next session.

October 22, 1991

X came to town. We talked a lot about remote viewing. He had asked me to do a remote viewing of the Tunguska explosion and I shared my perceptions with him. We decided to ask for a conscious Visitor Interface, but we were not sure if this happened. We were up very late talking. Before he left I did a rune reading for him. X felt that the reading was accurate and reflected some property negotiations he was taking part in early next week. I advised him to use the masculine rather than the feminine side of his nature, to be firm in the negotiations.

After he left this afternoon, I came back home and took a nap. I experienced some vivid hypnogogic imagery as I was relaxing. One image consisted of a wide band of light divided into several bands. Each band flowed in a different direction and contained plus and minus symbols. The plus symbols flashed on and off. What this symbolizes, I have no idea. It resembled other times when I have experienced this sort of imagery. Then I was looking at a golden, metallic surface that contained raised images. Most of these images were unknown to me. It looked like an art form. I found the stream of symbols and the golden surface captivating.

October 23, 1991

Earlier in this journal I recorded that I had met a woman, Betty-Sue, at a New Jersey UFO club and realized that she and I had shared some similar experiences. She and I had been befriended at a local psychophysics lab by a researcher, Helen, who had performed hypnotic regressions with us. At that time I looked back at my own experiences and felt these hypnotic sessions could have been used by Helen to scan for UFO information as part of a larger investigation. Betty-Sue also had this impression.

At the weekend, X mentioned that he had been in touch with Betty-Sue and gave me her new telephone number in Florida. He said she was going through some troubling times and that I should give her a call. Betty-Sue and I talked on the phone and I decided to share my psychophysics lab experiences with her. However, I still feel some reserve in interacting with her. Betty-Sue and her husband were active in the navy, and although she is now divorced, she still seems to have dealings with navy personnel. I want to maintain the integrity of my own experiences and do not want to have them influenced by someone else's interpretations. I will send my recollections to her marked "Absolutely Confidential." I have also come to the point of admitting that Betty-Sue's "Destiny Man" and my X are the same person.

October 25, 1991

Last night, I experienced a real dream that centered around a group meeting. X was there.

In the dream, I was being questioned about my perceptions of the future, which I have called the Exodus. I had told X about this when he visited. My perceptions indicated that in the year 2030 the quality of our atmosphere deteriorates rapidly and there is a mass exodus of people to the Mediterranean regions for about fifty years. I remember someone in the dream questioning me: "How soon does this happen?" During the dream, I was aware of X sitting on a couch with other people.

In normal waking consciousness I would have had no reservations about going over and greeting him. When we met last week, there were no reservations between us and we talked openly about the Visitors and how they affect our lives. The dream interrogation followed a pattern that started this summer.

October 26, 1991

I received a note from Betty-Sue with some puzzling comments. She thanked me for sending a package of my written materials, but she took issue with some of my remarks. She felt that I was "radically incorrect" in my concern that she was planning to sue Helen and the psychophysics lab for the things that had happened to her. I know that I was correct in hearing her say this, when she initially phoned me. Betty-Sue felt that the idea that she was going to sue was "implanted or induced into my mind while under hypnosis." She complained that Chuck, our mutual airline pilot friend, had "leanings" that disturbed his ability to translate her experiences correctly. She felt that he meant well but that he had a tendency to "twist the facts." I disagree with her evaluation of Chuck, as I have always found him to be honest.

Last Monday I made a decision to look for an apartment of my own, rather than continue to share Emily's house. Emily has become distressed by the possibility that the Visitors have been appearing in her house. Since the incident, where her house guest saw the Visitors in the night, Emily has voiced concern that these events might be real. Like me, she has long denied that the Interfaces have a reality, and the events of the past few months have caused her increasing angst. It has been four years since I moved in with Emily, and the sharing of the house has worked pretty well, until recently. It would not be fair to subject her to more Visitor experiences.

This week I located a small apartment near the center of the town and closer to the parapsychology lab. It consists of a bed-sitting room, eat-in-kitchen, and a bathroom. It is located in an old large house that was subdivided into private apartments. When I told Emily of my decision, she seemed relieved and said that she was looking forward to moving her home office, and maybe even her bedroom, upstairs. I am not sure whether the Visitor contacts will continue when I have moved. I have to ask myself, are the Interfaces tied to the house or to the individual?

October 30, 1991

Today, I had a second hypnotic regression session with Dr. V. We decided to look at an incidence that occurred in England when Alan and I were disturbed by bright lights in our bedrooms. I was sixteen; he was thirteen. Alan said a UFO had landed in the meadow at the bottom of our garden. He said that "figures" got out. The light stayed on for some time as I hid under the bedclothes. Then the light went out suddenly, and I thought the experience had ended. A few years ago, I did a visualization exercise to see if I could recover any memories of this event. I felt Alan and I had left the house to visit the UFO.

Dr. V and I looked again at this event and, from the hypnotic regression, it appeared that the action began once the lights went out. At that point, Alan and I and three "golden" people held a five-way telepathic conversation that was difficult to describe. As I was describing this experience to Dr. V, I experienced severe pain in my pelvic region. This became stronger as I was talking about the Interfaces and the invasion of my body that occurred. As the session progressed, the pain disappeared. Dr. V and I planned our next session, where I want to look back at earlier Interfaces. I somehow feel that I gave permission for these Interfaces to take place, and I would like to remember that event.

November 13, 1991

I decided to use this session with Dr. V to look back at some of the earliest Interfaces with the Visitors. I was able to access several events: one when I was fourteen months of age, and two more when I was two years old. The following is what I remember of the sessions:

When I was fourteen months old, we lived in a prefabricated bungalow in Bristol, England. It was postwar housing erected for the many new families being formed after the war. One afternoon my father took my mother and me for a ride on his motorbike and sidecar. We went up to Penpole, a local nature spot, from where you can look out over the Bristol Channel and into Wales. Suddenly, it was dark and my parents were standing on the hill, my father holding me very tightly. It seems that my mother and father had been abducted and we were kept there for several hours. I was allowed to play with what I thought were other children but who were actually small grays. Several tall, golden Visitors took my parents away. I was happily playing until I realized my parents were not there and I started crying for my Mummy and Daddy. My next memory is of standing on the hill. We were surrounded by the Visitors: the grays. I wanted to get down to play and I kept saying, "Get down. Get down." But my father would not let me go. He was holding me very tight. I do not recall how we got home. There is another fragmented memory of my parents talking to several "golden" Visitors by a sundial. It was during these sessions with Dr. V that I encountered both the grays and the "goldens."

The second Interface occurred in the bungalow. My mother was in the kitchen with the door closed. I was about two years old. My mother could watch me through a glass window that separated the kitchen from the living room. I was playing with some soft blocks and wanted someone to play with. A tall person appeared with a smaller person. I thought that another mother had come with her little girl. The tall one seemed to be shiny. The small gray one sat opposite me and we looked at each other and "communicated." It seemed to be fun.

The third event took place in our backyard at the bungalow. I was still around two years of age, trying to ride a tricycle and not doing well. I was getting frustrated. My mother was in the house with my baby brother, Michael.

Two tall, golden people appeared and asked me to go with them. They had asked me to go with them during the earlier Interface, but I had refused because my mother said I must not leave the house without her. This time I agreed to go, because I was bored with the tricycle. I found myself in something like a doctor's office, where I was sitting naked on an examining table. I stood up and walked around, showing off. I cried a bit for my Mummy and wanted to go home. I was only allowed to go home after they had physically examined me, mostly by touch, no instruments at this stage. The words that came to mind to explain why I was chosen were "estimation of potential."

The main reason for wanting to look back at these early

Interfaces was to see when and where I had given my permission for all the ensuing Interfaces. Two answers emerged: first, permission was not given by me until a later age and these remembered events were too early. I was perhaps too young to give permission. Or second, perhaps permission was never overtly given but there was a gradual familiarization with the goldens and the grays over the years. As Interfaces took place over the ensuing years, I was not able to refuse to interact either physically or mentally.

Although a lot of material is being uncovered in these regressions, the events still retain a sense of unrealness. Like past-life regressions, lots of material is produced, but there is no way to corroborate the details. However, I plan to continue with Dr. V and see what future regressions reveal.

November 20, 1991

There has been a continuation of the interrogation real dreams in which I am being questioned about my Interface experiences. I dreamed that I was talking to someone, a man who resembled X, and telling him that I could write things down much better than I could explain them. He said, "Well, why don't you do that then?" Interestingly, a Russian colleague at the psi lab told me that yesterday he dreamed he was being questioned by President Bush about his work at the parapsychology lab.

November 21, 1991

I have been sleeping over at Emily's house to look after her cats while she is away. This morning I discovered a large scratch in the soft, upper part of my right ear. It looks new and inflamed. It was not caused by the cats, because they were out all night and I let them in early this morning. I will monitor my dreams for the next few nights and see if there is any memory retrieval. If the scratch is an actual trauma from an Interface, some dream memories might surface over the next few nights.

November 24, 1991

Medical dreams: I was lying on an examination table undergoing a procedure. I was groaning. Someone was telling me it would not last long. Then there was a short break where I was lying on my right side and resting. Then there was another examination that did not hurt. During all these examinations, I was feeling embarrassed and anxious. I was in actual discomfort during the first part of the examination. The examiners were human, not Visitors.

November 28, 1991

I went for a fourth regression session with Dr. V. There were two events I wanted to explore. First, I wanted to find out if a remembered abduction by a human had actually happened or whether it was a disguised Interface. I had read that some individuals remembered being taken away as children when, in fact, they might have been abducted by aliens. On a family trip in England when my brother was five years old and I was eight, a man enticed us into the woods. We were picking wild flowers and he told us that he had lots of flowers at his cottage, which was further into the woods. My brother went with him and I ran back to find my parents. We found my brother safe and he had not been harmed. This turned out to be a completely terrestrial event.

The second event I wanted to explore took place in Scotland. In 1969 or 1970, I went on a trip to Scotland for a two-week stay on Iona. Iona has a tradition as the birthplace of Scottish kings. It is also the birthplace of Scottish Christianity and has much older, pagan traditions. Iona is a tiny, magical island. While I was staying on Iona, I went by boat with some fellow travelers to visit Seal Island.

What emerged during the hypnosis was that I remembered a large, shiny craft came floating into the bay. It was not touching the water but hovered just above it. We watched with amazement and with some anxiety as this thing came closer. It did not come all the way to the beach but stopped in the shallows. My next memories are of wading out to the craft and watching lots of tiny silvery fish darting about in the water. We climbed up onto the rim of a metal doorway. A hard, bony hand helped me up into the craft. Inside, the group of us, young and old, male and female, were subjected to an experience in which devastating emotions, real and contrived, were elicited.

A young couple I had befriended on Iona was there. On board the craft the two seemed very upset and confused. She sat on a chair in a small room sobbing uncontrollably, while her husband was standing with his arms around her, also looking angry and upset. The couple was subjected to mental manipulation, eliciting real memories and emotions, and generating false emotions. For example: the Visitors would show the couple movies of real events, to which they reacted emotionally. Then the Visitors would show the couple scenes of the Earth blowing up and life being extinguished. This caused the couple even more distress. I suppose that this procedure was for the grays' knowledge and information.

Then we were back on the beach, anxiously waiting for the boat. We did not want to stay on the island any longer and complained that the boat was late, when in fact it was not. We didn't discuss our experiences on the craft and we kept some distance from each other. We were all very quiet. I was pretty vulnerable during this experience, because it had only been a year since I had separated from my first husband. Other memories also emerged from this regression.

I did not investigate the trip back to Iona during the hypnosis session, but I believe we were picked up again. For the rest of the Iona vacation, we tended to go around in groups instead of exploring Iona alone. I think that our common experience caused us to group together for safety. During this regression I expressed anger at the experience but acknowledged that the Visitors have a different concept of what is right or wrong, that their "morality" is different from ours.

December 8, 1991

During the last two weeks, I have had three dreams where I have been physically attacked and had to fight for my survival. In the first dream I was running away from an individual who was wielding a large "probe." It looked as if it was made from some white ceramic material. I did not want this probe to enter me. I had to stop running and I kept falling over. In the second dream, I was on a bus and sitting in front of me was a large, black woman in a navy uniform. There was a fight on the bus. The third dream also involved fighting back at people who were attacking me. I discussed these dreams with Dr. V, and I felt her interpretation was right—that I am fighting back against the process of being a victim. She felt that this was a healthy process.

December 31, 1991

1991 has been an interesting year in terms of personal development and discovery. The year involved some interesting travel to Russia, England, and around the States. I have been meeting new people, making new friends, and reestablishing old ones. 1991 also saw a change to a new apartment, with a renewed sense of harmony and peace in my personal environment, despite a continuation of the real dreams. I needed to establish my own space away from Emily's house. During the past six months I have been doing hypnotic regressions sessions with Dr. V. During these I have been exploring and examining some of the anomalous Interfaces that have occurred over the years. Some dramatic material has emerged that indicates that for me the Interfaces began as early as when I was fourteen months old. It appears that all of my family have been involved: my parents and my brothers. However, the regression sessions have been a luxury in terms of time and money and I have taken a break until the spring, when I might resume them.

12

Covert Surveillance

"I strongly recommend that there be a committee investigation of the UFO phenomena. I think I owe it to the people to establish credibility regarding UFOs and to produce the greatest enlightenment on the subject."

—President Gerald Ford, in a letter he sent as a congressman to the chairman of the Armed Services Committee, March 28, 1966.

January 1, 1992

Another year has come and gone and here we are in 1992. What exciting things lie ahead this year? Socially there have been many group events for me, but only sporadic romantic encounters. Andy, my friend in California, found a permanent girlfriend, but I may continue to see him on a platonic basis when I go out to San Francisco.

There is the possibility of a new friendship closer to home. Yesterday, I got a call from Gregor, the leader of a local Scottish dancing group, who said that I was recommended to him by a colleague. Somehow he knew that I used to enjoy Scottish country dancing when I was living in England. Gregor invited me to attend the next dance at the university.

I have come to a new understanding about the Visitor

Interfaces. I recently completed a series of sessions with Dr. V and discovered that the Interfaces have been occurring on a regular basis since childhood and have involved the whole family. These Interfaces have involved not only the grays but also a tall, golden type of entity. I have taken a break from the regression sessions to assimilate what has emerged so far.

Early in November of 1991, I decided to find my own apartment. I shared Emily's home for four years but needed more privacy. I found a small apartment in the town, and this has become my sanctuary. Interestingly, the Interfaces *have* declined a little since the move. I wonder whether Emily's home acted as some sort of focal point. The fact is that the Interfaces have become less frequent and less intense.

January 6, 1992

I had a telephone call today from Betty-Sue. It was an interesting call. Betty-Sue feels that she is being harassed because of her Interface knowledge. She also feels that there is government involvement and intervention. She told me she has not been able to find employment. Jobs she had previously have ended abruptly when her bosses received phone calls about her. I feel that, however paranoid she sounds, she has no one to turn to and actually fears for her life. She gave me the name and address of a friend of hers in California to call if anything happened to her.

I received an interesting paper from Dr. Richard F. Haines entitled "The Human Response to Abduction: A Research Methodology toward an Alien Abduction Taxonomy (AAT)." Dr. Haines acknowledges the enormous task we are facing in considering the array and ramifications of human reaction to alien abduction. He states how the serious investigator is faced with such a broad range of reported effects that "it is very difficult to see whether patterns actually exist within and between individuals." His paper is an attempt to "offer a methodology that will lead to the development of a flexible taxonomy of human responses to abduction." It is serious researchers like Dr. Haines who might eventually shed light on the topic. Dr. Haines has developed a "Three Stage Technique (TST) to avoid biasing effects during hypnotic regression." In stage one of TST, Dr. Haines lets the subjects hypnotically recall their abduction experience: everything they can remember seeing, feeling, and hearing. During stage two, he instructs the subjects to describe everything they see, feel, hear, say out loud, and think to themselves during the abduction experience. Then in stage three, he asks them once again to go through the experience from beginning to end, during which Dr. Haines is then able to question and probe the subjects' experience with minimal biasing.

January 21, 1992

I had a strange dream at the weekend about a stocky man who wanted me to live in Washington, D.C. I dreamed that this man was being very friendly to me and asked me to marry him. He was trying to convince me to move to D.C. and to live with him on "South Second." He said that I could apply for grants to continue my school studies. However, in the dream I kept thinking, "Who is this man? I do not know him. Why would I want to marry him?"

I was sleeping at Emily's house last week to watch her cats while she was away. I believe that several Interfaces happened. I woke up one morning with a puncture trauma to my left hand and the memory of a tall man gently saying, "Wake up, Angela."

On Sunday, I had another long conversation with Betty-Sue. We exchanged details about a lot of personal experiences, trying to find pieces of the puzzle and to find some answers to these intriguing questions. It seems that she has met a male companion through an Internet service. Her new companion is in the air force, and she may go to live at his house in Virginia. He told her that he also had Interface experiences and sent her some poems he said came from an Interface experience. She sounded excited, but I feel very concerned for her. We talked for some time but really got no nearer to any answers.

February 1, 1992

Very scary real dream last night when I "awoke" to find an intravenous infusion in progress. There were about five small IV bags dripping into a larger reservoir. One of them was yellow. I was the recipient of this infusion. A woman asked me if the IV was okay, as I was kneeling up and looking at the bags. They had labels and one said "Xanax," which I recognized as a modern tranquilizer. There was a colleague present who was looking at a copy of the *American Pharmacopeia.*

When I awoke, I felt alarmed but dismissed the experience until I noticed a red puncture mark on the back of my right hand, over a major vein. This has filled me with a great deal of emotional conflict. The door to my apartment is locked and chained at night. However, I have a recollection of seeing two tall figures by the door last night. The needle mark is a red puncture hole with a slightly inflamed area around it. I also noticed that the top of my head was very sore today, as if I had knocked it, but I know I haven't.

As I was writing this, another dream memory emerged. Last week there was another real dream when I woke to find a medical colleague examining my lower abdomen and wiping off the area with warm water or lotion.

March 1, 1992

I have been at the new apartment now for about four months, and the Interface experiences have definitely lessened. Since I left Emily's house, I have had no further experiences of seeing the grays. The real dreams have contained humans rather than the entities. However, the Interfaces are still occurring. I have been talking with other women and I am finding many similarities in our experiences.

On Friday I talked on the phone with Betty-Sue, and she told me about a recent experience in which a large, black, unmarked helicopter hovered for several hours over a gazebo near her home. She felt that there may have been some missing time. The next day she discovered that the two business managers for her housing complex had become very sick overnight: one had a nervous breakdown and the other a heart attack. They lived in a house near the gazebo. Betty-Sue was in the process of evaluating her own experiences to help her understand them. She asked me who I was able to trust and I told her that these days I only trusted myself and my intuitions. I live by the Sufi maxim: "Love all, trust none."

This week, I had an evening phone call from something called the Mathematica Institute. They said that they were dong a telephone survey dealing with employment, family stress, and health. I felt that these were important topics, and although I don't usually do these kinds of surveys, I complied. The survey lasted about forty-five minutes, and the majority of the questions were of the type you would find in a survey of this kind. However, there were other questions, such as my loyalty to my profession, my supervisors, my colleagues, and about personal health issues, that seemed unusual. They also asked for the name and telephone number of a friend or relative they could contact if they wanted to contact me for follow-up interviews. I gave them Emily's name and address. The next morning I looked them up in the phone book but they were not listed. I mentioned the call and the name of the company at the parapsychology lab, and one of my colleagues said that he had heard of them. They had recently been bought out by Martin-Marietta, a defense industry firm that specializes in Department of Defense technology and space exploration.

Early yesterday morning I awoke with the feeling that an Interface had occurred but drifted back to sleep. I was awakened at 9:30 A.M. by Heather at the door. She was extremely agitated about a "dream" that had taken place early that morning. She said she had been taken to another location to be medically examined. She saw medical attendants in white and people on tables having examinations. She said that there were lots of tubes and equipment. She panicked and decided she was not going to be examined. She picked up a pair of surgical scissors and fought back. Then she found herself back in her own bed. She was very distressed. I don't think I was able to help her much. I counseled her that she should not see herself as a victim but should fight back, as she had done, to record her experiences, and to look for patterns in them.

After Heather left, I got a call from Gregor asking if I was planning to attend the Scottish country dancing this evening. The last time I went I met an interesting man, Michael, who seemed very attentive. He had turned up at the dance in full Scottish regalia, including kilt, and a dagger in his sock. We danced as partners for several dances. After the phone call, I remembered one of last night's dreams. I remember seeing Michael in my dream. He was sitting on a hard-back chair. He was just sitting and not doing anything special. In fact, he looked bored. At the memory of this, I experienced a strange physical attack. I became very cold and shivery and felt very weak. I went back to bed and slept until the late afternoon. What could have caused such a reaction?

In the evening, I felt much better and went to the Scottish country dancing. We had a great time learning new dances. Michael kept looking at his watch and appeared anxious about something. Then he said, "Do you know it is Sadie Hawkins Day and a woman has the option of asking a man out on a date? Do you have the same custom in England?" We danced for a while and then I replied, "Michael, do you want to go out on a date?" He said, "Yes," and I gave him my telephone number and address. He said he would call. Michael is an interesting man: he was in the army for many years and now is in the medical reserves. He lives in the next town. My paranoia kicks in, knowing that he is ex-military, but he seems nice. I will see what happens. I wonder if he will call?

March 3, 1992

Over the past couple of years, I have been corresponding and visiting with several people who have had Interface experiences—X, Mariah Folger, B, and Betty-Sue—in an effort to provide mutual support. I have also been looking for answers to my own experiences. During this time, I have been reading, networking, and analyzing my experiences, trying to make sense of them. I have added this information to a memory data-sorting process, letting it all mull around in my subconscious, allowing insights to emerge spontaneously.

Until today, I have kept the option open to the possibility that aliens were involved in my Interfaces. However, I am beginning to feel that there are no aliens, at least not visiting Earth yet, and that therefore the Interface experiences are something else. The alternatives to the alien hypothesis are that some people are more susceptible than others to alternative realities and perceive the Visitors as an altered-state experience, or that as a human race we share a collective unconscious that includes the Interface experiences, or that there may be human experimentation happening that is cloaked as Visitor interactions.

Cannon wrote at length about his theory that there are no aliens and that the abduction scenarios are staged events, probably orchestrated by certain factions of the government. Until recently, I was willing to discount his claims. Now, I feel that I have to include his ideas in the evaluation of my own experiences.

I wrote to Mariah Folger, X, Betty-Sue, and others:

> Dear folks, This is a long-overdue letter to you patient folks, although I have talked to some of you by phone. I haven't written to you guys about my Interface experiences since I moved to my new address four months ago as I wanted to see if my new location and circumstances changed anything. I have also been back to my old address to house-sit and wanted to compare my experiences there and here. I have also been

> doing a lot of reading on ELF and microwave research, listening to other women's experiences, and keeping a journal of my dreams and Interfaces.
>
> Here is my evaluation. Since I moved to the new address, I have had no dreams of grays or other aliens. There have been Interface dreams, but these have involved humans. I have come to the conclusion that the old house might be a focal point for gray experiences. I have taken steps to further protect myself and have reinforced my attitude of not seeing myself as a victim but working toward active, conscious participation in these events. I have come to the conclusion that there are no aliens (sorry, Mariah and Betty-Sue), just people, and people I can deal with.
>
> Before the holidays, I was working with a psychologist, and a lot of interesting and bizarre material came to light. But I am not satisfied that this was the right way for me to go. I have read that in an altered state the mind can fabricate and alter perceptions. I know that during my hypnotic regressions, I was not deliberately fabricating. However, the sessions left me with the same feeling as when I did guided imagery exercises, that everything was very colorful and interesting but afterwards there was confusion and self-doubt. So I decided not to continue with the regressions at this time.
>
> I would appreciate your reactions to this letter. I plan to continue evaluating my own experiences, to continue reading and networking with other experiencers, and to perhaps find some more pieces of the jigsaw.

There is a Hans Christian Anderson story called "The Emperor's New Clothes." The people do not challenge anything the king does or says. One day the king is visited by a group of tailors who fit him with an imaginary suit of clothes. They say that this suit can only be seen by intelligent, knowing people. The king and all his servants pretend to see the clothes. When the king parades around the town, all the people pretend to see the new suit of clothes. However, one little boy sees the king and proclaims, "The king has no clothes on!" Whereupon all the townspeople see things as they really are and see the king without his clothes. I feel like that little boy, but proclaiming "There are no aliens!"

March 6, 1992

Despite my proclamations of a few days ago, I had a bizarre dream in which I was taken to a house where I met some strange entities.

I was with Michael and I remember laughing with him about something. Then I was introduced to two tall, thin people who had long, thin hands. They resembled Lladro figurines. (Lladro figurines are tall, thin ceramic figures popular with collectors.) One was male, the other female. I was not sure which hand to shake first, as they both put out their hands simultaneously. I saw a colleague across the room, sitting, meditating on a pillow. The room was very noisy and I had to call him several times to get his attention.

At the side of this dream house, I found a secret doorway that was open, and I looked in. There was a flight of wooden stairs going up several stories. Upstairs, I found myself with the meditating colleague and we were in a big, barnlike space. There was an enormous pool with a UFO at the bottom of the water. The colleague said that this was where the aliens lived, and I understood that they were allowed to live in their craft with their own life-support and food-producing systems. The water was to provide buoyancy for their fragile physiology against Earth's gravity. They could leave the craft if they wanted to. Behind us was another, empty, pool.

March 7, 1992

This week I obtained two very interesting papers on the theme of government intervention in the abduction scenario. The first paper was written by Mark Phillips, a deprogrammer of abductees, and is entitled "The Top Secret Monarch Project: The U. S. Defense Intelligence Agency Project for Radically Modifying Human Behavior through Mind Control." As I was reading these papers, several ideas came to mind, and I felt that it would be worth recording them. Regarding the Monarch Project:

1. Is the Monarch Project the same as MJ12?
2. It seems that Mark Phillips used to be associated directly with the intelligence community up until the Carter era. How does he claim impartiality?
3. The paper mentions that a Revised Monarch Project was under the direction of a U. S. Army colonel, Michael Angelo Aquino. I remember Betty-Sue was asking me about a South American colonel when we talked the other day. This colonel had appeared in her Interfaces. Is this the same Latin American military-medical type who has appeared in my Interfaces, too?

4. Mind control programming, according to Phillips, encompasses four areas: alpha, beta, delta, and theta. Alpha is regular programming and basic control, which could be accompanied and accomplished through brain entrainent; beta involves the primitive mind and conditioned sexual involvement and conditioning; delta achieves a psychopathic condition, killer instincts and self destruction; and theta involves psychic programming to develop latent abilities. Do these four areas correspond to brain wave states? According to Phillips, theta was generated by the Monarch Group by the cerebral implantation of "sodium/lithium-powered high-frequency receivers/transducers coupled to a range discharge capacitor." This would induce the brain into certain states.

5. Phillips also states that the Monarch Group used such equipment in "sound and light-proof sensory deprivation, isolation chambers, and fluid suspension tanks." This environment sounds like the psi lab studies I participated in and the Monterey studies in which Andy was involved.

6. Near the end of the paper, Phillips lists professionals who are knowledgeable about the U. S. Department of Defense Monarch Project, including one at the UCLA School of Psychiatry in Los Angeles. Incidentally, this is where my medical colleague, John, is completing his psychiatry internship. John has been working on brain-mapping research and electromagnetic effects on the brain. He has also worked with another UCLA researcher who is into ELF and its effects on the brain and behavior. The last time my colleague was visiting us, he seemed withdrawn, almost depressed, and it makes me wonder what he has gotten himself into and how he is coping. Two years ago, I shared my Angel Island real dream with John. In this experience I was told that I had been chosen to be involved in a special project but if I shared information concerning it, I would be killed. My medical colleague had commented at the time that he had a similar experience and death threat. I feel that he is into something where he feels way out of his depth. Before going out to UCLA, John was working with an orthopedic surgeon in New York, ostensibly developing an electromagnetic treatment for bone fractures and osteoporosis. This surgeon, according to my friend was formerly a navy surgeon, who had been sent tissue,

ostensibly from the Roswell UFO crash. The surgeon had found it to be an animal/plant matrix. Interestingly, John has been one of the individuals I have recognized in my Interface experiences.

7. Mark Phillips lists characteristics of mind-control victims: they are usually 94 percent female; 100 percent of them suffer from multiple personality disorder; 100 percent of them have been involved in childhood pornography and were victims of childhood sexual abuse. Some of the early victims have a tattoo or scar resembling a blue Monarch butterfly. Victims were also given gifts of butterfly barrettes, earrings, and pins. From an early age I have had a fascination with butterflies, but I do not feel that this reflects in any way my involvement with mind control. My personal feelings about butterflies are that they symbolize transformation and metamorphosis, personal growth, and development.

The second paper I received analyzes the career history of X and claims that because of X's long and ongoing interaction with military, government, and defense agencies, his claims of "not knowing anything" about the UFO abduction scenario should be regarded as false. The author of the paper claims that X knows a great deal about federal involvement with the UFO problem and that his assertion to the contrary is preposterous. He theorizes that "when one combines Big Money plus backing from a key congressman, plus Pentagon and intelligence community interest . . . very positive actions will result." The paper, written by my pilot colleague, Chuck, lists several "rumors" that have circulated regarding X:

1. He has approached psi researchers about the best way to recruit and use psychics for intelligence gathering.

2. He has visited many psychics for readings, has taken psychic development courses, and has spent much time with alleged abductees.

3. For many years, X has been involved with classified research on electronic mind control.

I refuse to become paranoid about this material. I will add it to my mental database, and I will continue to do an intuitive data-sorting process. What will transpire from all this who knows, but each piece adds more information to the whole picture. Sorting out information from *dis*information is not easy. In the meantime, I will take steps to protect my own person, thoughts, and integrity.

March 15, 1992

For several years I have been looking for a male friend who would not be threatened by my intellectual and intuitive abilities. I have dated many men but have not found the right one. I thought that Gregor might be an interesting person to link up with, but he is going through a particularly tough divorce and seems preoccupied with this. Then I had a date with Michael from the Scottish country dancing group, and we seem to have hit it off. We share a medical background and an interest in things Scottish and English. I hope it will continue. We went to see the movie *Lawnmower Man* on Thursday. It was about virtual reality and mind control. The graphics are fantastic and the story line is similar to Cannon's and Phillip's theories of government involvement in human development and mind control. Michael dismissed it as science fiction.

March 19, 1992

I dreamed that I was holding Heather's two-and-a-half-year-old son on my lap. My blood pressure was taken. Then they wanted to take the little boy's blood pressure, and they asked me to hold his hand because he was afraid.

April 10, 1992

I visited with Mariah in California and we had some fun times together. We talked a lot about our Interface experiences. I mentioned to her that if government involvement was an issue in these experiences, I wished they would approach me directly, rather than run cloak-and-dagger activities in the night. I would be very happy to cooperate and help them, and to learn about the Interfaces.

Mariah and I drove to Bodega Bay and stopped for lunch at an old, renovated restaurant. We sat at a side table where the sunlight was streaming in. It was very pleasant to sit there and eat our lunch. At one point, I looked up to find a man photographing us from outside the restaurant front window. He was an older man in a coat and hat. He took a lot of pictures without saying anything to us. I felt embarrassed. I tried to ignore him and eventually he went away. I have since heard from other women who have had similar experiences of people photographing and videotaping them without their permission.

April 12, 1992

Back on April 9, I had a dream that someone was going through my purse and commenting on the things in it. This turned out to be a precognitive dream, because my purse was stolen last night. I am attending a school session at a conference center. I accidentally left my purse in the dining room, and when I returned it was gone. We had been talking about "empowerment" at dinner, but this incident has made me feel very vulnerable! I went to bed and cried for the loss of identity that losing the purse represented. I wondered what would be next: would I lose my luggage on the plane, would I find my apartment burned down? My mind went through various stages of loss, and I cried some more. Actually, I had dreams of my apartment burning down before I came out to California, so that is why I brought my passport and naturalization papers with me. Now they are gone. Then I rationalized that my real identity is who I know I am, not what my documents say I am. Documents can be replaced.

April 18, 1992

Last week, I remember that I awoke from an Interface dream in which I was saying "Good night" to several humans who were leaving my room. I was still at the conference center. The next morning when I showered I noticed a large red puncture mark on the inner side of my right elbow (where blood is drawn). My right shoulder and hip hurt.

This Thursday night I woke in the night and found that Michael and I were talking, but I fell asleep again. When I woke in the morning, I felt terrible that I should have fallen asleep, but Michael did not remember it happening, so it must have been a dream. However, I did have a huge bruise on the back of my left thigh that was not there the night before. Michael pointed it out to me. It was about two inches across and doughnut shaped, with a clear center. It was a fresh bruise, but it did not hurt.

April 22, 1992

Before going out to California this month, I had a precognitive dream and a sense of unease about my apartment. I felt that maybe there would be a fire while I was away. I decided to take my passport and green card with me to California; then they both got stolen with my purse. The precognitive unease was correct. A young man the landlord had evicted from one of the bottom apartments had decided to get revenge. Before he left, he had piled cushions and papers into the middle of the living room and set fire to them. Fortunately, they did not stay lit and the house did not get burned down.

Last night I had a wonderful dream about unconditional love.

First I was at a second-floor hall, where a group of us were discussing unconditional love as a theme and title for a talk. About fifty people were at this first meeting; then they went away. Then hundreds more turned up. Then I was out in a beautiful valley on a stage addressing thousands! I was amazed how clearly I spoke. Someone asked me why I was talking about love when Jesus had done the same thing. My reply was that nobody was listening any more. I asked the crowd to do an exercise in which one person in each pair closed his eyes, the other one covered her ears. They tried to lead each other around. I addressed their sense of frustration and incompleteness. How we should be helping each other to see and hear and be whole. It was a wonderful dream.

April 25, 1992

Earlier this year I had been telling people I did not have time for a relationship. However, I was in need of a social life, so I joined the local Scottish country dancing group at the university. There I met Michael, who came to the first dance. We flirted and discovered that we had a lot in common. At the end of February, we decided to date and have seen each other a couple times a week, and we talk on the phone every day. The relationship has been good for both of us.

Michael has felt self-confident enough to finally land a great job that recognizes his managerial skills. We have been exploring each other, mentally, physically, emotionally, and spiritually. His self-esteem has also been bolstered by the news that he will be made a major next January. He is still in the army reserves and wears his dog tags everywhere under his shirt. He is looking for a medical unit to join. I have not told him too much about my Interface experiences. I do not want him to think I am too weird.

May 9, 1992

Lots of anxiety dreams early this morning. The dreams were about being lost in a large building and trying to find my way back to my room. Then I was outside and trying to find a bus to get home. During part of an earlier real dream, I was being examined, and it was extremely uncomfortable. I commented to myself that I was not dreaming and that this was a real experience. A human male and female were doing the examination. After they left, I wriggled so that I was hanging over the end of the bed. Someone was looking for me. They looked in and saw only a heap of bedclothes and thought I was gone. I think that was when I left the room, got lost among all the rooms, and got outside.

I want to mention here a strange experience that occurred after Michael and I had been dating for a while. Michael is a big man who lifts weights and runs. I am a large woman, but he can easily lift me. One day, he lifted me and I felt incredibly light. He almost dropped me as he was expecting me to be my usual weight. He said "What just happened?" I could not explain why I had suddenly, but temporarily, become very much lighter in weight. Was this a side effect of the Visitor experiences? We were both very puzzled by this incident.

I had a phone call from the airline pilot, Chuck. He had attended Dr. Z's abduction conference in April and had heard an interesting talk by DE of a Virginia-based remote viewing group. It seems that DE and his viewers have been remote viewing alien bases on the Moon, Earth, and Mars. They claim that these aliens transport minerals to the Earth, mainly for nourishment, and have zombie-like people for their slaves. I had to laugh out loud at this! It also appears that there are three types of aliens, according to DE: small grays who are practically robotlike; larger grays who are the pilots; and another kind, who are mystical "shape-shifters."

Chuck also reported from DE's talk that he considers that there are "implanted" humans who are maybe unknowingly acting as advocates or missionaries for the aliens. These advocates act as liaisons between humans and aliens. I asked Chuck whether DE did all the remote viewing himself or whether his perceptions were a consensus of several viewers. DE views abductions as a form of out-of-body-experience, or OBE. If this is so, how does he account for the physical trauma such as bruises, cuts, and scars that result from the experiences? Also what about physical traces left over from UFO touchdowns?

May 19, 1992

On TV for several nights this week there was a dramatization of the work of Dr. John Mack. Mack is a psychiatrist who has been investigating the phenomenon of alien abductions. The movie *Intruders* was well done and illustrates many of the phenomena that abductees experience. The main purpose of the documentary seems to have been the generation of public interest. Yesterday morning they were discussing the topic on the local radio station. It has also generated interest from experiencers, who have been calling the parapsychology lab and sharing their stories. One lady had experiences going back to 1962, which resulted in her becoming psychically sensitive. I will go over to Heather's house this evening to see the concluding part of the documentary.

May 20, 1992

Last night I watched the end of the *Intruders* documentary. It was without exaggeration. After watching the movie, I had a nightmare in which I was surrounded by grays. I was fighting them physically, striking out and hitting them. However, the grays were passive and unemotional, coping with my aggression by either standing near me or by gently taking my arms. I awoke very frightened, and even though I wanted to go to the bathroom, I did not want to move or get out of bed. I do not know if this was a new Interface or a dream recall of an earlier one.

May 23, 1992

Over this last week, I have been reading Raymond Fowler's recent book *The Watchers,* which documents the abduction experiences of Betty Andreason. There are some similarities between her experiences and mine that are worth recording. Betty describes a clear, glasslike sphere that is capable of independent movement and direction. These balls of light sometimes glow and are between the size of a basketball and a baseball. One hit her between the eyes when she was a child and was the size of a marble. This ball of light sounds like the bubblelike ball that Bev and I saw a few years ago. That one seemed to have the ability to change direction. Betty Andreason had some of her alien contacts while experiencing the OBE state with her husband. Most of my Interfaces have taken place in an altered state of consciousness.

May 27, 1992

This morning I noticed a red area on my right wrist. Looking at it closer, I saw that I had a triangular trauma, about a quarter inch in diameter in size on the back of my right wrist. The trauma does not hurt, but the area is red and it looks like a top layer of skin has been removed. It is now partially healed with no oozing or bleeding. My apartment door was locked and chained last night.

May 28, 1992

It has been four and a half years since I started working at the lab. For the latter half of that time we have been aware that funding for the lab has been declining and it was possible that my position would be phased out. Also, I have grown far more skilled than the job requires and feel the need to look around for something more academic and challenging. So, like Mary Poppins, who let the east wind carry her away when she had completed a cycle of being needed at a particular location, I will let the cosmos carry me to a new adventure.

Several ideas for a science fiction story were sparked by a newspaper article about Hispanics as illegal aliens in Los Angeles. What would be the immigration status of ETs landing on American soil? Would they be classified as "illegal aliens"? Would they have to go through the immigration process, and where would we deport them to? If they were allowed to stay, what kind of work would they do? What would be their qualifications for a green card? Would the ETs end up working at fast food restaurants because they had no Earth-educational background? Would there be a prejudice against them because of their race and color? It would make an interesting science fiction story. If the ETs were given special treatment because of their novelty or their access to special skills and technology, would there be reprisals from other minority groups? What about language and food? Would telepathy become accepted because the aliens communicated this way? Would specialty ET food stores spring up that specialized in alien food, such as chlorophyll soup or cow's blood sausage? Would ET-type restaurants become fashionable? I believe that the ETs might be secreted away and their special knowledge used for the advancement of the human race.

June 13, 1992

I got a letter from a psychotherapist colleague, and she

enclosed a report that she had previously told me about. It is entitled "A Roper Survey of Abduction Experiences." The report was mailed to nearly one hundred thousand psychiatrists, psychologists, and other mental health professionals. It contains the combined data from three national surveys of nearly six thousand adults. The report was initiated by Ron Westrum, professor of sociology at Eastern Michigan University; David Jacobs, professor of history at Temple University in Pennsylvania; John Carpenter, psychotherapist; and Budd Hopkins, artist and abduction researcher. The report was financed jointly by an anonymous donor and Robert Bigelow of Las Vegas. According to the report, the surveys dealt with the relationship between unusual personal experiences and what the researchers called the "UFO abduction syndrome."

One of the indicator questions addressed the feeling that the persons had left their bodies. The poll respondents indicated that 14 percent of them had, at some time or another, felt that they had left their body, and 4 percent of the population polled said that this had happened to them more than once. Interestingly, a proportion of executive/professional and white collar workers reported more mental events than did other occupational levels. This group, identified by the Roper Organization as the "Influential Americans," reported the greatest number of OBE events. This group also answered positively to four or more of five key indicator questions in the poll suggesting that they may possibly have had other anomalous experiences.

The Roper report has generated a great deal of criticism from the scientific community. However, the figures stand by themselves to indicate that not only do a great number of people have paranormal experiences, but that the number increases with education level and social activity. This goes opposite to the popular idea that people who have these unusual experiences are uneducated and gullible.

June 15, 1992

This morning I dreamed about an alien device. In the dream I found this device in my bed, but someone retrieved it and took it away from me as I was inspecting it. I do not know its purpose. At one end was a long thin device like a vibrator. One end was rounded. From the other end extended a loosely constructed mesh of filaments and small metal balls. A star-shaped emblem or decal was woven into the mesh.

June 16, 1992

Last night I had a real dream in which I was in a military setting. I remember looking at a bulletin board with soldiers around me. I was in some sort of group setting.

June 24, 1992

During the early hours in a real dream, I felt and saw a man at the right side of my bed. He said, "Come with me." I think I was reluctant to go at first, but then I went with him. I have been away attending graduate school for this past week and am still in California.

June 29, 1992

I flew back to New Jersey and Michael picked me up at the airport last night. We drove back to my apartment, where we celebrated a romantic homecoming. However, this morning Michael was behaving very strangely. He was searching through the papers and books on the shelves by the bed. When I came in, he asked if he could take his Scottish catalogs back. I said, "okay," and found them for him. Then he was going through the magazines on the coffee table, as if he was still looking for something. After that, he was in the bathroom searching. Then in the kitchen, searching through a small glass container where I keep earrings and other "odds and ends." Michael found a pair of earrings that matched and said, "Wear these." I was already wearing earrings. What was he looking for?

This evening after Michael had left, I settled down to watch TV. I put my cup on the shelves by my bed and noticed a small gray piece of plastic, like the lid of a tiny box. It was only a few centimeters across and attached to a piece of masking tape. It had the letters "TETRAD" on the top. The letters were long and thin. The cross section of the device or lid was designed so that it could slide over another small piece. The lid was open at both ends and manufactured from Earth-type gray plastic. There were two rounded projections on the underside of the container with the letter *R* in the middle. Perhaps it contained two other things? Masking tape that was one centimeter wide was attached to the object. Was this what Michael was looking for? This makes me feel very nervous and paranoid and I do not like these feelings! I hid the lid and tape in my secret place and plan to find out what the trademark

"TETRAD" stands for. My guess is that it is something medical or electronic.

June 30, 1992

There was a funny message on the Psi Skeptic Internet News Group today. The posting related to a letter that was found in the *Boston Globe* "Letters to the Editor" for June 30, 1992. The letter was from a Dr. Fred L. Whipple of the Smithsonian Astrophysical Observatory of Cambridge, Massachusetts. He was speculating on a possible source for the common abductee experience. His conclusion is that someday this will be recognized as a primal remembrance of a baby's first visit to the doctor's office!

July 3, 1992

After discovering the gray, plastic cover in my apartment, I decided to try and find out what it was. I took it to an electrical engineer and asked him if he knew what it was. Yes, he knew. It turned out to be a cover for a microchip. According to the electrical engineer, it protected the microchip in transit and the cover was usually discarded when the chip was installed. I asked him what kind of chip would have been contained in the cover? He was not sure but thought maybe a computer chip. I don't know enough about computers to tell if anything has changed in my computer. I am reminded of something that Mariah Folger said. She was told by an army colonel that personal computers were not secure any more but could easily be accessed over the phone lines. This does not worry me, because all I do on my computer is schoolwork and play games. I recently got "on-line" but have no secrets to share over the Internet. My feeling is that if "someone" wants to monitor what I am doing on my computer and phone, they are going to be pretty bored.

Yesterday, I had a telephone conversation with a philanthropist in Nevada named Mr. T, and we had a fascinating talk about my going to work for him and his new foundation. I was directed to Mr. T through a job "headhunter" who had represented the job as "interviewing abductees." The job, however, has a much larger scope. Mr. T is setting up a chair of anomalies research at the University of Nevada at Las Vegas. Mr. T wanted to set up a laboratory at the university to coordinate with the parapsychology lab, to replicate their psi work. I would be the liaison between the two labs and would travel back and forth between Nevada and

New Jersey. Mr. T is interested in all areas of anomalies research, including psi, UFOs, abductions, and crop circles. He and his team from Nevada are planning to visit New Jersey toward the end of July. I will also get to meet him when I attend the Parapsychology Association meeting, which is to be held in Las Vegas this year.

July 14, 1992

I dreamed that Michael and I were on a bed and a contraption was being lowered over us. It was large, rectangular and of a tubular design, like an oblong neon-tube arrangement. It was about three feet (on its longest side) by two feet. It came down over the top part of our bodies, and I was worried that it was hot and would burn us, because it was glowing red.

July 16, 1992

Last night, I awoke having difficulty breathing. My lungs felt heavy and full as if my chest muscles would not work properly. There were significant dreams that contributed to this condition, but I could not remember them. As I woke, I felt as if my left sinus was draining, but it turned out to be a heavy nosebleed. After the nosebleed stopped, I put the tissues in the trash can. There may have been an Interface last night. Michael was with me during the night, but he did not remember anything happening.

This evening, I decided to put out the garbage and get rid of the bloody tissues from this morning's nosebleed. Strangely, I could not find them. I do not remember flushing them away, as there were too many of them. I know that the nosebleed was real but where have the tissues gone? Had Michael taken them?

July 17, 1992

This last weekend, I attended the Mutual UFO Network (MUFON) Symposium in Albuquerque, New Mexico. I roomed with my friend B, and the day before the conference we drove to Santa Fe to see the ghost towns, rock formations, and lots of traditional sights along the way. In the evening we drove out to the desert to look for UFOs and found a wonderful frog pond, swelled by the recent rainstorms. The noise was tremendous as thousands of frogs sang the night away. We were a little disappointed that we did not see any UFOs. The MUFON talks were on a wide variety of topics, ranging from the serious to the ridiculous. (I was still going through extreme pendulum swings: sometimes renouncing the reality of the aliens, then looking for them to appear. It was a time of denial interspersed with the need to accept the aliens' reality.)

The speakers included Linda Moulton Howe, Dick Haines, Jacques Vallee, Stanton Friedman, Budd Hopkins, and many others. Specific topics ranged from UFO sightings, foreign research, physiological effects, abductions, MJ-12, and crop circles. Budd Hopkins was the only representative of the abduction scenario. Most of the people attending the symposium were MUFON members, state directors or assistant state directors—good, ordinary people—but there was no spark to the meeting at all. I waited three years to attend this one and will probably wait three years before I attend another one.

The main highlight of the MUFON Symposium was an interesting presentation by Budd Hopkins. He presented a woman who had experienced an abduction out of the thirteenth-story window of her Manhattan apartment. This was witnessed by two "policemen," a "dignitary," and a woman whose car had stalled on the Brooklyn Bridge at the time of the abduction. However, although Budd and the woman appeared to believe their story and that of the witnesses, the whole story seems contrived and fails to convince me. It just did not ring true.

After the woman had reported the abduction to Budd, she underwent some investigations with him. The two "policemen" then contacted Budd with their story, but it seems that they were not policemen but from the Secret Service. The woman was physically abducted by these two men. They grabbed her off the street, tried to put her into their car, and the poor woman almost got run over in the process. They interrogated her in the car, insisting that she was an alien. She seemed more frightened by this experience than by the alien abduction.

I felt angry at Budd for putting this woman on the stage when he had promised to protect her identity. The woman was bombarded with questions by the audience and later by the media. Budd said that he could not reveal the identities of the two agents, the dignitary, or the woman on the bridge. It is highly possible that the two agents accessed information about the abductee from Budd's records and may have fabricated the witness story. It is also possible that the whole thing is a setup to discredit Budd and his long-standing work with abductees. It will be interesting to follow this story and see how it plays out.

13

The Abduction Jigsaw

"We had a job to do, whether right or wrong, to keep the public from getting excited."

—Dr. J. Allen Hynek, scientific consultant for Air Force Project Blue Book, on camera shortly before his death in 1985.

July 18, 1992

What a bumpy ride this past six months have been, both exciting and eventful. The major issues that have emerged are the necessity to find another position because of the parapsychology lab's funding situation. I also felt the need to find my own apartment after living with Emily for over four years. It was not fair to continue to submit her to unwanted Visitor intrusions. I have had several leads in the job market, the best one being with a new foundation in Nevada. This group is funded by a local philanthropist, Mr. T. The parapsychology lab in New Jersey will act as a model for the new group in Nevada. My role will be to act as a liaison between the two labs.

The Interfaces have continued on a reduced basis but still have a combined medical and technical aspect to them. Physical effects such as bruising and biopsy-like skin lesions have resulted. There is the possibility of human surveillance of the Interface experiences. I returned from California earlier this month to find a device on my bookshelf, obviously forgotten by someone. I took it in to an electronics expert, who identified it as the cover for a microchip. The company produces similar microchips for covert surveillance. This is scary stuff, but I cannot let this knowledge stop me from living my life fully. Basically, I have nothing to hide, therefore nothing to fear. Maybe, someday, I will find out who has been so interested in my activities.

July 27, 1992

Last weekend, Michael and I drove down to Virginia so that we could attend the Scottish Games. We stayed at a motel in Laurel, Maryland. By the second night we were both absolutely exhausted from all the games. I think there was an Interface that second night. There was a real dream. In the first part of this dream I was traveling by car with other people. In the second part, a medical procedure was taking place.

The Friday night Michael and I arrived in Virginia we had dinner with DE, who has a business group that is promoting remote viewing to business and industry. I was impressed with him and his presentation of his company. Michael was quite skeptical, but DE was able to assure him of the validity of remote viewing and its applications. DE said that other viewers had been very complimentary of my remote perception skills. He also told me that he was very proud of his team and that he had the "cream of the talent" working for his company. They were relocating to Albuquerque, New Mexico. I had heard that McDonnell Douglas was interested in funding his group. DE asked me to be a part of his team. I feel that this is a great honor. To be asked to be part of this team is fantastic. A while back I was meditating on the need for recognition of my psi abilities—and here it is. DE said that he would call me in New Jersey and I would act as a remote viewing consultant for his group.

July 28, 1992

A real dream in which I have a memory of blood going into a syringe and watching it with fascination. This morning I noticed a slight red trauma inside my left elbow but ignored it at first, which seems to be the pattern with these experiences.

July 31, 1992

An interesting symbolic dream. I was handed a small, computer-like device, about the size of a small book. It had several windows to the right and several push buttons. I saw a picture in the top right-hand window of an alien-type craft. It was on a runway and ready to take off. Out of curiosity, I pressed the button next to the window. The craft took off. In the second window, there were more and faster craft. I pushed the button again and the craft took off at a faster rate. Then the third window showed hundreds of craft, and again, out of curiosity, I pushed another button, and all the craft took off. Then to my horror I realized that with my curiosity, I had launched a battalion of alien craft. Then to my relief I realized that this was a test and a warning, that I should be careful what buttons I press and what I initiate.

August 14, 1992

Well, here I am, checked out of the Hacienda Hotel in Las Vegas, waiting for my ride to the airport to catch my flight back to New Jersey. What a whirlwind of a week! My meeting with Mr. T went very well and we seemed to get on well. We spent a lot of time talking, attending the parapsychology meeting, visiting with the departments at the university, and networking with colleagues. Mr. T took me out to look at some apartments and found rooms where I could live temporarily. Mr. T's office building is a lovely old house built on the style of an old mansion. I will have my own office downstairs, where we are going to put together a library and computerized database of psi resources. We will also be liaising with the university to set up research groups in several departments. I will move out to Las Vegas at the end of September.

September 2, 1992

Since my return from Las Vegas and the conference, a lot has been happening. I am glad that I have a job confirmation but feel sad at leaving the parapsychology lab, which has been my home for five years. The new job at the foundation should be very interesting. My dreams have been colorful, dynamic, and symbolic. They have involved a child, which is symbolic of new beginnings for me. The Interface dreams have also continued. The other night I dreamed I heard two loud knocks, and a woman's voice clearly said "Angela?" in a questioning tone. The voice was young, energetic, and unknown to me. I woke up, but nobody was there and no one was out in the hallway.

An interesting paper has come across my desk entitled "A Pilot Study: Of the Extent and Nature of Extraterrestrial Contact," authored by Dr. James A. Harder of Berkeley, California. He and his colleagues have found through questioning abductees that their subjects report a very different description of extraterrestrial contact than those described in recent popular books. Harder supposes that this may be the result of a serious bias that has affected what has been called abduction studies. The bias, he says, may have entered the studies in at least three ways:

1. Persons with bad experiences tend to be found more easily by those who offer relief.

2. Persons with positive experiences seldom come forward to talk about them out of fear of ridicule.

3. A very large number of contacts are hidden even from the subjects themselves by a veil of amnesia. When this is reversed, it is generally found that the amnesia is not the result of suppressing memories of traumatic events but rather an agreement not to talk about sensitive matters with the media and disbelievers.

Harder's main conclusions from his study are that: "Perhaps it is not surprising that a large population of these subjects report a physical extraterrestrial contact. What may be surprising to those new to the subject is the seeming pervasive influence the contact has had on their lives: these persons tend to be far more concerned about social issues and world peace than the general public, to be more psychic, and to report a much greater interest in spiritual matters."

I have been packing boxes, selling furniture, and tying up projects at the parapsychology lab. All in all, things are moving pretty smoothly, and I should have everything completed by the time I leave New Jersey at the end of September. One of the sad things is that I will miss seeing Michael. Despite all my suspicions about his involvement with Interface, we have had some very enjoyable times together. We have enjoyed Scottish dancing, the beaches of New Jersey, movies, trips, and an exotic personal relationship. However, I feel that his need to be with me is greater than my need to be with him.

September 22, 1992

During the past couple of weeks, I haven't had many real dreams, but the following is one I remember clearly. In the dream, I was directed to lie on a bed. Someone moved something off the bed, like case notes. I was encouraged to lie on the bed, which I did and went to sleep. In a second part of this real dream, I was holding a gas mask that led to a cylinder. It was an anesthetic-type gas mask, and a humidified gas came out of it. I kept letting my arm relax and the mask would drop from my face. Someone told me to keep the mask up near my face. In both parts of the real dream, the ambiance was warm and nonthreatening. The attendants wore blue overalls and were friendly but professional. There was no physical trauma attached to these real dreams.

Here I am in Las Vegas after a month of planning, preparation, and packing. Everything went fairly smoothly and Sophia (my cat) and I are safely arrived in Nevada. We are staying at the Sun Harbor Apartments. We have a small box of an apartment, but it is enough for me and my kitty. I arrived on Wednesday night and went to work on Thursday morning. I spent the rest of the week unpacking boxes, putting my books into the foundation library, buying additional books, and sorting out household items to bring to the apartment. Even though I sold all of my large furniture, there were still a lot of boxes to ship to Nevada.

When I arrived on Wednesday night, I had a disturbed night, waking every few hours. I had an interesting symbolic dream in which I met a "golden woman." She was head of a household in a large house. She was tall, very pale, and thin. Her hair was very fine and stood up around her head in a style resembling Nefertiti. It glowed golden when the light hit it but the bottom part looked like solid gold. The top looked feathery. She was very beautiful. She drew my attention to a clock calendar on a mantle shelf. It seemed like one of those clocks where numbers flip over. The clock calendar showed a series of numbers. I was told that this symbolized the end of an era and the nearing of a new one, when we would encounter other realities and revelations. It was a mystical, magical dream.

Last night I dreamed I was at a place where I had volunteered to help at some medical program. There were two large tentlike enclosures, and most of the people were in the other tent. I was resting on a narrow camp bed before going to help. A doctor came in and explained that I needed to have an injection of an antibiotic before I could help. He gave me a shot in the deltoid muscle of my left arm. I asked him what it was and he said, "streptomycin." The shot was given in a standard Earth-type plastic syringe. The dream had a real feel to it.

On Thursday evening, Mr. T and I had planned to attend a meeting of a psychic group in Las Vegas. This group meets on an informal basis. The leader, Alan, works as an engineering specialist for EG&G Energy Measurements, a government contractor for the Department of Energy (DOE). Alan runs a group called Para-Physics, which meets every few weeks for the purpose of research and exploration. He has been running this group for about twenty years. Unfortunately, Mr. T could not attend, so I did and had an interesting evening. Alan has one wall of his house taken up with a huge computer/TV screen. The group consisted of Alan, a psychology professor, several intuitives, and some work associates. The evening was taken up mostly with Alan's psychic friends doing "readings," which Alan recorded. One man there, David, was very intuitive. He gave me a very good description of Michael. I am curious about Alan and his DOE connections, but he seems to have a genuine interest in parapsychology and says that he isn't doing psi research for the government.

October 24, 1992

My friend B faxed me a copy of a paper that has been circulating in the UFO community. Basically, the paper is a critique of a recent case being investigated by UFO researcher Budd Hopkins. Hansen briefly recaps the case, which involved an incident that occurred at about 3:15 A.M. on November 30, 1989, when a woman was floated out of her thirteenth-floor apartment in lower Manhattan. According to Hansen, three witnesses in a car about two blocks away observed the woman and three humanoid figures emerge from a window and ascend into a craft hovering over her building. Two of the witnesses were government security officers who were guarding a third witness, a dignitary. More than a year after the case, the two agents wrote to Hopkins, stating what they saw, and a few weeks later they visited the woman in her apartment. After the visit, the agents began a series of physical abductions and harassment of the woman. Hansen criticizes the way the case was managed, as follows:

"UFO abductee, Linda Napolitano claims that she was kidnapped, assaulted, battered, harassed, and nearly drowned by two agents of the U. S. government. Prominent ufologists Budd Hopkins, John E. Mack, David M. Jacobs, Jerome Clark and Walter H. Andrus accept these claims. Hopkins has collected extensive materials that could be used to help apprehend and convict the agents. Yet, Hopkins, Clark, and Andrus have vigorously argued that these crimes should not be reported to law enforcement authorities: they indicate that such could be 'politically damaging' to UFO research. These ufologists are asked to defend their decision and priorities."

To date, Hansen states that he has not been given a satisfactory explanation for their views. He concludes: "At risk is not only the safety of Linda but also that of the general public. If federal agents have engaged in kidnapping and attempted murder, they should be brought to justice. The matter is of great concern for the general citizenry and for the conduct of UFO abduction research."

I have been doing a lot of dreaming lately but most have been forgotten as soon as I awake. However, in one real dream I remembered, I was being asked to sign a consent form. A man was explaining to me that this form was similar to a surgical consent form but was not for surgery. I think that I signed it, but what did I sign?

I took a nap this afternoon and in my dream I asked to see an angel. A car pulled up and a family got out. They were beautiful, delicately featured, with pale, beautiful eyes. There were a man and woman, and a baby in an infant seat. They asked if I was expecting them. I said, "Yes, I was expecting an angel." They said, "That's us." "But you have a family and a car." "Yes, we're modern angels!" They took me to a location called the "waiting room" and we discussed spirituality. They were the most beautiful people/angels I have ever seen.

While buying books for the foundation library, I came across two interesting books. The first one by Leah Haley is entitled *Lost Was the Key,* which seems to have parallels to my own experiences. In Leah's book, she writes about alien abduction and abduction by military personnel. Katharina Wilson tells a similar story in her book *The Alien Jigsaw.* The flyer for her book reads: "*The Alien Jigsaw* chronicles the first thirty-two years of Katharina Wilson's life. With over one hundred entries from her journal you will learn about the many different types of alien beings, unusual crafts, and possible military/government involvement."

It is interesting that someone else has thought to keep a journal of her abduction experiences and refers to the unfolding story as a "jigsaw." I too have used that term in referring to the pieces of the puzzle I have been putting together of my own experiences.

October 31, 1992

Mariah Folger was here to attend a convention. On Monday night we both dreamed we were aboard an aerial craft. Mariah reported flying near the ground and going over a bridge, while I was looking out of the cockpit, seeing the ground coming up very rapidly. I thought we were going to crash and felt resigned to that. Then I was at a meeting at long trestle tables. My doctor colleague John was there and we were having a discussion. The dream moved onto a medical setting, where a doctor was examining a woman. He was looking at the area behind her left ear.

In the morning I noticed that the electrical sign at the entrance to the apartments was malfunctioning and men were up on a cherry picker making repairs. It looked like every third neon tube had blown out. They seemed okay last night. It seems that when Mariah and I get together anomalous things start to happen.

November 15, 1992

Last weekend I went to Texas to meet up with the "ffolks." This expanding group of people have been networking for mutual support and information regarding their Interface experiences. We are all professional, intelligent people. A dozen of us met up at a retreat site in central Texas. The retreat was a horse ranch and the home of one of the ffolks. We talked and shared experiences for two days. We had a wonderful time. When we went out to walk, we were accompanied by horses, dogs, cats, and guinea fowl. As well as myself, also present were Mariah and her adult son, X, a businesswoman from New York, another businesswoman from Texas, a female hypnotherapist, a male psychologist, a female writer, and her male friend. Later a local, female psychologist and her son joined us. We had a productive weekend. There may have been Interfaces on both evenings, according to some of the participants, but I had no dream memories at the time. I did, however, remember this dream on the last day: There was a dream memory of Mariah's adult son getting up from a narrow bed. This was not the couch he slept on at the retreat. He was distracted and disoriented.

The second day of the retreat I had a ringing in my ears, a tingling in the center of my forehead, and pressure in my right eye. It gave me a headache. However, I had lots of energy over the weekend. The morning after the first night I woke with the thought that the night's interactions were just "stocktaking," a taking inventory of who was at the retreat. I had a flash memory of watching people being taken down the stairs by grays. I was watching from the balcony rail by my bed. Then there was a gray to my right. I saw Mariah and the hypnotherapist going down the stairs.

During the week after the retreat, I had dreams of being in medical settings and waiting to be examined as part of something routine. One dream involved my lying on a narrow bed as a doctor placed his hands on various parts of my body. Each time his hands were on opposite sides of my body there seemed to be energy that passed between them. I sent off these dreams and impressions to the other members of the group to see if they remember anything more.

Yesterday, I flew with Mr. T and another colleague to Los Angeles, where we took part in a one-day conference for mental health professionals. The topic was UFO abductions. About one hundred and fifty psychologists, psychiatrists, and others attended. Professor David Jacobs, Budd Hopkins, and John Carpenter gave presentations. Professor Michael Swords officiated. The meeting flowed and they were very professional. This was the first conference of its type that was specifically targeted at mental health professionals, and there was a great interest in the topic.

One of the great things to happen after my move to Las Vegas was meeting David Smith. I met Dave at the Para-Physics Group. He works with Alan at EG&G as a computer technician. He is also very intuitive and does readings at Alan's group. We hit it off the first night and have been seeing each other since. We had dinner last Thursday before the Psych Club meeting. Next weekend we are going to camp at some hot spring in California. A nice guy, he is in the middle of a separation from a long marriage. I do not know how far this will go. It may remain just a pleasant friendship, and that would be great.

November 26, 1992

An exciting couple of weeks have gone by. They have been a great mixture of getting settled into the foundation office, starting a new relationship with David Smith, doing some remote viewing for DE's group, and getting more settled into my new Las Vegas location.

Dave and I have decided to do some experiments when we go out camping in the desert to try and "vector" in some UFOs using some of Dr. Steven Greer's methods and protocols. Dr. Steven Greer, a trauma surgeon, has set up an organization called CSETI (Center for the Search for Extra-Terrestrial Intelligence), which advocates full-consciousness interaction with the Visitors.

Mr. T and I just got back from a trip to some small towns north of Las Vegas. He had heard that many of the people there had seen UFOs and that there had been cattle mutilations and alien abductions. We interviewed people about their experiences and made a lot of interesting contacts. We had decided to conduct a "snowball" sociological study, guaranteeing that no names would be used, and asking each person to recommend us to other witnesses. At first people were very reluctant to talk, but gradually we convinced them that we were not reporters or from the government, and they opened up to us.

The interviews were very interesting. For example, there was a local cafe owner and her husband who reported that several months ago they saw a huge, black, triangular craft fly silently down the canyon and over the town. The craft was accompanied by two military helicopters. The sighting was repeated every night at the same time, with such regularity that the woman and her husband brought out lawn chairs every evening to watch the flights. Other townspeople had seen the same black triangular craft flying low over the valleys between Caliente and Pioche. We heard from another woman who reported seeing a similar black, triangular craft flying low over Caliente. She said that it was as big as the hotel it was flying over. She was with a group of three other people when the sighting occurred. Dave and I have a suspicion that what these people might be seeing is advanced *terrestrial* technology being tested locally.

One case that got my attention was a woman who claimed to have been burned by a strange light from the sky. She showed us a portion of her arm that was devoid of pigment. When she was seventeen, she and her fiancé were riding horses in a local wood in one of the Midwestern states. Suddenly, they were knocked off their horses. She said it was like the iris of a camera opening up in the sky and extremely bright light shot out. She lay on the ground with a portion of her upper arm burned to the bone. When she returned home, her mother took her to their local doctor. She could not say how she had been burned and the doctor treated the burn with dressings. She and her mother returned home.

In the middle of the night, there was a telephone call for the mother to bring her daughter back to the doctor's office. There, she and her mother were questioned for hours by two professional men in dark suits. They questioned her over and over again about her burned arm and how she had received the burn. They took X-rays and blood tests. She reports that the injury, although it was initially burned down to the bone, healed very rapidly. For the following few years, she was recalled periodically to the hospital for medical testing, X-rays, and blood tests. When she became an adult, she became very nervous about these visits. Whenever she moved, it seemed that the Veterans Administration (VA) tracked her down and contacted each new doctor to send her back to the VA for testing. Now, she was living in an undisclosed location and seemed in fear that she would be tracked down again. When Mr. T heard the story, he wanted the woman to have her arm reexamined, but she was so frightened that she told us there was no way that she would submit to an examination.

December 1, 1992

On November 14 I attended the Los Angeles meeting held to educate mental health professionals about the abduction phenomenon. After the meeting, several people came up to me to give me their cards and to ask if there was anything they could do to help the project.

I found an interesting article in *OMNI* regarding an experiment conducted by Dr. Michael Persinger of Laurentian University in Ontario, Canada. He suggested that reports of alien impregnation were highly exaggerated, if not completely false. According to his research, false pregnancies are more common than thought and the women who experience them appear to be more "fantasy prone" that other women in the population. Persinger asked 106 college coeds if they had ever suffered from missed periods, abdominal enlargement, morning sickness, and breast changes that they had mistaken for pregnancy. A total of 22 percent of the women replied affirmatively. When Persinger tested these women, he found that they held more unusual beliefs in phenomena like poltergeists and UFOs and were more imaginative than most women. However, they also experienced more memory blanks and night paralysis. As I scientist, I know that correlation does not mean causation, and Persinger's study, while interesting, is not the definitive answer.

January 27, 1993

I am beginning to wonder if I made the right decision to come to Nevada. One of the great things that has come out of the move was meeting Dave Smith. We share a lot of love as well as mutual interests like sky-watching for UFOs, psi, and computers. Since my move to the new condo, he has been so sweet in helping me locate and move furniture. We have been on the same "wavelength" several times, picking each up each other's thoughts and ideas.

My major dilemma about the move to Las Vegas centers around the foundation. Before the move, Mr. T assured me that the job would involve research and I would be liaising between the New Jersey lab and the local university. I was assured that my job would not be administrative but would entail research and exploration. However, there seems to be very little research involved and the majority of my time is taken up with administrative duties. I am not treated like a professional colleague but more as an administrative assistant. I have come to the conclusion that the business environment is not conducive to research.

Consequently, I have sent my résumé to the university to see what is available. It is all very disappointing, as I thought the position would be a wonderful opportunity. My skills and experience are being greatly underused and I feel very frustrated. There is an impasse between the New Jersey group and Mr. T. Neither will take the time to call the other and discuss the proposed joint project. I also miss working as part of a team and feel isolated down here in my back office. So, the search is now under way.

There was a period of time, when I came to Las Vegas, that the Interface dreams lessened. However, since I moved to the condo, there have been several interesting real dreams. In one dream a colonel who has a strong interest in UFOs and parapsychology and X were talking with Mr. T about a physics project. We were at a building, like a motel. I looked out of the window and said to myself, "I will remember this place when I next see it." In a later dream, I was watching UFOs of all shapes and sizes. They were flying down a long valley accompanied by helicopters. The dream had a realistic quality to it, as if I was watching a video.

There were several medical real dreams in which I was an observer. In the first one, I saw a blue-coated medical technician sitting in front of a bank of dials and screens. She was monitoring a woman who sat in a dentist's chair. The chair was to the right of the bank of equipment. The woman in the chair was partially covered with a blue blanket and she was semiconscious. She had a ventilator tube in her mouth and I could hear her raspy breathing. I watched as the medical technician put an IV into her hand. There were several IV solutions hanging up. The woman in the dentist's chair had some sort of goggles on. I asked the technician who the woman was and she replied, "She is an abductee." I tried to tell the technician some of my experiences, but the words would not come out properly. I was very anxious about all the medical equipment.

There was another medical real dream this past Monday night, in the early morning. In this real dream I was watching another blue-uniformed woman medic examining a semiconscious woman who lay flat on a gurney. The medic was to the person's right, and she was examining and doing something to the woman's ears. I saw an Earth-type instrument—an otoscope. The medic mixed some kind of compound or cement and put it into the woman's ears. The medic asked me why I was there, and I answered, "I have to have a physical," which was accepted as a matter of fact by the medic and me. Again, I was just an observer.

On the weekend, I dreamed that I was given a rifle to see how I would use it. I believe that I shot off a round into a room.

Several times during the past few weeks, I have observed a red puncture mark inside my right elbow, as if blood has been drawn, but there is no bruising or pain.

I have discovered that it is a small world we live in. It turns out that Dave's brother, Paul, is also a remote viewer. When I mentioned this to DE, he said, "No way!" He went away and did some checking and then said, "Yes, you're right." Dave says that DE told Paul I was one of his best viewers.

Many people have asked me why I was selected by the Visitors for contacts. I have thought about this and have concluded that there are several factors that might have brought me to the Visitors' attention. The first is that I am a woman. Many abduction researchers and therapists have found that women outnumber men in reporting contact with the Visitors. This may be because women are socialized to be less aggressive and less territorial than men, and the Visitors may find it easier to communicate with women than with men. Another probability is that women may have been selected to fulfill certain hybrid breeding needs of the Visitors.

The second factor may be my intelligence. I am not an average woman. I have a high intelligence, as tested on IQ tests. Many of my contact experiences have centered around solving puzzles and problems. My feeling is that the Visitors are trying hard to understand humans and how we think, feel, and act. I am not sure if my intelligence would be a factor for their choosing me for hybrid breeding, but by our human standards, that would be a plus.

The third factor might be that I come from a Celtic background, of sturdy farming stock. My brothers and I are rarely sick as adults and when we do get ill, we seem to recover faster than others. We tend to look after our own health issues and rarely visit the doctor. If the Visitors are interested in breeding hybrids, they would want healthy humans for their needs. There may be a family history of contact with the Visitors. My great-grandfather Frank was born in Bratton, in Wiltshire, England, where many crop circles have been reported. Also, that area in Wiltshire has many local legends of UFO sightings.

Finally, my high level of intuitive skills would be a definite factor in my being chosen for contact by the Visitors. There have been many reports of the Visitors communicating with abductees on an intuitive or psychic level. Since childhood, I have been very intuitive. From about eight years old I remember having out-of-body experiences and being telepathic. There have been many psychokinetic events in my life, where mind and matter seemed to merge for a short time, resulting in objects being moved or changed. During my thirties and forties I focused on bringing many of these innate abilities under control and applying them. Over the years, I have trained with good teachers and have become a skilled remote viewer. So I am not an average woman and that is perhaps why the Visitors chose me for contact.

Dave and I have discovered that we know another person in common. Dr. A is a physicist who is interested in alternative technologies. Dave says that Dr. A goes out into the desert with a vanload of detection equipment looking for UFOs. Dave has been in contact with Dr. A to get some electromagnetic data, because Dave is building two UFO detectors for Mr. T.

Dave and I have been out in the Nevada desert several times

but have not seen anything substantial. Last week we went with a local UFO club to sky-watch at Blue Diamond, just outside Las Vegas. Supposedly many people have seen UFOs out there. While we were there, Dave recognized lights from several airplanes the club insisted were UFOs. The UFO group also gathered in a circle and aimed their flashlights at the Andromeda galaxy. They were hoping that the Andromedans would see them and respond! We did see a tiny red light doing maneuvering around the mountains, but it was too small and too far away to say what it was.

January 29, 1993

During the past six months, I have been hearing more of the knocks and electronic-sounding beeps that other experiencers have reported. The one I experienced in New Jersey consisted of three knocks followed by a woman's voice calling my name. There have been times when I have heard series of three beeps. Some have occurred when I was falling asleep and other beeps have awakened me from sleep. Last week I distinctly heard three metallic-sounding beeps in my left ear, which was down on the pillow. It went "beep, beep, BEEP." M, a local UFO investigator, called me on Wednesday to tell me about the beeps she has heard in relation to her Interface experiences. Basically, they are the same as mine.

I have been thinking about my decision to change jobs and have decided to stay here at the foundation for a few more months. If something better comes along in the meantime, I plan to reconsider. The following is some advice I wrote down for myself before taking the Las Vegas position, and it applies equally well now: Be a strong decision maker. To reach your goal you must gather all of your resources together and organize them. Carefully consider the long-range consequences of temptation. They might not be so bad. Being more perceptive and courageous will put you in a position of power.

Last night I had a symbolic dream about Mr. T and my current employment. I dreamed that I was nurturing a flower garden. I had grown a beautiful plant, which was about two feet tall. It had white bell-shaped flowers and a beautiful perfume. I went to do something else, and when I got back, a man had chopped down all of my flowers. He shrugged and would not give me a reason.

I awoke and thought about the dream. I believe that the dream reflects my work with Mr. T, which was represented by the garden and the beautiful flowers. Mr. T continually takes over my projects and denies my competence and reliability. He symbolically mows down my garden. So I have decided to "grow my flowers" at home, where I can nurture and develop my own projects. If Mr. T wants a sterile world with no flowers, it is fine with me, but I will make a life filled with beauty and richness.

February 3, 1993

This week I went to a meeting of abduction experiencers whose group is a branch of the UFO Contact Center International (UFOCCI). The head office is located in Washington State. It was interesting to meet with this group and make some new contacts. It seems that most of the group have had local Interface experiences. Dr. O, a woman psychologist at the meeting, asked me to start a new abductees group with her, but I do not have the time at the moment. Also, I am still trying to understand my own experiences.

UFOCCI puts out a listing of medical anomalies that are exhibited by abductees. The group points out that some people may have one or more of these medical anomalies, but that does not mean they are abductees:

1. Abnormal blood cell types
2. Implants—eye, skin, nose, and so forth
3. Shoulder pain that comes and goes
4. Lower back pain—three vertebrae above tail bone
5. Knee pain—in dip of knee under knee cap
6. Rashes after contact
7. Lump in dip of collar bone at connection to neck, may cause paralysis of arm
8. Artery in the wrong place—implant in arteries
9. Pregnancy connected with abduction time period—unusually small fetus or no fetus at all after three months
10. Baby has unusual appearance
11. Child has ESP and is advanced beyond its age
12. Eyes may be able to see through closed eyelids
13. Marks, abrasions, or bruises on body
14. Scars in geometric form on body
15. Scar on back of leg for people born in 1943 (seems to indicate skin sample taken)
16. Buzz-beep or modulated tone in ear
17. Last breath feeling—may be out-of-body experience

18. Shaking of bed in conjunction with limbs of body floating rising
19. Geometric symbols seen in mind
20. Tiredness in morning after sleeping all night
21. Feel as though you are worn out—indicates sleep learning
22. Out-of-body experiences
23. Sudden development of ESP
24. Extra vertebrae in neck
25. Egg-size lump on bottom rib—doctors say nothing is there when examined
26. Warts form a geometric shape—may be from some instrument
27. Sleeplessness or insomnia
28. Do not need to sleep—plenty of energy

In addition there are other symptoms that UFOCCI report are exhibited by a large percentage of abductees:

1. Lower than normal body temperature
2. Low blood pressure
3. Sensitivity to light
4. Sensitivity to touch
5. Sensitivity to emotions
6. Troubled by chronic sinusitis
7. Suffer from swollen or painful joints
8. Pain in the back of the neck
9. Adversely affected by high humidity
10. Best mental work done after sundown
11. Favorite music is classical
12. Prefer metaphysical books
13. Science fiction movies are favorite
14. Television viewing is often composed of talk shows, documentaries, and science fiction
15. Some 90 percent say they have never sampled hallucinogenic drugs
16. All had an activating visionary experience at about age five, and most endured a traumatic event at around age eleven
17. Most have had an experience with an angel, elves, or lights
18. Have had an unseen playmate or friend
19. Felt that their parents were not their true parents; many felt they were adopted
20. Yearned for a place they consider their "true home," somewhere other than Earth
21. Alien ancestry has always been suspected by large percentage

22. Most have maintained at least a sporadic contact with a guiding entity or have continued to receive messages and visions at various times in their lives
23. Most hear a whine, a click, or a buzzing sound preceding psychic events
24. Most consider themselves natural empaths who take on the problems and pain of others
25. Experience a great feeling of urgency
26. Envision themselves as working against some cosmic time-table in order to complete important goals

For the past three or four days, I have had a pain in my lower back. It particularly hurts on the left side when I lie on my back. Yesterday, I asked Dave to look at my back, expecting him to see a bruise, even though I cannot remember bumping myself there. To my surprise, he said that I had a two-and-a-half-inch-long white line scar across the area. It hurt when he pressed on the scar. He said that the scar was centered between two folds of skin and disappeared when I moved but it was definitely there. I showed him another curved scar on my left forearm: a thin, hairline scar that would not tan last summer. I wonder how and why I could be acquiring these long white scars when there was no injury to account for them?

February 11, 1993

Yesterday, Mr. T and I joined a group from the university to visit the Nevada Test Site. There has been much speculation that certain areas of the Test Site, such as Areas 51 and S2, house alien craft that have been back-engineered to aid human technology. However, the parts of the test site that we visited were not anywhere near these controversial areas. Because we were a university-sponsored group, we were given special privileges and shown many areas of the test site that are off-limits to the general public. We visited some of the labs, one of which contained a total body radiation counter. We lunched at the Mercury staff restaurant and watched videos of the early underground bomb tests. It was impressive to see the ground rippling and the eventual cave-in of the blast holes.

During the afternoon, we visited the P Tunnels, where devices had been blasted with radiation to test their effectiveness. Later we went to Sedan Crater, which was mind-boggling in its depth and volume. The crater was blasted out to test the nuclear potential for peaceful engineering projects. Last, as the light was waning, we visited Frenchman's Flat, where the first aboveground nuclear tests were conducted. It was all intriguing and fascinating yet unsettling. There are plans to put the test site to peaceful purposes such as the development of solar energy.

This morning I called John Carpenter, an abduction investigator, and told him about the line scars on my back and elbow. I told him how much consternation they caused me. He suggested that I call an abduction group in Los Angeles that operates a network of professional people, including doctors and psychologists. One of the MDs is an emergency room physician whom I have met twice at different conferences. I am unsure what to tell him if he calls. I suppose I could just tell him the chronology of the scars and see if he has come across any other cases.

February 17, 1993

I heard from some of our Caliente friends that there were sightings of a large triangular craft that hung in the sky around the Eagle Valley area near Pioche. We need to go up there soon and check this out.

I came across an article in *Astronautics and Aeronautics Journal* (July, 1971, vol. 9, no. 6: 66, 67) with a reference to certain frequencies that have been associated with UFO sightings. I am not an engineer, so I have no idea what all this means, but the frequencies were reported as follows:

> EMC reconnaissance operator #2 of Lacey 17, RB-47H aircraft, intercepted at approximately Meridian, Mississippi, a signal with the following characteristics: frequency 2995 mc to 3000 mc; pulse width of 2.0 microseconds; pulse repetition frequency of 600 cps; sweep rate of r rpm; vertical polarity. Signal moved rapidly up the D/F scope indicating a rapidly moving signal source.

The skeptics claim that there are no physical traces of UFOs, especially radar or electromagnetic readings. This proves them to be mistaken.

February 22, 1993

My pilot friend, Chuck, decided to write a paper to disprove the numbers contained in the Roper Survey. This report suggests that 2 percent of the adult American population has had "a constellation of experiences consistent with an abduction history." That is, one in every fifty Americans may have had UFO abduction experiences. Chuck tried to do the statistics to prove that this number of abductions would be unfeasible. However, what he came up with was that these numbers could actually take place just as described. His paper actually proved the report numbers to be feasible!

We have heard that Professor John Mack is looking for grants. John Mack's group plans to look for alternative explanations to the abduction experience and will focus on the intercultural and spiritual dimensions of the experience. The group plans to invite many of the world's religious and spiritual leaders to a conference in Washington, D.C.

February 26, 1993

A real dream in which I was sitting next to a narrow bed that had white sheets on it. I was facing the bed. Before the dream I heard a voice saying, "It is three A.M. Get up." To my right was an open oblong window. I am not sure if there was glass in the window. A human figure was talking to me through the window.

In another real dream, I saw a tall black man with a radio receiver in his ear. He was standing, waiting for something, not talking, showing no emotion. He looked like he belonged to the Secret Service. He was dressed in a dark overcoat. I saw him several times throughout the real dream, and I said to myself, "I will remember him if I see him again."

March 1, 1993

During the past month or so, I have had many hospital-type dreams, where I am visiting very crowded medical centers, with beds crammed next to each other and medical equipment all over the place. Last night I dreamed I was at an outpatient clinic. There were long, narrow rooms off a long corridor. Each room contained beds crowded together down the left wall, and to the right were wheeled instrument trays. The inconsistency of this dream was that the instruments were made of a dark, metallic gray rather than the shiny, silvery metal common to terrestrial instruments. Also, the wheeled trays were very light. I was in one room and wandered out into the hall, but a tall, thin doctor, who spoke with a foreign accent, ushered me back into the long, narrow room. I had to be careful when I made my way down the row of beds so I would not upset the trays of instruments.

In another real dream, I was at a medical installation, trying to find a vacant bed. I wandered past many crowded rooms and I think I was escorted. The people in the rooms were fully clothed and seemed to be waiting around.

I talked to several other Las Vegas women who experienced the abduction phenomena, and they have all been having similar dreams: crowded medical facilities with many men, women, and children waiting to be examined. It seems that the Visitors have speeded up their process in Las Vegas and are managing more people. Why? Is it because of all the millions of human visitors that fill the city every week? Is there a deadline or some date to get something done? I can just see the headlines, "Come to Las Vegas and Get Abducted!"

March 8, 1993

The foundation has received some more information about interesting UFOs and other anomalies happening in the small towns north of Las Vegas. We heard about a ranch fifty miles north of Pioche where there have been reports of both ghosts and UFO sightings. The ranch was, historically, the site of many gunfights and early deaths. One ranch occupant tells an interesting story of a UFO sighting. He and his partner were in their pickup truck and saw unusual lights: seven lights in a boomerang configuration. The two men thought that each light was an individual object and that all the lights moved in unison. The colors were off-white and yellow-white. The men estimated that the lights were about one hundred yards away from them; there was no noise and no static on their radio. Later, they had another sighting of several lights over a dry lake bed. The lights were moving erratically and kicking up a lot of dust from the lake bed. A third sighting was of a single light that seemed to dart up and down above a mountain.

Another ranch worker in the area saw a UFO near his ranch for four or five nights in a row, but we didn't get any further details. According to this ranch worker, there is a bar in Caliente that has a chunk of aluminum alloy that is incredibly light. It is about two and a half inches thick and four inches square. It has been analyzed, but the results were inconclusive. It is discolored on one side and has a bubble effect. The finder was hunting deer about twelve years ago, near Bend, Oregon, in an area of lodge pole pines growing closely packed together. He came to a clearing, where he noticed that the tops of the trees had been broken off at a forty-five-degree angle. He looked around the area but could not find anything to account for the damage. Then he sat down on a bed of pine needles and sat on the chunk of alloy. He made a guess that the area had been searched but that the chunk was missed because it was hidden by the pine needles.

March 15, 1993

Lately I have had several mental experiences (remote viewing), backed up by real dreams, where I have been viewing and interacting with the Visitors in an underground facility. In these real dreams, I am taken to a facility, which is built from concrete and which has a bunkerlike quality. The corridor to the viewing and holding rooms is narrow and dark and to the right of the major rooms. The first room is raised up and has an angled viewing mirror that overlooks another lower room, where one or two aliens are held.

In the real dream, I am led down the corridor to an area at the end where there are bathrooms and cots and where I am allowed to rest until they need me. Then I am brought up to the first room, up some steps and into a lighted room, which is filled with electronic instruments. I am instructed to look down into the lower room, which contains a child's wading pool and sometimes one, sometimes two Visitors. The Visitors seem alone and bereft. I am instructed to interact with the Visitors and find out what they need. I tell the technicians that they have to put liquid chlorophyll in the water in the wading pool.

March 19, 1993

Several dreams last night including a medical real dream involving a small gray man and a human woman.

I dreamed that I was at an apartment and interacting with Dave and a small gray man. The small gray man was in and out of the scene. Then we were in bed, watching TV. The bottom of the screen displayed our blood pressures and pulse rates. They seemed normal. I do not know why we were watching TV, but the sound was either off or very low. Then a human woman came in. She was wearing a neutral-color uniform, not white like a nurse, nor a lab coat like a technician. She was carrying a device. The device had a spring-loaded needle at the bottom right. The main part of the device was square and black, and it had several buttons and dials. She pressed the box to Dave's right groin area, then to mine. The spring-loaded needle surprised me but did not hurt. Dave did not seem very surprised. I asked the woman, "Why did you do that?" She replied, "Don't you remember? We said we would be back to take some blood before you left us." I did have a vague memory of her saying this. We then got up and left together. I looked back at the TV to see if it was still displaying our vital signs. The numbers were there, but they were static. The woman turned off the TV set. We were in a trailer of some sort.

There was a small, red puncture mark in my right groin this morning and a small bruise on my left thigh.

Last month, when Mr. T and I visited the Nevada Test Site, someone asked a question about whether cattle had been ranched at the test site during the nuclear tests. We were told that there had been cattle there and that various parts of the animals were removed when they died. The rest of the animal was barbecued! There are no longer test cattle at the test site, but multiple unusual cattle deaths, called cattle mutilations, have been occurring all over the country, including the counties surrounding the test site. It seems that many of these unusual cattle deaths have occurred near military and government installations, according to researcher Linda Moulton Howe.

The deaths of these cattle are accompanied by unusual circumstances: strange lights and black, unmarked helicopters have been observed in the sky; the cattle seem to be spooked by "something"; body parts have been removed from the dead animals, including glandular and mucous organs; and the animals have been found bloodless and without decomposition. UFOs and satanic cults have been blamed for the mutilations. It is highly possible that some branch of government is still secretly monitoring cattle. Perhaps cattle are being used to measure biological reactions to the environment. Some government labs have shown that cow blood can be used as a substitute for human blood in an emergency. Also, there has been ongoing research into hormones and enzymes, and these cattle could be providing the raw research materials.

I have been thinking about the condition of these animals:

they are found bloodless, but with their veins uncollapsed, and they do not putrefy as quickly as other dead animals. This condition could be achieved if another substance, like saline, was circulated through them at the time the blood was drained. This would keep the animals' blood vessels hydrated. Then the saline would be absorbed into the animals' bodies after death. The saline might contain preservatives that could slow down the animals' decomposition.

Mr. T is adamant that the cattle mutilations are the result of extraterrestrial interference. He will not envisage any other explanation. I prefer to keep an open mind. His argument is that we have no technology that can account for the cauterized cuts and open wounds on these animals, or if we did, the equipment would be too heavy to carry out into the field. I know he is wrong, because I have seen devices in engineering magazines reflecting new medical technologies. For example, Phillips Laboratories, located at Kirtland Air Force Base, in New Mexico, has recently developed a device called the Medpen. It is described as follows: "Doctors and paramedics on the battlefield or at the scene of an emergency such as a highway accident will one day be able to cut and cauterize wounded patients with the laser Medical Pen, developed by the Air Force's Phillips Laboratory. The Medpen, as it's also known, is about 12 inches long and less than an inch in diameter, and weighs one pound. The 5-watt device is powered by 3-volt lithium batteries."

On Tuesday night, Dave and I attended a meeting held by Dr. B and the CSETI Group. CSETI was founded by Dr. Steven Greer, a trauma room physician, in an effort to conduct UFO contact on a conscious level. They even prepare for the eventuality of boarding a UFO. The CSETI representatives told us about the organization and its goal to "extend a peaceful invitation to the Visitors to our solar system." Greer goes out with groups of volunteers to "sky watch" and "vector" in craft. The group brought a videotape of lights that had been observed on such an outing, but the lights weren't very impressive.

Dave and I would be assets to their organization in terms of our psychic development, Dave's technical abilities, and my knowledge of the UFO field. But we decided not to join the group. We felt that Greer's demands that his volunteers attend a compulsory five-day training course at their own cost was beyond our means. We also learned that Greer keeps his volunteers up most of the night and then expects them to attend classes during the day for the full five days. There is also a militaristic and cultish ambiance about the group, which discourages personal, emotional involvement in the phenomena and with other members of the group. For example, when the videotaped group cheered and "whooped" as the "UFO lights" came in, one of the CSETI representatives jumped up and said, "That was a No-No!" Dave and I have decided to go out sky-watching on our own and to use our own skills and abilities to look for and "vector in" UFOs.

March 22, 1993

I remembered two parts of a much longer real dream. I was in a dark room, looking at a lighted doorway. I saw the shapes of two Visitors in the doorway. I was having difficulty breathing, but this was happening before I saw the Visitors. Then I sat at a conference table with several human people, including ex-president George Bush. We were discussing psi and remote viewing. Bush got up to leave, saying, "Unless you can produce, on demand, each time, I am not interested." I said, "What if I could produce on demand every time?" He sat down again. The dream was very fuzzy from then on, and I would have liked to remember the rest of it.

March 23, 1993

I was browsing the MUFON bulletin board system on the Internet and came across a law that was passed back in 1982 called the Extraterrestrial Exposure Law. It seems that on October 5, 1982, Dr. Brian T. Clifford of the Pentagon announced at a press conference that contact between U. S. citizens and extraterrestrials or their vehicles is "strictly illegal." This talk was reported on October 5, 1982. It seems that this law was originally intended to apply to astronauts returning from space flights. Anybody found guilty of such contact automatically becomes a wanted criminal to be jailed for one year and fined $5,000. According to the article by John Komar: "The NASA administrator is empowered to determine with or without a hearing that a person or object has been 'extraterrestrially exposed' and impose an indeterminate quarantine under armed guard, which could not be broken even by court order. There is no limit placed on the number of individuals who could thus be arbitrarily quarantined. The definition of 'extraterrestrial exposure' is left entirely up to the NASA administrator."

The public has been assured for the past thirty-nine years that UFOs are nothing more than hoaxes and delusions, yet Dr. Clifford says, "This is really no joke, it's a very serious matter." According to Komar, the legislation was buried in the 1,211th subsection of the fourteenth section of a batch of regulations and very few members of government probably bothered to read it. It was the proverbial "needle in a haystack" and was slipped onto the books without public debate. Thus, says Komar, we learn that without having informed the public, the government of the United States has created a new criminal class: UFO contactees and abductees.

Komar continues by quoting NASA spokesman, Fletcher Reel, that the law as it stands is not immediately applicable, but in case of need could quickly be made applicable. The relevant law is contained under Title 14, Section 1211 of the *Code of Federal Regulations,* adopted on July 6, 1969, before the Apollo Moon shots. In my opinion, this law is probably unenforceable. By implementing this law on a public citizen, NASA would be overtly admitting the existence of extraterrestrial contact, something it and other agencies have worked for years to cover up and deny.

April 10, 1993

Mr. T has asked me to travel to Huntsville, Alabama, to follow up on some UFO sightings and cattle mutilations that have been happening in this area. According to a Fyffe, Alabama, press release dated April 7: "Over thirty animals have been found dead in pastures around Fyffe, with various internal and external organs missing. The incisions examined on these animals exhibit precise surgical cutting. In many of the cases, there has been evidence of extremely high heat at the tissue incisions."

There were several interesting things about these cattle mutilations:

1. There were no footprints, tracks, or marks found anywhere near the animals, which were often found in muddy pasture-land.
2. Many of the animals' internal and external organs were missing.
3. Throughout all the cases, the farmers and their neighbors reported seeing or hearing helicopters in the vicinity either before or shortly after the mutilated cattle were discovered.
4. There was no evidence of blood at the mutilation site.
5. A white, flaky substance was found near one animal and was

composed of high concentrations of titanium, aluminum, oxygen, and silicon.

6. This material dissolved the brass tip of a ball point pen.
7. The incisions into the animals are straight, clean, often square and circular cuts with serrated edges or stepped, with notches at the base.
8. On examination, these incision marks reveal that they have been exposed to high heat and that the meat has been cooked.

These factors have been showing up in cattle mutilations across the United States. Before I left Nevada, I was able to download several articles from the MUFON bulletin board system that documented mutilations of cattle, sheep, horses, and big-horn sheep in and around Nevada. For example, someone found a pile of thirteen desert bighorn sheep in the Mormon Mountains, sixty-five miles northeast of Las Vegas. The sheep had been piled on top of a previously burned area, but the sheep were not burned. The animals looked as if they had been dropped from a great height.

The first evening in Huntsville, I met with the local MUFON group and gave them a talk about Mr. T's interest in UFOs. I met some very interesting people: First was an "Al Harrison," who claimed that he, his wife, and his two children had constant contact with an alien group called the Dracos. The younger daughter, aged four, had once been found inexplicably locked out of the house. She drew me pictures of the large-headed, large-eyed grays. This child appeared very self-confident, bright, and affectionate. "Mr. Harrison" wanted to meet with me privately to discuss his contacts. Then I met "Angelo," a Cherokee who received information from the Visitors and who told me "By the time you leave, you will know!" Other people in the MUFON group told me that he plays mind games.

There was another young man at the group, half Cherokee, who has a healing spring on his property, and petroglyphs nearby. He said that he conducts "spirit fires" and claims that he has met and communicated with the "little people" on his property. There were several other people at the group who seemed very sane and sensible and had interesting stories:

> A family of three: mother, father and son who lived on a ranch outside of Huntsville. They had their first UFO sighting in 1989 and since then have experienced cattle mutilations at

the ranch, abductions of the mother and son, and paranormal activity in the house.

A young man from Birmingham, Alabama, an artist, who had a UFO sighting in 1988 and possibly some abduction experiences.

A relative of the family at the ranch, a young woman who had a multiple UFO sighting with ten other people in 1989. Dr. James Harder, an abduction researcher, had regressed this young woman and uncovered her abduction experiences.

An elderly gentleman, an ex-NASA scientist and engineer, who had several UFO sightings around Madison, Alabama, in 1951.

A young woman currently working with a local psychologist to uncover her early experiences. One of her earliest memories is of being punished by her father for spending the night sitting in a cattle trough of water. This was witnessed by her brother. She says that during the night, two men in white came and put her in the trough.

An elderly retired gentleman who had UFO sighting and communications with entities in 1981. He had some interesting theories regarding the physics of UFO flight.

A young couple that had both sightings and abduction experiences.

An older professional woman who had recently retired from Huntsville's NASA Space Facility.

A couple of local newspaper owners, the Bakers, who had reported extensively on the UFO flap over Fyffe, Alabama, and a local policeman, Ted Oliphant, who was investigating the sightings. The MUFON directors and I spent most of the first evening at the home of the newspaper reporters and saw some of their video footage of local cattle mutilations. The footage was gruesome, with the cattle missing udders and genitalia and other parts of their bodies.

On our way back from the MUFON meeting, one of the passengers in the car noted that a white car had been following us all the way. Our driver deliberately made several turns off his normal route, and the car continued to follow us.

When we reached Fyffe, we stopped at the local police station where Ted Oliphant was on duty. We found Ted, and he opened up the nearby community center so that we would have a place to meet and talk. We were joined by two abductees who were visiting Fyffe. Ted was initially suspicious of my interest but said he had already checked me out through the police station and by talking with mutual colleagues. After we had talked for a while, he opened up and talked very frankly about the UFO sightings, cattle mutilations, and abductions that were happening in Alabama.

During my initial interactions with the locals, I was able to confirm my impressions that the locality and characteristics of Fyffe closely matched those of Caliente, Nevada, where Mr. T and I had heard similar tales of mutilations and abduction:

1. Both Fyffe and Caliente are rural, isolated areas with cattle ranches.
2. Both have nearby mountains, bodies of water, and limestone caves.
3. Both have nearby military installations. Caliente is close to the Nevada Test Site (including Areas 51 and S2) and the Tonapah Test Range. Fyffe is close to Redstone Arsenal, which includes the NASA/Marshall Flight Center, the NASA Space and Rocket Center, and the U. S. Space Camp at Huntsville.
4. At both localities, the residents are conservative, private, and religious.
5. Both have Native American populations: Cherokee in Alabama and the Payutes and Utes around Southern and Central Nevada.
6. Both have a history of UFO sightings and cattle mutilations.

According to local Alabama history, in the early part of the twentieth century, the Cherokees were forced off their traditional lands by white Americans, and relocated on out-of-state reservations, a journey known as the "Trail of Tears." Before that time, the Cherokees had occupied the lush green valleys, hunting the local game. The Cherokee history maintains that silver discs came down out of the sky and that the Visitors taught the Cherokee chief a written language. Until then, the Cherokee communicated and passed down traditions orally. The chief decreed that all the young people of the tribe were to be schooled in the new written language.

April 11, 1993

I stayed overnight at the Lake Guntersville State Lodge, a wonderful retreat site that overlooks Lake Guntersville. During the day, eagles flew over the lodge and all the cherry trees around the lodge were blossoming. Around noon, I met with "Al Harrison," who came out to the lodge. Unfortunately, even though he has an interesting story, he admits to having major emotional, social, and financial problems. The bulk of his rambling two-hour monologue centered around his meeting with humanoid entities and the Draco. He said he would send me his writing under an alias, because he is frightened of the government and seems very immersed in government conspiracy theories.

Later in the afternoon, a mother and her seven-year-old son, both of whom had experienced cattle mutilations at their ranch, came to the lodge. The mother had run the gamut of unusual experiences. Her son was a "test-tube" baby, conceived after multiple miscarriages, and she described him as her "miracle."

Some of her experiences included:

1. A UFO sighting in 1989, which was also seen by her sister, her husband, and several members of the police force who were called to the scene.

2. Cattle mutilations on her ranch, which included two cows and a calf. Ted Oliphant later showed me his photographs of the dead cattle. They had been classically mutilated and drained of blood.

3. Two scoop scars on her forehead that had no remembered origin. Many abductees report such scoop marks on their legs and other parts of their body. She also had a triangular marking that appears from time to time on her lower abdomen. As she is very religious, she is reluctant to investigate the origins of these scars.

4. Her young son has talked about "the doctors" who visit his room in a red light and take ducks from the pond by the house. When he was four years old, he was found downstairs at night with wet feet and grass on his feet, as if he had been outside. When he was six, he drew a picture of a UFO and abductions, along with helicopters and aliens. He told his mother that they were "all connected." The child is unusually bright and self-confident, with a sense of social responsibility beyond his years.

5. A great deal of paranormal activity in the house has consisted of lights coming on by themselves and a mechanical toy bear switching itself on in the night.

While this woman and her son were visiting the lodge and telling me their story, we may have had a UFO sighting. From the balcony of my room we saw a large, round red and white light rise up vertically about four or five miles away. It did not wink like strobe lights and soon disappeared into the clouds.

April 13, 1993

I visited again with Ted Oliphant in Fyffe, Alabama. We traveled to Lookout Mountain, Sand Mountain, and Mentone, because those areas are rumored to have had multiple UFO sightings. I took pictures of the area but did not see anything unusual. Ted has made a video about the Fyffe sightings called "UFOs: A Need to Know." He showed me his photo collection of local cattle mutilations. They seemed to be identical with the cattle mutilations that have been occurring around Pioche in Nevada.

April 14, 1993

I talked with the young lady who had scoop marks and other marks on her body resulting from her abduction experiences. She showed me a scoop mark and a lump on her right shin that she thinks is an implant. She also told me an interesting story. After we were followed by the white car on my first day in town, she was harassed at her place of work by strange messages on her answering machine. The next day she and a male friend were at her shop and were harassed by a man in uniform. He parked in an old car across the street from the shop. Whenever either one of them left the shop to drive anywhere, the man in the car followed them. Eventually, they got tired of this happening. They came out of the shop, stood in the doorway, and waved wildly at the uniformed man, whereupon he drove away, and they did not see him again. I could possibly write off her experiences as paranoid, except that I have been coming up against similar stories time and time again. These people cannot all be paranoid.

April 19, 1993

I just returned from Alabama. I did not have any Visitor experiences myself while I was there, but it was a fascinating trip. I enjoyed talking to all the individuals who had experienced the events at Fyffe. It is interesting that the circumstances and surroundings at Fyffe are very similar to those around Caliente and other small towns in Nevada. Dave and I want to travel up to the Eagle Valley area where they have had numerous sightings, but the area is still snowed in.

I downloaded an interesting notice from the Internet that was generated by the UFO Research Institute of Canada (UFORIC). They are researching cases that have the following medical aspects:

1. high white blood cell count
2. missing ovary
3. unusual organs
4. fibromyalgia
5. chronic fatigue syndrome
6. massive hair loss at an early age
7. unexplained visual blind spot or black spot in visual range not understood by ophthalmologist.

They do not say why they are looking for these cases, but the suspicion is that they have several abductees who are claiming these effects and looking for specific medical answers before assuming them to be the result of abduction.

Many cultures and traditions have myths and stories of meeting with the Visitors. I wondered if Canada had such a history. In Daniel Cohen's book *Encyclopedia of Monsters* (1982), I found the following regarding a creature called the "Mannegishi" of the Cree Indians: "the Mannegishi creature, from the mythology of the Cree Indians of Canada. They were supposed to be little people with big round heads, small skinny bodies, big eyes and no noses. Their main purpose in life, according to the legends, was to play jokes on the big people." The similarity of the "Mannegishi" to the appearance of the "gray" type of entity is interesting.

Recently, I have been attending an abduction support meeting run by M, a local who has had experiences herself. The group has about six or seven women, who attend every two weeks. It has been helpful to hear about other people's experiences.

My own Interface experiences have been fairly quiet, although there have been some "busy nights" and some mornings when I feel I have been up all night. I am generally an early riser and have lots of energy.

A few weekends ago, Dave and I went out to the Saline Valley Hot Springs again. It is wonderful there, a green oasis in a valley of volcanic tuff and rock, surrounded by extinct volcanoes and rocky mountains. We did not have any sightings or even dreams of sightings this time. When Dave and I last went to the hot springs in November last year, we both had dreams about UFOs. However, while at the hot springs, I dreamed that I woke up and went outside our tent. I saw UFOs coming from the southeast, and they lit up the sky with colored lights. They were so beautiful. Dave dreamed that he was aboard a craft. He was going around it, feeling the surfaces. I recently learned that China Lake Weapons Base is located southeast of Saline Valley. There have been rumors that alien craft are stored and flown there. Earlier in the evening, I had told Dave before the UFO dream that I expected a sighting to come from behind us.

As we left Saline Valley this time, we noticed a big barrier across the road leading into the valley, which had not been there a few days earlier when we came in. The barrier had a large "Road Closed" sign on it, which was odd, because there had been no activities such as storms or road works that would have warranted closing the road.

April 28, 1993

Yesterday, Mr. T asked if I would like to go to New York City in a few weeks to stay with Budd Hopkins to help him with his Intruders Foundation. Budd Hopkins is a well-known abduction researcher, artist, and writer. Since Budd's recent illness and travels, he has got behind with much of the foundation work. There may be correspondence in his boxes of mail that could be relevant to several of his ongoing cases.

Budd was the first researcher to work with UFO abductees and to use hypnosis to uncover their experiences. He has written several books on the topic, including *Intruders*, and he recently conducted an abduction survey in *OMNI*. Consequently, he has been inundated with mail. It will be a privilege to work with Budd. I view him as a mentor. It will be educational to talk to him about his work and methods, to sit in on some of his groups, and to learn from him. I particularly want to ask him about his work with children and their abduction experiences. I call them "enhanced children," because they appear to have a higher IQ than normal, feel a stewardship with the Earth, and express a social responsibility far beyond their years.

May 3, 1993

There have been some interesting real dreams over the past

few weeks related to Interface experiences. I "woke" during the night and was interacting with people who were giving me some information. This information was sandwiched between layers of consciousness. When I eventually woke to normal consciousness, only the awareness of the information remained. Last week on Thursday night I had a scary dream, which repeated itself twice during the night. In the dream, I was outside at night near some trees. A helicopter landed, and a man in dark clothes got out. He came toward me. I started to panic and scream.

Dave said he did not hear me scream in the night. But he reported to me that he had an interesting dream of his own, involving levitation. Before I awoke this morning, I had another strange dream. In this dream I was able to send messages from my computer to a TV announcer. There were several "official" people present, including one man from the CIA. This dream was followed by a dream in which I was breathing through a face mask. I realized that I was getting some kind of anesthetic gas, but I did not care.

Whether all these dreams have any reality, I do not know. However, dreams that produce physical trauma, such as bruises and needle marks, are hard to dismiss. As I was reading through this journal, I reread the dream of March 19, where blood was taken with a handheld device. I have a vague recollection of another dream in a medical situation and discussing things with a medic. I asked about the blood collection device and it was confirmed that it took place. It was also confirmed that the same procedure would take place at the end of this particular dream.

I received an article marked "Confidential" from William La Parl, a UFO researcher. It was entitled "Something Wicked This Way Comes or My Mind Was Gang Raped by the Office of Naval Intelligence." As this paper has become widely distributed in the UFO community, I want to write up the gist of it for my journal. Basically, the four-page article outlines material that La Parl gleaned while attending a five-day abduction conference in Atlanta.

It seems that during DE's formal presentation at the conference, he reported that his group had viewed green fireballs (allegedly from something called Project Twinkle). These fireballs were actually saucer-shaped craft that appeared to be ball-shaped because they had gone through "different phases." DE claimed that his group was aware of underground extraterrestrial facilities where ETs and "preserved" humans were stored; his group was also aware of an underground "contact site." According to La Parl, DE claims that the in-house name for this UFO project is ZARDOZ.

DE claimed that his group had remote viewed the Roswell incident and that it was a "mass brainwave entrainment conducted by the aliens." The soldiers did not really see wreckage and alien bodies. Overall, the writer of the article found DE to be "a very intelligent and personable individual." However, the writer is a member of a loose-knit group that has made a point of debunking the UFO and abduction field, so despite his protestations, it is possible that he is spreading disinformation.

May 4, 1993

Today, I had a call from the families in Caliente who owned the horse ranch. They have been having Interfaces for several years, and a new phenomenon has occurred: their teeth have started to fall out. The father asked if I had come across this phenomenon before, and we discussed some of the possible causes. Their dentist says that there is "no reason" for their teeth to be falling out. I had never heard of this effect from the Interfaces. One of the possibilities we discussed was that the physical trauma involved in the Interfaces, such as the insertion of tubes and devices in their mouths, may have loosened their teeth.

May 14, 1993

On Sunday May 9, Dave and I drove up to the Rose Valley area and camped at Warm Springs on the way. Warm Springs is located way out in the desert, up the valley from Rachel, Nevada, at the crossroads between Tonapah and Ely, and at the top right-hand corner of the Nevada Test Site on public land. Apart from the occasional passing vehicle, the area is quite deserted. Thermal water at scalding temperatures comes out of the ground and surges down the hill in white, calcite channels. It eventually arrives at a building that contains a swimming pool. However, the building and pool are locked, with "Keep Out" notices posted.

About eight P.M. I suddenly became incredibly tired, and all I wanted to do was to crawl into my sleeping bag and sleep. Warm Springs overlooks the Tonapah Range, and I wanted to stay awake to see if I could spot any UFOs, but I could not keep awake. During the night, I had a real dream that a very bright light was shining on us. I awoke to see the outline of our little blue truck, which we had parked in front of us. Dave reported that he dreamed he was visiting with the family from the horse ranch. In his dream, he and the teenage daughter, K, were doing mental tests, and he was helping her.

We spent the next two nights at the Caliente Hot Springs Motel, because Dave got sick with a throat infection. However, we did get to interview two new people in the area who had UFO sightings.

On Wednesday we drove up to the Eagle Valley to camp near Pioche. We learned there were more UFO sightings, but we did not see anything. On our return through Caliente, we met the family from the horse ranch. They reported that K had dreams about me while Dave and I camped at Warm Springs. She dreamed that she saw me drive to the front of their house in a white car. I was in the car with a very fat man with dark hair. He took up the whole front half of the car. In her dream she was doing tests and puzzles.

May 15, 1993

There may have been an Interface last night, because I awoke in the early hours to hear a clicking sound and, a little later, electronic-like beeping. The clicking sound was continuous for several seconds, and I realized that I had heard it before recently at night.

May 17, 1993

The first night at Budd Hopkins's in New York City, I slept in his daughter's room. I locked my doors, reasoning that if there were Interfaces, it would be the Visitors rather than the house occupants. I had a dream the first night. I was stopping people coming into my room and locking the doors. They were disappointed that they could not come in.

May 21, 1993

I have come to the end of my first week with Budd Hopkins and it has been a fruitful week. We have gotten quite a lot of his office work caught up. I have also participated in Budd's support group and sat in on two hypnotic sessions. Budd regressed two women who were part of a possible mass abduction of six people, including three males and three females. Budd has offered to do some regressions with me too, and we will probably do one tomorrow. Greenwich Village has been a surprise and I have been out walking to the stores every day. I also go to the post office every day for Budd.

I wasn't sure if any Interfaces would occur while I was in Manhattan, but I think that something happened on Wednesday night. The previous two nights, I had kept the hook bolts on the doors for privacy, but on Wednesday, I decided that I was being too paranoid. I felt that I really did not need them and that I was safe in Budd's house. During the night, I dreamed that someone was doing something with my left foot. I was thinking, "I am glad I washed my feet."

On Thursday afternoon, when I was putting on my boots, I noticed that I had a small lump on my left shin surrounded by a small, reddish, circular area. The hard lump is still there today, although the redness has disappeared. I told Budd about the lump and showed it to him. He said that we would examine the incident in a regression tomorrow.

May 22, 1993

Today, Budd regressed me to the dream surrounding the hard lump in my left shin. In the regression, I remembered waking up in the night to find someone sitting at the end of my bed; my left foot was being manipulated then lowered onto something that felt like a human thigh. A piece of magnetic curved metal was placed over my left shin and the area felt numb "as if part of it wasn't there." Then I felt, rather than heard, a "pop," and a little thing was implanted into the front of my left leg.

Budd told me that I am the seventeenth person to have something like this happen while staying at his house. One man felt his leg drop from being held at a height and the drop woke him up. Others have seen grays in Budd's studio. Budd thinks these events are staged by the grays to let him know that they are aware of his activities with abductees and to keep track of his Visitors. However, in my regression, the person who implanted the device was not a gray but a human person.

May 29, 1993

During the two weeks I spent with Budd, I helped him respond to over one hundred pieces of mail. Responses usually included a reprint of information for abductees and, if possible, a referral. During the week, Budd and I worked on his extensive card file, and he worked on his two new papers about the Linda Napolitano case and a case that involved an Australian family becoming "invisible." It seems that a family went to the local park and noticed a UFO. When developed, photographs the father took of his family showed just the lake and an empty foreground.

During my stay, Budd traveled to Chicago to meet with the "Third Man," a dignitary who, with two government agents, had witnessed Linda Napolitano being abducted from her thirteenth-floor Manhattan apartment building. Budd shared the name of the individual with me and showed me pictures of him from recent magazines. However, I promised Budd that I would not share the Third Man's identity with anybody until that individual was ready. Budd met with the Third Man in Chicago's O'Hare airport and conveyed letters to the Third Man from himself and Linda, plus a videotape. These were accepted by the Third Man, without question, thus establishing that the Third Man had some knowledge of who Linda was, according to Budd.

14

Confirmations and Conundrums

"Unknown objects are operating under intelligent control. . . . It is imperative that we learn where UFOs come from and what their purpose is."

—Admiral Roscoe Hillenkoetter, first director of the Central Intelligence Agency, 1947–50, in a statement for the National Investigation Committee on Aerial Phenomena in 1960.

June 4, 1993

This new chapter of my life in Las Vegas has introduced me to the beauty and wonders of the Nevada desert, mountains, and thermal springs; has brought me a host of new friends, including David Smith; and has given me an interesting job as research coordinator with Mr. T's foundation. This pays enough for me to continue attending school and provides a nice place for me to live. I also have time to do my writing. I am in the process of writing a book about OBEs and remote viewing. My disappointment with the job has eased somewhat. When I came out to Las Vegas, it was on the understanding that I would be a liaison between the parapsychology lab in New Jersey and a department of the local university in Las Vegas. However, that never panned out. Instead, I have been assisting Mr. T with many of his UFO investigations in and around Las Vegas.

Yesterday, the foundation had a phone call from Ted Oliphant in Alabama. He wanted to give us some updates on the Fyffe sightings and cattle mutilations. He told us about one dead cow that had been severely mutilated and was found lying next to an electronic wire fence. On one side of the fence was half of a rotated thirty-foot crop circle. The electronic fence was melted in two places away from the post and the electronic relay was burned out.

Last May 9, Dave and I were camping at Warm Springs near Tonapah, and we had some unusual experiences and dreams. These included us and a family that lived on a nearby horse ranch in Caliente. While I was visiting with Budd Hopkins, he hypnotically regressed me, and the following is what I "remembered":

> After we arrived at the Warm Springs site, I became extremely tired and all I wanted to do was sleep. I remembered waking in the night, feeling wide awake. Dave was also awake and shivering violently. He was sick with a throat infection the next day.
>
> I then remembered that there was a "very bright light" and "something" landed on the flat space beyond the blue truck. I couldn't see what it was because the truck was in the way. The next thing I remember was that Dave and I were approaching the back of the horse ranch. The teenage daughter, K, was sitting on the wooden steps. There was a single light above her and she was wearing what I thought then was an old long coat. When I got nearer, I saw that it was actually a man's plaid dressing gown with the sleeves rolled up. I was wearing my pinkish-red sweat suit.
>
> We proceeded to play a game on the steps, watched by two "golden people," who were off to the side. K's parents were "switched off" and were standing in the darkened kitchen. In the game, one of us would pick a card. On the card would be a design and we would telepathically share the design with the other two. Then we would mentally construct the design, three-dimensionally with marble-sized "balls of light." If one of us "lost the design," the balls would fall, but we got quite good at it. Then, I remembered going back to the mountain but could not remember how we got there.

Following the regression, I called the horse ranch family to say hello and to confirm some of my observations under hypnosis. It seems that their back steps are lit by one bulb. K does sit out on the back steps, and she often wears a man's oversized robe, with the sleeves rolled up. In fact, the mother and daughter fight over who wears it, as it is so soft and comfortable. So, it is possible that I could have seen K waiting for us, wearing such a robe.

I did not tell Dave the details of my regression or follow-up investigation, as I wanted him to remember his own version. Tonight, we went to Alan's house, where at a Para-Physics meeting, he hypnotically regressed Dave. First, he took Dave back through several previous lifetimes: as a dolphin and as a clockmaker named Fred Saunders. Alan then brought him forward to May 9 and to the "dream" on the mountain. Here is Dave's memory of those events: Dave saw a light filling the sky, coming in streaks over the truck and filling up the truck. There was a flash. He remembers me asking, "What was that?" Then Dave saw himself at the horse ranch and he was helping K to assemble a corral to keep in the horses. He was bothered by mosquitoes. He said to himself in the dream, "How did I get here?" He did not remember getting from the mountain to the horse ranch. After his regression, Dave commented that while he remembered building the wooden coral with K, he also had a sense that he was taking part in a mental task with her. I then mentioned the "light ball" game to him and he said that sounded right.

What to make of all this? It could well be that Dave, K, and I shared a mutual dream. It could be that we telepathically shared information in the dream state. Or, we could have been abducted from the mountain by either Visitor or human agencies and taken to the horse ranch at night. Another explanation is that there is no explanation—just that Dave dreamed, that I dreamed, and that K dreamed, but there is really no connection. We had already planned to visit the horse ranch in a few days and they were anxiously waiting for our visit. However, the fact that Dave and I both recalled the light and its location, under hypnosis, that we both remembered mental tasks, and the fact about the porch and K wearing a man's robe with the sleeves rolled up—all this leaves us with many unanswered questions.

June 7, 1993

According to the MUFON computer bulletin board, it seems that a remote viewing professional, DE, is claiming that there will be a major UFO event in New Mexico between now and August of this year. Dick N., a clinical psychologist, has proclaimed on the Internet that DE and his company have played a major role in misinforming the public about upcoming major manifestations of the extraterrestrial presence on Earth. The event in New Mexico is supposed to happen in Chaco Canyon. According to DE, "Jason scientists are reported to be standing by, as well as the media and medics, ready for the event." (Jason scientists are professionals from many areas of science, engineering, physics, and so forth, who meet once a year at a government facility to form a "think tank" and evaluate some of society's concerns.) However, Dick N. thinks that Chaco Canyon is not the location but that the event will occur in the Four Corners area of New Mexico. It seems that the Native American population that now occupies the Four Corners area has been hit by a mysterious viral disease that has killed several young people.

I came back from New York to find a backlog of mail and e-mail, which I have been working my way through. I found some interesting messages from Dick N. regarding Mr. T and his foundation. It seems that Dick N. has got a "bee in his bonnet," saying that some of the newly published books on alien abduction are all disinformation, that many of the abduction researchers are in a plot with black-budget disinformation types, and that Mr. T is laundering "black money" through the foundation to the abduction researchers! I passed this information onto Mr. T. He will find it very amusing.

June 10, 1993

On June 23 Dave and I will be attending a conference on scientific anomalies and will be traveling to New Mexico. DE has offered to meet us at the airport and drive us to Santa Fe, where the conference will be held. I hope that DE and I will get to talk about his current remote viewing ventures and that we will hear more about the August alien events that he predicted.

June 11, 1993

I woke in the early hours after a nightmare of seeing UFOs rising rapidly up into the air, and a later dream in which I was with two tall, thin people who were doing medical procedures. The UFO dream consisted of watching a UFO from inside a building, then being outside and looking at one as it moved over the rooftops. It was partially hidden at times, and I had to move to get a good look at it. At one point, I decided to fly up in the air and it seemed so easy. I awoke feeling very afraid and breathing heavily, and it took me a while to go back to sleep. Then, I was dreaming that I was with the tall, thin people. They told me about a process I was being prepared for, but I do not remember the procedure.

Today as I was working, I remembered something. Just as I was falling asleep, before the two dreams, there was something—a memory or a sound or a feeling that caused me to wake briefly and experience a bodily spasm or recoil. It was not like a jerk or a jump that occurs when your body is relaxing to sleep. This was a conscious reaction to whatever it was that I was experiencing. Whatever it was, it was not remembered. I am not sure if the two events, the recoil and the dreams, are connected, but it is possible. There were no physical marks on my body this morning.

June 18, 1993

Wednesday, I had a call from a female abductee who has worked with Dr. Dave Jacobs. She was featured in his new book, but under an assumed name. She works as a naturopath and has been seeking answers to the UFO phenomena, abductions, and crop circles. On Monday she is off to England to try an experiment with colored lights and music in some of the crop circles and plans to do acupuncture on subjects inside and outside the circles. She has written several papers on the mathematical measurements of the crop circles and their relationship to musical measurements.

This woman's UFO sightings and abduction experiences occurred on the Delmar Flats on the way back to Nevada from California. She is fairly disillusioned and critical of most of the UFO community and tells some interesting stories. For example, in England a German crew turned up to measure and film a crop circle with sophisticated equipment, only to find there was no place to plug in their equipment when they were out in the cornfield. We had dinner together and shared a lot of information about the field. I also shared with her the information that my great-grandfather's family came from Bratton in Wiltshire. Bratton is near Alton Barnes, where most of the latest crop circles have formed. She will contact us again when she comes back from England.

On the MUFON bulletin board, I found some information about crop circles from the Center for North American Crop Circle Studies. Their 1993 Crop Circle Report outlines recent crop circles in England. Most have occurred in the southwest corner of the country, particularly in Wiltshire. Most of the crop circles have been circular, but there have been some D shapes and some have had a rippled or radiating effect.

Scientific work is being done on crop circles such as continued observations, measurements of the circles both from the land and the air, and measurements of the energy within the circles. The report also contains an account of a recent mile-and-a-half-wide crop circle reported by a tourist and filmed from his plane. The circle consist of five concentric circles, each about twenty to thirty feet in width.

Today, I had a call from Linda Moulton Howe asking if I had any information regarding recent UFO sightings and activity last night in the Clearlake, California, area. I called MUFON headquarters in Seguin, Texas, but they did not have any information. I then contacted the local MUFON representative in California and located MUFON representatives and a state director who were on top of the investigation. It struck me as strange that the head of MUFON was not aware of these ongoing and fascinating events.

According to Linda Moulton Howe, a resident of Guerneville, California, along with four other witnesses, had sightings for three to four nights running of about a hundred, dollar-coin-size objects (as seen from the ground). These objects were seen between four and six A.M. on these nights; they had multicolored lights and performed unusual maneuvers in the sky.

When the witnesses made calls to the local police, they were told that the lines were "jammed with calls about UFOs." However, when I called the Guerneville police, they told me that they had "no reports made to them the night before or previous nights." When I called the Santa Rosa police station (the nearest large town to Guerneville), they said that they had received no calls about UFOs. Similarly, when I called the Guerneville police, they again stated that they had no reports made to them the night before, or previous nights, about UFOs, strange lights in the sky, or other unusual phenomena. They did tell me that all police reports for the Sonoma Valley were routed to the Sonoma County Sheriff's office. I called them, but they also said that they did not have any reports from Guerneville of any usual phenomena. Then I called the Marin County Sheriff's office and got a similar response. What was going on?

Following another track, I called local newspapers in the Sonoma Valley area, including the *Clearlake Observer,* the *Record Bee,* the *Middleton Star Times,* and the *Russian River News* (which covers Guerneville). None of them admitted to receiving any recent reports of UFO activity or unusual sightings. Later, I contacted a local reporter, who informed me that he had a police colleague "on the inside" who said that there were police reports made but they were not available to the public. When I talked to residents of the area, they said they were reluctant to share their sightings with the police and the media for fear of ridicule. I can see why!

Yesterday, Mr. T and I had a meeting regarding his idea about setting up a weekly radio program dedicated to the anomalies field, in particular, UFOs. He has finally located a talk-show host, Art Bell, who has agreed to air Mr. T's program on Sunday evenings. George Knapp and Linda Moulton Howe have agreed to do on-air news about recent UFO sightings. We are working on a title for the show, and I am collecting a directory of potential speakers.

Tuesday, Dave said that he had a strange dream just before he woke that I should call one of our contacts in Caliente. This is the lady who viewed the large black triangular craft flying down the Caliente canyon. I tried calling her on Wednesday, but she was out of town. I finally reached her on Thursday, and she had an interesting story to tell. It seems that she had hired a woman who also works at the "Y" at Panaca. About a year ago, she was going between Caliente and Panaca and saw a UFO hovering over the valley. She did not tell anyone, because she did not want to be thought crazy. However, she decided to tell the woman who ran the bar and grill on Monday night. Our friend at the bar and grill showed her a copy of the photograph I had sent of the 1974 UFO sighting in Fyffe, Alabama. The woman recognized the UFO as identical to the one she saw near Panaca. She was quite astonished. When I talked to our friend, she asked when we would be up to Caliente again. I told her that we were planning to come sometime in late July or early August but we would come earlier if there were any local sightings.

Last week I got a call from our pilot friend, Chuck, in New Jersey. He is very disappointed with his colleagues in the UFO field and is preparing a debunking of Budd Hopkins's Manhattan abduction case. The pilot was calling to introduce me to a woman in Berkeley who he feels has some interesting ideas to share. I thanked him for the referral but told him I had already talked with her when I was living in New Jersey. However, I called her again and talked about her ideas regarding remote viewing, UFOs, and inventions. She was very cagey and cautious but said that she had several ideas she wanted to share with Mr. T. However, she would not go into specific details. She is going to send Mr. T a proposal but is worried about government theft of her ideas.

June 30, 1993

There has been quite a bit of speculation in the UFO field about DE's proclamation that a UFO event of historic proportion will take place in August this year. When Dave and I were in Santa Fe earlier this year, we were able to talk with DE at length. He alluded to a "Federation star ship" that was bringing alien hybrid babies to New Mexico. These babies were refugees from some extraterrestrial event, according to DE. We asked him what they looked like, and he replied that if you took a picture of a young iguana and "morphed" it with a picture of a female Caucasian, then "morphed" it again with a picture of an Asian person, this would give a fair representation of their appearance.

Dave and I talked about DE's prediction in great detail, staying awake until the early hours of the morning going over all the information. Dave feels that the probability that DE is delusional is greater than the probability of the arrival of the alien babies. DE seems committed to these ideas and could not be swayed from his beliefs.

DE said he would add me to his "short list" of contacts because of my work with orphans, premature babies, and developmental psychology. He will call me if these events occur. Dave and I have decided that if nothing happens, it has been an interesting mental adventure. If it does happen, and the alien babies arrive, it will be a mind-blowing, historical event.

When I was visiting New York a few months back, I had the opportunity to meet with Ingo Swann and had dinner with him. We talked about many things, including psychic children and children who had been involved in the UFO abduction experience. My observations of these children is that they are very bright and spiritual in nature. I refer to them as "enhanced" children. Ingo recommended that I write to Alice Bryant in New Mexico, because she has become interested in these special children.

July 2, 1993

I talked to some folks from the UFO world today and learned of a new crop circle that has appeared in Kennewick, Washington. The crop circle appeared in young winter wheat and is 36 feet across and 193 feet long. The crop circle is a pictogram, that is, it contains several symbolic shapes. For example, at about two o'clock on the main circle is a letter *F* shape that is fifty-seven feet long. At right angles to the circle is the symbol for "female," and there is a *T* shape at the end of the path that measures five feet across. There has been a lot of interest in the English crop circles but not much in the American press about circles that have been occurring all over the states.

July 21, 1993

Over the past few months, there have been several real dreams that could have been Interfaces: I dreamed several times that I was undergoing a medical procedure. The doctor was in her fifties, tall, with straight, graying hair. She wore a white coat and was very kind and gentle.

In addition, there have been dreams where I have been with my psychiatrist colleague John. The dreams have centered around my completing some mental task. Last Sunday at Dave's apartment, I became incredibly tired and had to take a nap. Dave and the boys had left for the afternoon, but I had the impression that someone came into the apartment.

July 26, 1993

Just got back from a wonderful weekend with Dave. He was attending a course in Burbank, California, and I flew out to spend the weekend with him. We drove to Galeta, near Santa Barbara, where we visited Ventura Harbor. It was lovely to see the ocean again after the desert of Nevada. We stayed at the Goleta Inn and had a romantic reunion. However, what was disturbing was to find multiple bruises on my body the next day. There were two bruises on the right of my lower abdomen, another on my right hip, one at the top of my left thigh, and another in the center of my right buttock. Only the one on my right hip hurt. Dave also had some small bruises inside his left, upper arm but he was not sure if they were there before or not.

July 28, 1993

According to astronomer Walter Webb, we should be in for a spectacular meteor shower in early August. The yearly flyby of the Perseid meteor shower is supposed to give a good show this year.

An increased number of meteors have been caught in the Earth's gravitational pull from their parent, the Swift-Tuttle comet. The early evening of August 11 until the morning of August 12, coming up, is supposed to be the best window for sighting. Alan of the Para-Physics group, Charles, Dave, several EG&G colleagues of Alan's, and I plan to camp out overnight to watch the shower.

August 3, 1993

Mariah Folger recommended that I contact David Purseglove, who is the director of a nonprofit group called the New Being Project. This group claims that humans are undergoing a profound change, or "rewiring," that will enable an evolutionary jump to take place. They outline several indications of these changes. They think these changes are already taking place in some people.

Their philosophy is that, because we are beings who can reflect on how we are changing, we might be able to facilitate parts of the transformation and help ourselves and each other through the changes. Also, we can modify the direction the changes take and can become coarchitects of our own evolutionary change. They claim that the types of evolutionary change that are taking place encompass many kinds of exceptional human abilities: physical, mental, and psychic. This seems to tie in with Alice Bryant's discovery of the "Super Children." Yesterday, I received a letter from Alice referring me to two other woman with interests similar to ours. The two women are interested in being "ambassadors" and meeting with the Visitors on a friendly basis. I have no idea what these ladies and I will do together. Perhaps we will form a sort of "Alien Welcome Wagon"!

August 12, 1993

Dave and I rendezvoused with his colleagues on Stewart Mountain and saw some spectacular meteors. They seemed to be shooting in all directions, in all parts of the sky. We were "oohing" and "ahhing" all evening. Finally, we settled down in our sleeping bags, and as we did not bring a tent, we stayed awake as long as we could, watching the meteor show directly above us. There may have been an Interface in the night. Even though I do not remember leaving my sleeping bag during the night, there was vegetation and dirt inside my bag this morning. I mentioned it to Dave, and he said I must have been sleepwalking. No way!

October 1, 1993

Today is an anniversary. One year ago today I moved to Las Vegas to begin working with Mr. T and the foundation. It is also one year to the day that I met Dave at Alan's Para-Physics meeting. A lot has happened during this past year, as well as many things continuing to happen. It is hard to believe that I have been with the foundation for a whole year. Since July 4, the focus of the foundation has been a radio show sponsored by Mr. T, featuring many well-known names in the UFO, parapsychology, and alternative health fields. I was a guest at one point and talked about the foundation and our UFO investigations in the small towns north of Las Vegas. While I was doing the two-hour interview, Dave stood by, supplying orange juice, love, and funny faces.

October 13, 1993

A few weeks ago, I had a phone call from a local psychotherapist, Roy, who expressed an interest in working with abductees, using regression and hypnosis therapy. Roy came to the foundation office several times, and we exchanged some audio and video segments on UFO shows from the radio and TV. At the third visit, he let slip that he had a brother in the military "back East" who had information that several members of the infamous MJ12 were about to retire. Roy seemed to want to tickle my interest with the information but would give me no more. He also mentioned that he had some friends working for the CIA.

At the next visit, Roy leaned forward in his chair and asked, "If someone wanted to give some information to the public about UFOs and the aliens without panicking them, how best could this be done?" My reply was that the information should be given to several top UFO researchers, ones who were professional in their dealings with the public and who let the "information" trickle down, until it was accepted into general knowledge base of the population. Roy leaned forward again and said, "Like through your radio show?" I said, "Maybe." However, the next time he came by he didn't want to talk about his ideas, but said he was off to Virginia to see his brother. I worry that his "information" might turn out to be disinformation.

When Dave and I were in Santa Fe in the summer, we talked at length with DE and discussed his predictions for an August "big event." According to him, this would be the start of a chain of events that would culminate in the landing of a group of alien hybrids, mostly mothers and infants. As August came and went and nothing happened, people began saying that the end-of-August prediction was a "flop." However, since then DE has been making some statements to the New Mexico *MUFON Newsletter* editor, Carolyn Duce-Ash, that the event did occur and that it was directly linked to the Mars *Explorer* disappearance. However, he added, the announcement of the event would be delayed for five or six weeks. Then the announcement would be given by a world-famous person "higher than the president of the United States." DE also announced that there was much more going on than anyone could imagine. He added, "and it is incredibly beautiful!" When asked to elaborate on the "strange things," DE contended that people would be "scared to death to see what is happening." DE continued that this was just the beginning of events. He gave Duce-Ash the reassurance that things would continue to happen. DE describes the beings he is interacting with as having "purity and innocence."

After reading this information, I got mad at DE. He had promised back in July that if the event occurred, I was on his "short list" of people he would call to be there to witness it. He said that my expertise with orphan and premature babies would be useful in helping the alien hybrids adapt. Now he says that the "alien hybrids desperately need to be taken care of." So why didn't DE call me and Dave?

I called DE immediately and left a message to let him know that I was prepared to fly out immediately. I was calling his bluff, as I now feel that Dave was right, that DE is leading everybody up the proverbial garden path. I was prepared to give DE the benefit of the doubt, but now I am not so sure. Either he puts up some proof that these events have happened or he shuts up! I feel very angry that he continues to lead people on this way. It would be wonderful if the aliens really had landed, but until an official announcement is made, I can no longer believe what DE does or says.

October 30, 1993

There is a group of us "experiencers," the "ffolks," who are professional people in established positions and functioning well in our daily lives. We found one another through various conferences and groups and we meet from time to time. The "ffolks" are contemplating a meeting in Las Vegas in January. There may be eight to ten of us, and I hope we will be able to get a conference room. Tentative invitees will be Dave and I, Mariah Folger and her son, X, and several of the "ffolks" who were at the Texas meeting.

Basically, our group (the "ffolks") are professional men and women who have had Interface experiences and realize they have had encounters with "another reality." We also realize that these experiences cannot dominate our lives. We have to get on with our daily living, learning, and loving while at the same time working to integrate memories and emotions regarding these issues. The purpose of the January meeting will be to share coping mechanisms and ways, other than through hypnosis, that we, as "ffolks," have been able to access suppressed memories. As we meet with others, we will add them to our group, but for now we will remain a small, exclusive group.

One of the purposes of Mr. T's radio show, called *Area 2000,* is to invite the public to call the foundation with accounts of their personal experiences. This has been moderately successful and it has brought me into contact with some fascinating people. There have been a fair share of fanatics, psychotics, and people on the "fringe of the fringe," but overall the calls have been from average people. These individuals have had some weird and wonderful experiences and usually want to share them with someone who will listen with an open, nonjudgmental ear. Many of the people having UFO sightings often see satellites going over or very bright planets, but others have seen the huge, black, triangular craft that have also been seen in Europe.

People call with reports of contact with nonhuman entities. One in particular was striking. Ten years ago, a woman in Yorba Linda, California, had a three-hour interaction with three entities outside her house. This meeting followed a week in which her family experienced strange lights and noises over their house. Her mother and daughter were witnesses, and the only other person she had told was her husband. The experiences left her with a sense of nostalgia and a yearning to see the entities again.

Then there are the people who have had experiences with Men in Black (MIBs). Seven years ago, one local resident had an MIB walk across her patio, return back across the patio, then disappear. Another lady in Reno saw nine Oriental-looking MIBs while waiting at an Australian airport. She says that she may have had missing time, too. She asked me, "How could I have spent three hours just writing postcards?" Generally, I am able to reassure people that they are not alone in their experiences. I am sometimes able to send them information, give them book lists, or refer them to support groups, if that is what they request. Mostly, all they want is for someone to listen to their experience.

One young woman, whom I will call Mary, desperately wanted to talk to someone. Several years previously she had had a hysterectomy but now she was testing positive for pregnancy. She had not had sex with anyone but had experienced alien contact. She was highly anxious and wanted to be referred to someone who could help her with this dilemma. I referred her to a professional group in California. She said that she had done a pregnancy test several times and each time it had come back positive. However, when I called her a few weeks later she reported that, following another abduction experience, she was no longer pregnant.

Sometimes people call with ideas that they want the foundation to fund, such as UFO novelty ideas and toys. One man wanted to open a UFO Pizza Parlor! Someone else wanted to set up a UFO and futuristic theme park.

Occasionally, interesting characters visit the foundation office, such as Fred, who had a possible implant behind his ear. He told me that about ten years ago he had an emergency surgery on his face at a Veterans Administration (VA) hospital in Loma Linda, California. The doctor operated on Fred's nose and placed a piece of "something" behind his ear. He told Fred that it was a piece of cartilage. Fred showed me the area behind his ear and there was a very distinct, triangular shape of "something" underneath the skin. Fred said that he had tried to locate his medical records from that surgery but they were missing. Since the surgery, he has had many abduction-type experiences and often wonders if he received an implant. Fred has worked all over the world, studied shamanism, and assisted conservation groups in Central America. It is interesting that his surgery took place at the Loma Linda VA hospital in California, where others have claimed to have had anomalous experiences and to have received possible implants. Loma Linda is also the location of a group that has conducted research on microwave effects on human physiology and behavior.

Fred also had the ability to "speak in tongues" (called glossolalia), and he taped some of this speech for me. When I and others heard his tape, we agreed that it sounded like an American Indian language. I wondered if I could get the tape analyzed. I played it over the phone to Mariah Folger, who is of New York State Oneida heritage. She said that it sounded like a Dakota Indian dialect. Within a few days, I had another interesting visitor to the foundation, a Native American powwow dancer. He agreed to listen to the tape. This charismatic man has his own dance troupe and has danced all over the world. He had just returned from Australia, where he discovered that the Australian Aborigines share very similar myths and history with the American Indians. The dancer had also studied Egyptian symbols and had found many similar references to UFOs and ETs in all three cultures—Native American, Australian Aborigine, and Egyptian.

The scariest person I met was a listener of *Area 2000,* who brought his gun to the office. He sat opposite me and when he opened up his attaché case, there was the biggest revolver I had ever seen. "Does it make you nervous?" he asked. I wondered how I should handle the situation. So I replied, "Well, I respect your right to have a weapon, but I would prefer that you keep it behind your chair while we talk." So he carefully placed it behind his seat while we continued our discussion. Las Vegas in many respects is still the Wild West!

15

Abduction One, Abduction Two

"I would like you to assume personally the initiative and central responsibility within the Government for the development of a program of substantive cooperation with the Soviet Union in the field of outer space, including the development of specific technical proposals."

—President John F. Kennedy. November 12, 1963. National Security Memorandum #271 sent to James Webb, administrator, NASA.

January 3, 1994

What another interesting year 1993 turned out to be. This time last year I was ready to quit my job at the foundation and had no idea what I was supposed to be doing here in Las Vegas. However, over the past year the position has become more interesting, especially with the development of the *Area 2000* radio program.

January 10, 1993

Mr. T announced last week that February 6 would be the last airing of the radio show. I was not too surprised, because he seemed to be losing interest in it over the past few months. He had decided it would be too difficult to get another six months of speakers, even though I had a roster of potential speakers available. Art Bell, who had been hosting the show, has decided to carry on with the show under another name, from his Pahrump studio. A great audience is following the show and he wants to syndicate it across the country. Mr. T was not too happy with this idea. His objections were that people would still associate the show with the foundation, that Art would not get quality guests for the show, and that the quality of the show would fall. However, I think Art will do well and all that will be needed is a change of name and an initial disclaimer. Despite its short six-month run, the show was very good for networking and getting to know new people.

Yesterday, Dave and I went to the afternoon showing of the movie *A Nightmare before Christmas.* I had heard that it was a pretty good animation movie and that the main character, the "Pumpkin King," was a good animation of an alien. Sure enough, the character has the round dome head, large black eyes, no nose or ears, and the long, spindly limbs and gait of a praying mantis insect. The artist gave him a mouth and teeth, but if he had made his mouth small and narrowed his chin to a point, he could have passed as a gray. The skin tone and the "neck too narrow to support the head" were other similar characteristics. I wonder of the moviemakers used the gray-type entity as their model. I was pleased to see that the character was portrayed as intelligent, caring, curious, and a leader and that he tried to get things right. His failures were attributed to his being different and from an alternative dimension. In the movie, when the military shot down his Halloween-style sled, the emphasis was on sympathy for the character rather than revenge. Overall, it wasn't a blockbuster movie, but it was very interesting, considering the conspiracy theorists' claim that the moviemakers are educating us to accept different alien types.

As mentioned earlier, Mr. T had decided to terminate the radio show *Area 2000.* Before he or I could discuss it with anybody else, I got a call from an anonymous "listener" who asked about the show closing in mid-February. I asked him how he knew about the show closing, and he said, "You told me when we last talked." I denied this and said that he was mistaken. During the twenty-minute phone call, he basically interrogated me about the show and the foundation. He said that he was head of another "foundation that studied human potential" and he was very skilled at questioning. I decided to go along with his questioning, being honest, without being indiscreet. At one point he asked, "If you were to find out some information that would prove UFOs were real, would you put it on the air?" (This was the same sort of question Roy had put forward last year.) I told the caller that putting such information on the air "wasn't my decision to make," but I would discuss it with a few key people in the UFO field. He seemed satisfied with that.

We also talked about Richard Hoagland's *Area 2000* interview, and the caller said he was dismayed Hoagland was making predictions about the date the Mars *Explorer* would come back on line. Richard Hoagland is a researcher who claimed that photos taken of the surface of Mars show a human-looking face, as well as pyramid-shaped structures. This was a very strange call and one that makes me suspect that the foundation's activities and phone lines are not as private as we would think. Another remark that this caller made confirmed my suspicions. The caller referred to a publication on the mathematics of the face on Mars and similar artifacts. We had been sent a copy by the author, Stanley V. McDaniel. The caller remarked that he had a fully bound version, not the ring-bound version we had in our files. How did he know what we had in our files?

January 17, 1994

I had an interesting weekend with our group of professional "ffolks": Mariah and her son came from California; X from Washington, D.C.; Viv from Texas; and Joan from Oregon. Along with Dave and me, our group had an interesting weekend talking about the Interface experiences, coping mechanisms, and memory access. We took a couple of side trips to Red Rock Canyon and the Ethel M. chocolate factory, which is located on the outskirts of Las Vegas, as well as spending a lot of time sitting and talking. Joan was a new addition to the group. She had recently "remembered" her Interface experiences and was writing a book. We felt like we had known her forever.

The last morning five of us got together: Mariah, Viv, Joan, X, and me. We decided we would write a book together and that we would each write a section about the Interface experience from our own viewpoint. I said I could write on the paranormal aspects of the Interfaces. It would be an interesting book for us all to participate in writing. But I have my doubts about it taking place. Joan is already writing her own book, Viv expressed concern that she would not have time, Mariah is suffering from ill health, and X is under secrecy oaths about much of his knowledge.

April 1, 1994

Over the past few years I keep meeting people who claim they have received implants in their nasal and sinus cavities. Depending on whom you talk to, the implants are put in place by either the aliens or the government. I have mentioned the possible implication of the government in these operations to other people but always receive the same argument, which goes: If the government was doing this to people, and considering the number of people this is happening to, a vast number of medical personnel would be involved. All of these people would never be able to keep something like this a secret and it would leak out to the general public. The reach of this kind of operation would be on the scale of the Holocaust. It could not be performed without someone "blowing the whistle."

I reminded them that, during the time the Nazis were exterminating Jewish people in Germany and Poland, there were people and groups who knew about the atrocities but chose to keep it secret. When people heard about the terrible things happening in the camps, they chose to ignore and deny the facts.

Today, in the *Las Vegas Sun,* I read an interesting article that showed it is possible to medically interfere with the health of thousands of civilians yet have the "treatment" go unnoticed and unaccounted-for for decades. Entitled "Nasal Treatment May Be Nightmare for 400,000," the article was written by Laurence Spohn of the Scripps News Service. He writes:

> Decades ago, about 400,000 Americans may have received potentially dangerous radioactive nasal treatments now suspected of significant health problems, including head and neck cancers. Although no one knows the actual numbers, a Navy internal medical review in 1991 found evidence that suggests the number of people treated was more than double original estimates. The radium applicators used in the treatments are now believed to have exposed patients to significant doses of radiation. . . . Farber [one of the researchers investigating this problem] said now that the military exposures, originally thought to involve as many as 15,000 army and navy servicemen, would be dwarfed by the number of civilians who may have gotten the treatment from well-meaning physicians. "If

each radiator sold through 1961, was used to treat only 200 people, that total population of exposed people would equal about 400,000," Farber said, "and probably they were mostly children at the time."

According to the article, the treatment, typically given to patients who had hearing or chronic nasal infection problems, involved having a small, radioactive radium capsule placed up each nostril for several minutes. Also according to the article, medical authorities at the time warned of the potential problems, Spohn continues: "'Concerns for immediate and delayed adverse effects were voiced by nearly every author on the subject,' wrote Navy Commander Steven Warlick, who conducted a Navy literature search on the treatment in 1991."

Also according to the article: "The Navy report states the treatment used during World War II in the military 'became widespread' in civilian medicine in postwar years. That was partly because of the successful experience of military doctors and the commercial availability of the radium applicator."

Another type of device—an implant—that has recently become commercially available, designed to keep tabs on laboratory mice, is called the DAS-4001 Electronic Laboratory Animal Monitoring System, or ELAMS. Produced by BioMedic Data Systems of Maywood, New Jersey, ELAMS is a new application of microcomputer technology. A radio transmitter, as small as a grain of rice, is "harmlessly" implanted under the skin. When a wand is waved over the device, it energizes the transmitter, which sends an encoded number to a handheld data recorder. According to the BioMedic advertisement, "For at least the next 34 billion subjects, of any species, no two individuals can ever have the same moniker (identity number)." Scanners come in a handy "pocket size" or a handheld, notebook computer size. Will this type of device ever become available for use on humans?

I wrote to BioMedic and received a package of information related to the research, development, and applications for the ELAMS implant. For example, their material states:

"An unalterable, permanently encoded microchip (transponder) is hermetically sealed in a bio-compatible glass capsule with a patented anti-migration feature. This transponder is injected subcutaneously [under the skin] into any animal subject. A scanner connected to the unit activates the transponder when it is within the scanner's field, broadcasts the encoded number through the scanner and into the processor." The implant is placed in the animal with a handheld device, which inserts a needle under the skin, placing the microchip in place. According to a clinical paper that came with the package, "The transponders produced no adverse clinical or histopathological side effects in the rats."

A picture of one of the implants showed it to be about the size of a grain of rice (small enough to be injected with a 12-gauge subcutaneous needle). The implant itself was contained within a glass capsule contained within a polypropylene sheath. It was found that after several months of implantations, the implant was becoming enclosed in bands of connective tissue. Otherwise there were no local reactions.

However interesting this may be, is there any evidence that microchips have been implanted in humans? I am reluctant to accept just anybody's account of being "implanted," although I have heard many intriguing stories. I believe that a group in New York, headed by Whitley Strieber, has funded a CAT scan research of people who believe they have cerebral implants, but the data have yet to surface.

Another question that needs to be asked is if there is evidence that the "government" in its myriad forms has been involved in medical research that directly affects the public. In fact, "government" in its many forms appears to be seriously involved in many medical issues that affect the public's health. For example, the Department of Defense, as well as the National Institutes of Health, recently convened separate panels to discuss how to spend a twenty-million-dollar appropriation to test a specific AIDS vaccine. It seems logical to assume that any medical issues arising out of the abduction experience would draw interest from one or more branches of government and the military.

Life at the foundation has been very slow since we canceled the radio show, and there have been no new projects. Consequently, I have decided that, with my savings and my school loans, I will leave the foundation and work at home on my schoolwork and my writing.

About a month ago, I was approached by the head of MUFON to take on the role of assistant state director for the Nevada branch of the organization. I was interested in this and said I would give it some thought. I felt that this would give me an opportunity to generate some new local interest in the organization and, for myself, to have an autonomous position apart from the foundation.

However, I received another call from the head of MUFON advising me that Mr. T had "given his permission" for me to take on the position. This rankled me so much that I declined the position. I realized it had only been offered me in a ploy to be in favor with Mr. T and his possible funding of the organization.

July 1, 1994

Many changes have taken place since I last updated my journal. In April I resigned from the foundation to work at home on my schoolwork and writing projects. In early June I traveled to Austin, Texas, to attend a conference for explorer scientists, and it was good to meet all my old friends. The first night of the conference is always a cocktail party for folks to meet and get reacquainted. There I was approached by a young male physicist who did voluntary writing for the *MUFON Journal.* He asked me if I could do some newspaper searches in Las Vegas. It seemed that in the 1950s a UFO was spotted over Hoover Dam and that this was observed by many people and was reported in the local newspaper. I said I would think about it but would not promise anything, because I was very busy with my own projects. The young man seemed energetic and enthusiastic.

The next day during one of the conference talks, this young man keeled over in his seat, turned denim blue, and started bleeding from his nose and mouth. I went to him, and, because he was still breathing, tried to rouse him. He then stopped breathing and his heart stopped beating. Several doctors worked on him to no avail and he died. It was devastating and brought the conference to a full stop for the rest of the day. Everybody was in shock. Up to the point of his keeling over, the young physicist had been in good health. It was assumed that he had suffered a heart attack. The curious thing is, that when I went to him, he still had a heartbeat; it was fast and weak but regular. He was not gray and sweating like people do when they have a heart attack. He was also in his thirties, much too young for a lethal heart attack. He had received a satisfactory result on a physical just three months earlier. It was all so puzzling. We learned that he had been working with a senior physicist on technology to develop a new form of energy. Was this the cause of his death or something else? We later learned that there was an inconclusive autopsy and that it was decided that he probably died from a rare heart attack brought on by a virus.

Other strange events happened on that trip. We had a near

catastrophe when an evening boat ride ended with a sudden slam into the dock, knocking everyone off his feet. I went head over heels out of my chair but was not hurt. It seems that the captain "blanked out" for a few seconds as he was docking the boat.

Since I have been at home working on my studies and writing, I have felt much more relaxed, my paranormal abilities seem to have become enhanced, and my regular dreams have been vivid and memorable. However, there have been several really scary real dreams. The most scary experience took place on June 21, when I was at school in California. I was staying at the Red Lion Inn in Rohnert Park so I could attend school sessions and meetings. There was a prelude to the experience. I "woke" to feel myself being carried by several people. I remember saying to myself, over and over again, "I do not want to be here. I do not want to be here." I did not want to be awake in this situation where I was being carried somewhere.

Then I was lying on a couch or bed in a medical situation and a woman was sitting to the left of me, near my head. She was trying to put some cream or lotion on my face, mostly on my mouth and nose. I was resisting because of its chemical smell. I put my arms across my face. I heard someone say, "We will put some cotton balls up your nose and then you won't smell it." Then I was on my feet between two people and rapidly became fully and totally conscious. It was not a dream!

I saw people in blue scrub suits, with blue hats and masks. A man in scrubs and mask came back in through a swinging doorway carrying some cotton swabs that looked wet. He held them in his cupped hand. As I became conscious, I again said to myself, "I do not want to be here." I said this twice and then panicked. Ahead of me was a brown medical couch, up against a wall. On it were vials and medical equipment. It looked as if it was being readied for a procedure. As I became conscious, somebody decided that I should lie down on the couch. There were three people: two held me, another cleared off the couch, and they helped me lie down. The cotton balls were put into my nose, and they smelled like ether. I soon lost consciousness.

When I awoke, I was in a panic, because it had all seemed so real. I kept having flashbacks to the events of the night and felt a compulsion to know how long I had been conscious. I tried replaying the event in my mind, counting off the seconds between becoming semiconscious, as the noxious cream was applied to my face, and passing out on the medical couch. I mentally walked myself through the event three or four times and estimated that I was conscious for about thirty to forty seconds. It was long enough for me to open my eyes, know that I was conscious, and remember my surroundings.

What to make of this? I told a few people, but it sounded so much like a lucid dream that they dismissed my experience as "just a bad dream." I have had lucid dreams before. In these I *know* that I am asleep and dreaming and can manipulate the dream. On the night of June 21, I had been sleeping, became semiconscious, then fully conscious, only to relapse into unconsciousness. This was not a lucid awakening in a dream state. It was a full waking consciousness into a real situation.

July 2, 1994

About a month ago I had a dream in which someone was trying to put something in my mouth and down my throat. I was resisting, but a doctor reassured me that my mouth and throat had been numbed. I pressed my lips with my fingers, and my lips felt swollen and numb.

Then, last night I had a similar dream in which a medical person was examining my feet, asking me if they felt numb, which they did. It felt like I had some kind of spinal analgesia and it was working from my toes upward.

July 4, 1994

Perhaps related to the "spinal analgesic" dream of a few nights ago, my lower back suddenly and for no apparent reason started hurting terribly. Dave is away visiting his brother in Maryland and I had no one to help me when it started. The pain is so bad that I have to crawl between the living room floor, where I have made my bed, and the bathroom. I can barely stand to get a drink of water. I have never had a bad back like this; it came on so suddenly one morning that I had to roll out of bed onto the floor. Regular pain killers have no effect, and there is no diminishment of the pain. I have no medical insurance, so I cannot afford to go to a doctor. When Dave called, I told him that my back was hurt, but I don't think he realizes how much pain I am in. I am usually such a healthy person with a high energy level. It is hard for him to understand that I am sick, as I am rarely ill.

My guess is that the dream of the other night was of an actual medical intervention, in which I was given a spinal analgesia like the spinal epidural that is given to pregnant women during labor. A small catheter is placed near the spinal column, through a needle placed in the lower back, and a local anesthetic is injected to numb the lower body. I have heard that many women experienced similar back pain and disability following an epidural procedure. I have no impression of any implants being inserted, and there were no Visitors in the spinal dream, only humans.

July 16, 1994

Last weekend my back was feeling better and I was able to attend the MUFON conference in Austin, Texas. There was nothing new presented, as far as I knew, but they did let three abductees (Leah Haley, Carla Turner, and Linda Napolitano) speak. This was a breakthrough, because there used to be such a resistance to women speaking at MUFON meetings. My friend B, who lives in Texas, arranged for me to go to a massage therapist who has also had abduction experiences. She seemed able to soothe out most of the remaining pain in my back, and I was comfortable for the first time in weeks.

My friend B gave me a copy of the *Texas Morning News* for July 10, which featured an article on "lost memories." The author of the article, Bill Marvel, discussed the current arguments about personal memories of the past that are "recovered" under hypnosis. Lately, there has been a spate of court cases in which women have accused and sued their fathers and other male family members for allegedly sexually abusing them when they were children. Marvel cites some of these cases and points out the benefits and problems associated with hypnotically retrieved information.

The main argument is that the therapists have been blamed for using "leading" questions and that patients under hypnosis are especially susceptible to suggestion. This same argument has been aimed at the UFO abduction therapists. Claims have been made that the therapists have "led" their clients with questions that allow for a UFO or extraterrestrial explanation for their experiences. At least one abductee has warned me of a top abduction researcher who used this type of questioning. "Sometimes," she said, "if I could not remember an event, he would push me and push me and suggest things that might have happened, and I would agree just to get him to quit." I worry about this type of recall under hypnosis and would much rather believe an abductee who had personally remembered her experiences firsthand.

October 5, 1994

The summer of 1994 was wonderful. I took five months off to write and study and negotiated with a publisher to publish my first book. I am using my school loans to live on, and Dave and I are sharing all the house expenses. I love being at home, although Dave thinks I am "goofing off." I have enjoyed the chance to work at my own pace, to have time to think and plan, to read and study, and to be myself for a while.

I have not been in touch with many people in the UFO and abduction field for a while, although I have kept in touch with a few key people. The latest news in the UFO field is that the three largest UFO organizations, MUFON, CUFOS, and FUFOR, have formed a coalition with a research grant from Mr. T. They are soliciting research proposals for research projects. I have heard that all the proposals have to be formally approved by Mr. T, so I predict problems for the coalition.

Last Saturday a two-hour-long TV program, *Larry King Live,* was aired from Rachel, Nevada. The topic was Area 51 and the alleged UFO and government cover-up of UFO sightings. Kevin Randle, Steven Greer, Stanton Friedman, and Glen Campbell were interviewed. They aired the show twice on the same night and again the next day, but it did not say anything new.

January 21, 1995

Several colleagues have been monitoring the NASA Headquarters Public Affairs Office through the Internet. This is a newsgroup put out by NASA to educate the public about upcoming events and schedules. This latest bulletin, intended for the media, is entitled "NASA Kicks Off Seminar Series." The bulletin reads as follows:

> The first public seminar in a series designed to help shape a unified agenda for the future of NASA's space program will be held on January 23 at NASA Headquarters, Washington, D.C. "Signs of Life" featuring Dr. Lyn Margulis, University of Massachusetts, and Dr. Leslie Orgel, the Salt Institute for Biological Studies, will explore the definitions of life and how we can identify it elsewhere.

> The seminar series, initiated by NASA Chief Scientist Dr. Frances Ann Cordova and introduced on January 23 by NASA Administrator Daniel S. Goldin, will be scheduled over the next year to consider fundamental questions that bear on NASA's greatest challenges.

While this appears to be a bold step for NASA, the subject matter is not new to the agency. As early as 1965, NASA was considering the possibility of intelligent life existing in other parts of the galaxy. Publication NASA SP-7015 entitled "Extraterrestrial Life: A Bibliography. Part II: Published Literature" covers the 1900–65 period. The publication contains references to journal articles and books that have explored the extraterrestrial question.

I received a very interesting book written by Karla Turner, *Taken: Inside the Alien-Human Abduction Agenda.* The book recounts the abduction stories of eight women. There are many similarities between their stories but also individual differences in their perception of the events, which to me adds credibility to their stories. What is also very interesting is that all of them report real government and military interest in their experiences. One family, after experiencing a night of abduction events, found their farm overrun by men and women in military uniforms and protective clothing. Helicopter flyovers after an abduction event are commonplace. Sometimes, aliens and humans in military uniforms are seen together during an experience.

The common assumption is that the aliens and military have entered into a working partnership. I do not think it is that simple. There is a real phenomenon called alien abduction. It happens to at least one in fifty of the population, usually as repeated events over time, and is reported more often by women. The abductions are most often experienced while the abductee is in an altered state of consciousness but are followed by the finding of physical cuts, bruises, puncture marks, scoop marks, scars, and rashes, which are often in geometrical and unnatural shapes. I call this Abduction One. Overlaid on this scenario is Abduction Two: surveillance and physical intervention from some branches of the military and government.

What do we know about Abduction One and Abduction Two? The main characteristics of Abduction One are:

1. It may begin with the experience of awakening to find oneself paralyzed or unable to move a portion of the body. Mentally,

the individual feels wide awake, not dreaming or hallucinating. Before this, the individual may hear beeps, buzzes, or other repeated sounds in one or both ears. Whitley Strieber reports a series of three beeps. A strong light or arrangement of lights of varying colors may be perceived by the individual, either outside or inside the house.

2. It may proceed on the road or out in the open; when machinery is affected by an energy field, it is experienced as a feeling of heat or waves by the individual. Vehicles and other machinery become nonfunctional, as do lights, radios, and other electrical equipment. Strong static may be experienced over radios before Abduction One.

3. Lights in the sky, either over the road, countryside, or over individual houses are perceived by witnesses before Abduction One.

4. The individual may perceive a variety of nonhuman entities ranging from the short gray type (large head; large, dark eyes; short spindly body); tall, thin, golden entities; very tall Nordic types; or others. These entities may carry "wands," "prods," boxes, or other unknown equipment.

5. The entity and the individual communicate via telepathy, and other paranormal events are experienced, such as being drawn up by a beam of light into a craft and being levitated through windows and doorways. The interior of the craft is colorless, drab, plain, bare, and sparse. The examining tables and chairs appear to "grow" out of the floor or are integral with walls. There are no mattresses, pillows, blankets, or other comforts. Individuals are often brought before "councils or committees" of entities and questioned. Sometimes, individuals are given anomalous "food and drink." There are no bathrooms. There are rarely any items lying around; if there are, these are incongruous and unusual—for example, an ancient pair of spectacles.

6. It usually continues with a physical examination of the individual, and a "mind probe" where the individual and the entity are in eye-to-eye or telepathic contact. Sometimes a "virtual reality" scenario follows in which the individual perceives a video-type presentation of futuristic or cataclysmic scenarios. During the examinations, the individual is often soothed and told that everything is all right; the instrumentation and technology appear futuristic and

nonterrestrial. The Abduction One physical examination focuses on the head, spine, reproductive organs, and lower intestinal tract, and ignores the thorax, heart, lungs, and so forth. If physical pain is experienced during Abduction One, an entity often lays its hands on the individual's head and the pain subsides. The demeanor of the entities in Abduction One is generally emotionless and businesslike. Many individuals are told that they have been "chosen" and have a special purpose in life. Following Abduction One, some individuals may become more concerned about stewardship of the Earth, become more spiritual, and develop psychic abilities.

7. The individual is returned to his bed or car, often with amnesia of the events and missing time. No reported artifacts have ever been retained from Abduction One. Physical trauma is often noticed after Abduction One, in the form of bruises, scratches, punctures, burns, scoop marks, and geometric rashes, such as squares and triangles. Various problems may follow such as dry, red, itchy eyes; skin problems; compromised immune system function; missing pregnancies; and post-traumatic stress disorder syndrome.

Abduction Two may overlap in many ways with Abduction One and either might be mistaken for the other. Abduction One and Abduction Two have been reported by many women, including Debbie Jordan (*Intruders*), Linda Cortile (*Witnessed*), Karla Turner (*Taken*), and Katharina Wilson (*Alien Jigsaw*).

The main characteristics of Abduction Two are:

1. The individual is befriended, socializes with, or is even romantically courted by another individual (a "minder") who has recent links with the government or the military, especially with any of the intelligence agencies, military medical units, or government medical contractors. More often a male befriends and "minds" a female, although same-sex minders have been known. The minder may offer massages, or other New Age bodywork, to the individuals they are minding. If a romantic liaison occurs, the minder enters a sexual relationship with the individual early in the relationship.

2. The individual notices, and may become anxious and paranoid about, mail that appears to be tampered with, obvious telephone tapping, monitoring of computer mail and programs, and tailing

of his vehicle. If the individual seeks help at this point, he may be diagnosed as being paranoid and suffering from an emotional illness.

3. The individual reports physical abduction by real people, with whom she communicates in a normal manner (not telepathically) and by whom they are subjected to surreal events: drugging, interrogation, mental testing, and physical examination. The individuals may perceive real artifacts such as newspapers, backpacks, or discarded uniforms. The individuals may perceive being taken to medical facilities, underground locations, or military installations, at which they see uniformed and white-coated personnel. The rooms in which the individuals are examined are regular hospital-type rooms or are furnished with regular furniture. The individuals often meet key political or military personnel. The individual is often escorted to the bathroom and reports feeling embarrassed. The individual might recover artifacts that are left behind by personnel in the form of missed security stickers on mail and devices that are left behind following Abduction Two, such as implants. The medical equipment and devices are ones normally seen in a doctor's office or appear to be modifications of known technology.

4. The individual is aware that, even though there is selective amnesia of events, there has been physical sampling of his/her blood, urine, ova, semen, and hair and nails. Individuals are aware of IVs in progress, often being able to read the names of known drugs on labels. Individuals are often aware of catheterization, endoscopies, X-rays, vital signs being taken, gynecological and other internal examinations, tubes and instruments placed in their mouth, throat, ears, and other orifices. Face masks, with or without anesthetic agents, have been reported; oxygen via face mask appears to be given. Regular medical procedure tables, gurneys, and dental office-type examining chairs have been reported. Individuals may lie on mattresses, have their heads on pillows, and be covered with blankets.

Abduction One and Abduction Two are both real, but sometimes a screen memory of Abduction One may be hypnotically induced during Abduction Two. How has this license to monitor the American public come about and where has personal freedom gone? After my official entry into this country, I came to the realization that Americans are free to say and do whatever they choose, as long as they have a permit, license, authorization, or a piece of paper from an authority to allow them to carry out their everyday activities. In this controlled atmosphere, it is often difficult for individuals to act independently. The concept of an unknown, outside element, interacting in an uncontrolled way, with the citizenry of the United States, must be very worrying to the authorities who are charged with the security of the country. A program has been put into place to monitor these interactions. Many activities that would be deemed unethical in the normal medical and scientific field can be carried out under the guise of maintaining national security.

March 9, 1995

It's spring! In more ways than one. The trees have new green leaves on them, my rosebushes have buds, I have seen new birds in the yard, and the weather is getting warmer. I love this time of year. Last summer I left the foundation to work on my schooling and writing. I am now completing my final essay and getting ready to start my dissertation research. After taking off the summer, I had hoped to get back into full-time employment but found that I was overqualified for anything Las Vegas has to offer. I have been working part time conducting some classes for the Community College of Southern Nevada on business-related topics. The Interface experiences seem to have stopped for now. Time to get on with my life.

May, 1, 1995

There are ample historical records that relate stories of nonhuman entities that have interacted with humans throughout time. The appearance, behavior, and functions of some of these entities are very similar to those in modern accounts of contact and interaction with nonhuman entities. However, these records are ignored by modern historians and are relegated to the realm of myth and folk tales. What do we know of these historic encounters?

For example, Ezekiel of the Bible related seeing four humanoid forms that appeared in connection with a strange vehicle that came down out of the sky. Historical records of many cultures, from Ancient Babylon, Egypt, and Greece, contain records of Visitors from the stars.

January 4, 1996

After a year of dating, Dave and I moved in together and we have lived in a nice rented house in a development at the base of Sunrise Mountain. I can look out each morning and say "good morning" to the mountains! We have green around us, trees and grass, and I grow roses in my small yard. Life is good.

January 16, 1996

I have not been remembering all of my dreams, but there have seen some in which I have to solve a dilemma—much like real life. However, I did have one recent medical real dream in which I was told that a gynecological procedure had removed a small polyp and that an IUD had been put in place. What a weird thing to dream.

One early morning I awoke to see a low shadow pass in front of the chest of drawers on Dave's side of the bed. The shadow was shorter than the chest of drawers. I commented to myself, "Good, they are coming for Dave, so I can go back to sleep!" Dave has handled all this activity with humor and common sense. When I wake with bruises and puncture marks after a real dream we comment to each other, "Those damn aliens," and laugh.

February 10, 1996

I found an interesting article in *Science News* (vol. 149) entitled "Kids: Getting under Mom's Skin for Decades," by J. Travis. He reports: "Investigators have found that descendants of fetal cells, which escape into the maternal bloodstream during pregnancy, may persist for decades after the birth of the child." Diana W. Bianchi of the New England Medical Center in Boston says: "We are finding male DNA (among maternal blood cells) 27 years after the birth of a male child." Travis continues: "This unexpected discovery suggests that fetal cells can take up permanent residence in the mother and that pregnancy sometimes transforms a woman into a chimeric blend of mother and child." The researchers found that the persistent fetal cells had a distinctive profile of surface proteins. The most interesting fact about this article was women whose blood contained higher percentages of fetal cells often suffered from autoimmune diseases such as arthritis and lupus.

If alien impregnation is a reality, then it might be possible to detect alien DNA in the bloodstream of abductees. And, if alien impregnation is a reality, and alien DNA is isolated from the abductee's blood, might this explain the high incidence of autoimmune diseases, such as lupus, that are present in abductees?

April 18, 1996

In another twelve days I will hit the half-century mark: I will be turning fifty. I can honestly say that I have more energy and have better health now than when I was at my quarter century. The prospect of menopause does not hold any qualms for me, and if I should die tomorrow, I would have no regrets because I have lived a very full, active, interesting, and often exciting life. However, I hope to reach at least my three-quarter-century birthday before passing onto the next great adventure. I understand that during the next twenty-five years, my physiology and lifestyle might change—change is inevitable—but I plan to accommodate these changes. I hope that the next twenty-five (or maybe even fifty) years will be just as interesting as the last twenty-five.

When I was younger, I had a premonition that something final would happen to me when I turned forty. I thought that I might die or have a child late in life, but none of this happened. Instead, my forties turned out to be a wild ride: traveling, meeting new people and having new relationships. My goals for this fiftieth year of my life are to complete my studies and get my first book published. A lot of things have come full circle.

As I age, I have found that Interfaces with the Visitors have decreased considerably. It is possible that I am no longer useful in the supposed scenario that the Visitors are harvesting eggs and producing hybrids. I may have outlived my usefulness to them. If this is the case, I am glad, although I miss interacting with the Visitors.

September 13, 1996

Friday the thirteenth is an auspicious date to begin a new journal. At the end of September I will have been in Las Vegas four years—time has gone by so fast. It seems only yesterday that I was arriving to work for Mr. T and the foundation and met Dave at Alan's psi group meeting. Dave and I have lived near Sunrise Mountain now for almost three years, making a life for ourselves with his three sons.

I have been experimenting with various nutritional supplements.

I am the sort of person who does not take other people's word about a product. I have to try it for myself. For the past week I have been trying melatonin, a food supplement that has become popular, to see if it can enhance my dream recall. Melatonin is made naturally by the pineal gland, which some say is the "seat of the soul." This supplement is produced in large quantities in younger people but diminishes as we age. It has a role to play in sleep, dreams, and aging. Melatonin does appear to enhance my dreams. I have had very vivid dreams, some of them in exquisite detail. In my dreams, my mind feels as if it is a video recorder that can focus down on smaller and smaller detail, down to the cellular level. However, I find that the melatonin makes me feel very edgy and nervous during the day, so I've stopped taking it. Interestingly, the dreams did not revert to the Interfaces, which seemed to lessen considerably a year ago. I find that I am still missing the Visitors.

October 24, 1996

Today's local paper contains an article about Mr. T entitled "Las Vegas Millionaire Buys UFO Ranch in Eastern Utah." It seems that last July the owners of the ranch, the Shermans, broke years of silence and went public with tales of strange lights and UFOs on their 480-acre ranch. The article, by Zack Van Eyck, proceeds: "Sherman said he and other members of his family had seen lights emerging from circular 'doorways' that seemed to appear in mid-air, had three cows strangely mutilated and several others disappear. The rancher also reported unusual impressions in the soil and circles of flattened grass in a pasture."

Mr. T has reportedly bought the ranch for $200,000. He has erected an observation building and moved in a pair of scientists and a veterinarian. He has someone on the property twenty-four hours a day, recording anything out of the ordinary. However, as in all his ventures, he seems to have forgotten something important—the human element. The original owners have moved to a smaller ranch fifteen miles away, far removed from the activity, although Mr. Sherman has been hired to maintain the farm. From my own investigations, I have found that these types of incidents appear to be focused around an individual or a single family in one location. When the people move away, the incidents decline and stop. It will be interesting to follow this story and see what happens.

November 4, 1996

A lot happened over Halloween. First Dave and I got engaged. Dave is still a little uncertain about the deal, but I feel that it is a good step in our relationship. I did not know where I fit into his life. I was living the life of "wife" to Dave and "mom" to his boys but had no official recognition. I had always felt that a wedding license did not mean a great deal—it was just a piece of paper—but at this time in my life, I need the stability and recognition of my status as wife and mother. Dave and I had always said that we would need at least five good reasons to get married. We already had one, that we loved each other. So, I sat down at my computer to type up four more reasons. By the time I had finished, I had written one hundred and one reasons why Dave and I should marry! Some were very good reasons but there also were silly ones, odd ones, funny ones. I figured that even if Dave rejected 95 percent of these reasons, there would still be five good ones left. I printed up the "101 Reasons," rolled the papers into a scroll, tied it up with a blue ribbon, and presented it to Dave. He was very surprised.

December 9, 1996

In the fall, I was invited to speak at the Star Visions Conference in Estes Park, Colorado. It was a New Age and UFO conference with lots of interesting speakers. However, the audience seemed very naive and gullible. I attended one talk where the presenters were going to bring in the "Andromedans" to interact "in spirit" with the audience. The presenters gave preliminary instructions to the audience, saying, "Hold your hands like this (in prayer), hold your arms like this (in supplication), say after us—'I hereby give up my free will.'" At this point I got up and left the auditorium!

With each talk I attended I felt a growing conviction that I could present anything I liked to this audience. I could tell them I was the reincarnation of Mary, the mother of Jesus, come to take them up in a spaceship, and they would have believed me. However, I was raised to be honest and have tried to run my affairs ethically and morally. So I gave my presentation on the history and future of the remote viewing field and its applications to the UFO and abduction field, which was well received and generated some interesting, intelligent answers from the audience.

I had known for many years that I had a natural intuitive ability. Since childhood I had spontaneous psychic experiences, and in my twenties I began a journey to understand and control my experiences. I began a systematic quest of reading and personal experimentation that convinced me that my own psychic experiences were real. In the out-of-body state, I could perceive people, events, and things that I later verified as being at the location I visited.

In 1986 I had heard about the psychophysics laboratory in Princeton, New Jersey, and participated in their Ganzfeld studies, then volunteered at the parapsychology laboratory, where I became employed and stayed for nearly five years until 1992.

At the parapsychology lab, I learned about the remote viewing research that was being conducted at Stanford Research Institute (SRI) in Palo Alto, California, and met many of the key players at the Society for Scientific Research annual meetings. I also learned about an army unit at Fort Meade, Maryland, that was putting the SRI research into practical applications. Some of these individuals had retired from the unit, including DE, a retired army major, and were setting up businesses and training programs. Through contacts that I had made at the parapsychology lab, I was invited to meet DE and participate in his remote viewing applications as a consultant. Unfortunately, this gained me the reputation of "working for the government," because the firm made great claims about working targets for the military and the government. However, I was never tasked with any of these targets.

March 5, 1997

Such a lot has happened since my last entry. I have been working part time for a telecommunications company (to pay my bills) but resent the time away from my studies and my writing. At the beginning of the year, I finally took a leap of faith, left my part-time job, and started my own teaching group called Inner Vision Research Institute. Through marketing, with a brochure I designed, I recruited four students who are interested in learning remote viewing. The students did very well and surprised us with their rapid progress. What is interesting is that many of the students relate similar Interface experiences and want to use remote viewing to investigate their abduction experiences.

I have not done this for my own experiences, and I discourage my students from doing the same, for several reasons. Two of the factors critical in the definition of remote viewing are that:

(a) The viewer must have little up-front information about the target she is viewing (called frontloading), and

(b) The viewer is able to get feedback, after the fact, on what she perceives. Neither of these criteria would be satisfied for me to remote view my own experiences. There is also a schism within the remote viewing community as to the validity of remote viewing such intangibles as alien abduction.

I would like to add here a little about my own training in remote viewing. When I moved to Las Vegas, I discovered that David's brother, Paul Smith, was also working with Psi Tech (the parapsychology lab), even though he was still employed by the U. S. Army at the remote viewing unit at Fort Meade. I began training people in the remote perception skills I had developed over the years, giving the classes out of my home. Lyn Buchanan, another of the army's retired remote viewers, came to participate one weekend and gave my course a good recommendation in his monthly newsletter.

People had begun to ask me where I had been trained in remote viewing, so I decided to take some basic training in Controlled Remote Viewing (CRV) with Paul Smith. Taking this course has given me a structure on which to base my native skills and abilities and made me a much better remote viewer. Although this has allowed me to interact with some of the finest remote viewers in the world, it has also added to the rumors that I was working for the military. It is unfortunate that another woman, a civilian also named Angela, was brought into the army remote viewing unit toward its end. There have been many times when I have been mistaken for her and have been asked what it was like working with the psi spies.

June 11, 1997

Busy times. This evening I ate the first fruits of the year from our grapevine in the backyard—they were so sweet. It gives me a great deal of pleasure to grow things—grapes, roses, tomatoes. Talking of growing things, the boys have entered their growth spurt and are growing like young weeds. The scary Interfaces have stopped for the time being.

July 21, 1997

I have been working on some new book ideas. One book I have in mind would be about women, like myself, who have never given birth but who continue to lead rich and interesting lives. Infertility seems to be on the rise in developed countries, and the percentage of childless women is rising. Historically, barrenness has been seen as a social stigma, as if there is something wrong with not having borne children. I would like to interview women from all walks and ages of life and retell their stories in a positive light. It is possible that the rising infertility rates around the world are what have prompted the Visitors to interact with us.

Another topic that has been getting some publication is the concept of "multiple abduction abuse." It seems that, like myself, individuals who are involved in the "alien abduction" scenario are often under scrutiny and surveillance from governmental agencies. Too many individuals have come forward with similar stories for it all to be dismissed as paranoia and hysteria. Recently, I responded to a letter by Victoria Alexander in the February 1997 issue of the *MUFON Journal*, in which she claims that the abduction scenario consists of the "sexually repressed fantasies of lonely women." I responded with the following letter, published in the May 1997 issue:

> I have been following the ongoing debate in the Forum regarding Helmut Lammer's MILAB story and Victoria Alexander's comments. Unlike Victoria, I admire the courage of such women as Leah Haley, Debbie Jordan, Linda Cortile, Katharina Wilson and the late Dr. Karla Turner, for coming forward with their personal stories. I know that there are hundreds (maybe thousands) of women who could tell similar stories. I have spoken to many of them. As well as relating Interfaces involving other-dimensional entities, there has been obvious interference by humans in their lives from government surveillance, and even physical abduction. Unlike rape or abuse victims, these women do not have the luxury of appeal. And unlike rape victims (who can face and accuse their attackers), the abuse that women like Debbie Jordan experienced often takes place in a drugged state.
>
> Having experienced many of the same ordeals as Leah, Debbie, Linda, Katharina and Karla, I can understand their reticence in coming forward to the legal authorities. Despite assurances that the crimes committed against them will be

addressed, all that has been received by them is ridicule, disbelief, and loss of credibility.

You will find that women who have a life history of both alien and human interference in their lives may strive to make sense of their experiences by writing, either through published works or by keeping journals. Unlike other abuse victims whose lives fall apart, victims of Multiple Entity Abuse (MEA—my definition and which includes humans), often strive to excel in their fields, whether it be home-making, service to others, the arts, sciences, or humanities. The individual and combined strengths of these women are astounding.

I called Victoria, as we have been friends for many years, to let her know about my "Entity Abuse" letter, but she was unwilling to hear about my experiences at that time.

November 7, 1997

What a fitting place to upgrade my journal—sitting at a twinkling brook at a picnic table, surrounded by copper beeches, and the busyness of Woodstock, Vermont, passing by on the bridge up to my left. I am "on the road," visiting and giving a remote viewing course in Vermont. Last week I was in Helena, Montana, giving a similar course. Things have come a long way since the beginning of the year, when I gave up my part-time job to make teaching a full-time venture. Dave and I married in September and went to Australia to honeymoon. There I gave a remote viewing course to a group of adventurous Australians. Interesting that this group was also full of questions about the UFO and abduction scenario in the States. Many of the students in my class voluntarily reported abduction-type experiences.

When I was in Montana, I got a chance to see some of the wonderful mountains and scenery around Helena. While I was driving around with my host we took a shortcut by the National Guard Airfield and saw about fifty unmarked black helicopters sitting on the tarmac. I took particular note to see if there were any markings on these aircraft but could see none. Many abductees have complained of such helicopters that circle their homes and property. The military has always denied the existence of unmarked black helicopters, but here they were out in full view of the public. I have heard since that the U. S. Border Patrol also uses unmarked black helicopters.

This reminds me of another incident concerning a helicopter. About six months ago, I was walking down the street near my home to catch the bus. It was a lovely sunny day. I was in a summer dress and enjoying the walk. To my left, I noticed a helicopter hovering over the desert and wondered if it was one belonging to the city police. The main helicopters around our area are Metro (police service), various news helicopters, and Flight For Life, which services the city and the Lake Mead Recreational Area. The air force helicopters from the Nellis Air Force Base do not seem to fly over our area.

As I continued walking, the helicopter began to fly in my direction and then over my head. I noticed it was blue and white, one I had not seen before. It flew over, circled, came back, circled, again and again, in a figure-eight pattern. I kept walking and told myself not to be paranoid, even though I seemed to be the central point of its turning and circling. Then, the helicopter flew off, and there was a large white van keeping pace with me. I was becoming alarmed but told myself to keep calm. I was in a residential district, so all I had to do was scream if somebody bothered me. The van sped up, turned a corner, and I thought it had left. However, when I turned the corner, there it was, parked on the side of the road. I had to pass it to get to my destination. As I walked closer to the van, I saw through the back glass window that the rear of the van contained equipment, such as oscilloscopes and equipment with lots of dials. The sunlight coming in from the front window of the van highlighted the equipment. There was no intent to hide it. As I passed the van, I looked at the driver. He was an ordinary, middle-aged man, reading a magazine. As soon as I had passed the white van, it started up and drove past me and down the road. What was that all about?

Later, when I returned home, I asked Dave if his EG&G colleagues had been playing a joke on me. I told him about the incident. He said that the EG&G helicopter had been in the hangar all day. There could be many explanations for this experience. However, the reading I have been doing lately on implants and tracking of abductees makes me wonder if, perhaps, someone was tracking and measuring something about me.

This fall I read an interesting article in the *Journal of Scientific Exploration* entitled "Topographic Brain Mapping of UFO Experiencers." It has long been speculated that experiencers might have a different kind of brain activity as a result perhaps of implants or the experiences they have had when in contact with the Visitors.

This paper was of interest to me because researchers such as Michael Persinger in Canada have suggested that experiences with the Visitors might be a symptom of a mild epilepsy condition and could be brought on by stimulating the brain with electromagnets. Others have suggested that the Visitor experience is a psychopathological condition, that experiencers are mentally ill. The authors of the paper, Norman S. Don and Gilda Moura, found in this small sample that this was not the case.

November 10, 1997

Today I received an e-mail regarding a paper that Victoria Alexander is proposing to submit to the *MUFON Journal* entitled "What Would Freud Say?" The article was written in response to criticism raised over her initial comments regarding a MUFON article by Helmut Lammer entitled "Preliminary Findings of Project MILAB (Military Abductions)."

Victoria basically denounces the abduction concept by stating: "I propose that the 'abduction experience' in some way enriches the lives of abductees by either purging their troubled psyches or allowing them to undergo an 'arthritic sci-fi shamanic jaunt' (without the burden of leaving the comfort of bedroom and home). They undergo a self-described horrific ordeal which sets them apart, identifies them, and regardless of angry denials, makes them special, either to investigators, researchers, the media, or their circle of friends."

After regaling the reader with endless, selected quotes from the abduction literature regarding the sexual nature of the experience, and disregarding other aspects of the experience, Victoria leaves the reader hanging with no real conclusions.

I again called Victoria, whom I have known as a friend for many years, and again related some of my own experiences to her. I asked her if she thought I had a "troubled psyche." To the contrary, she sees me as a very capable and grounded woman. She thought that perhaps I was "mistaken" regarding my experiences. She showed a strong reluctance to discuss the fact that I had experienced the same things she denounced, yet she still accepted me as an intelligent, mentally healthy person.

Her real objective in the paper is to rebut Lammer's article in which he states that the alien abduction experience is a cover for abduction and experimentation by military and government personnel. Victoria writes:

> According to Lammer, authorities use three satellites to find or keep track of abductees. These "tracked lives" are in reality filled with numbing mediocrity and bone-chilling repetition. Believing that the U. S. government is monitoring your every move is not only comical, it is delusional. . . . Further, Lammer displays abysmal knowledge of the U. S. government's budgetary structure. To imply that in the eighties, SDI (Strategic Defense Initiative) funds were diverted to harass abductees belies the fact that there were abduction reports prior to that time. SDI was a high-visibility project. Lammer makes illogical assumptions about omniscient capabilities supported by unlimited funding In summary, Lammer's conclusions are totally unsubstantiated and therefore unreliable.

During my talk with Victoria, I mentioned that at an abduction conference in Connecticut in the late 1980s, I had met a woman who worked for an SDI facility. This woman had made no secret that she worked for SAIC (Science Applications International Corporation) in Virginia, and that she was working on SDI-related projects. She also made no secret of the fact that she was gathering information from abduction researchers and abductees about their experiences. Victoria felt I must be "mistaken." We agreed to differ in our views and remain friends.

At the end of Victoria's paper, she thanks her husband, John B. Alexander, Ph.D., "for his support, review, and insightful contributions to this article." John Alexander has long been written about in the conspiracy communities as a possible source of disinformation regarding the UFO and abduction phenomenon. Some conspiracy theorists have linked him with a fictional group called The Aviary that appears to have inside information on the abduction and UFO fields.

May 10, 1998

I am writing up my journal in one of the fifth-floor bedrooms of a lovely townhouse in Boston, Massachusetts, owned by two university professors. I have enjoyed listening to the Boston rain, which has been coming down most of the weekend, sometimes in a gentle, plant-growing drizzle, and sometimes pouring heavily. It reminds me of England.

I flew in Thursday to attend John Mack's Star Wisdom

Conference organized by Mack's PEER (Program for Extraordinary Experience Research) Group. On Friday, I attended a clinical workshop conducted by Mack. Almost half to two-thirds of the clinical participants were also experiencers. John Mack played video footage of an African shaman who had been abducted; he told his story with shock and puzzlement in his voice. Another video segment was of taped interviews with South African children who had collectively witnessed the landing of a group of UFOs and saw aliens as they exited their craft.

On the Friday evening, the Star Wisdom Conference began with an opening ceremony performed by Sequoia Trueblood, a Choctaw Indian shaman, followed by a talk from Edgar Mitchell, the sixth man to walk on the Moon. On Saturday, the conference consisted of several panels and workshops in which I participated. The conference was extremely interesting and featured a dialogue between two different cultures. The Star Wisdom brochure described this as "Exploring Contact with the Cosmos: A Native American/Western Science Conference and Dialogue on Extraordinary Experiences." I sat on two panels: as an experiencer who was talking from a Celtic perspective, and another panel on which I wore my scientist hat.

The audience ranged from serious scholars to unfocused New Agers. However, some interesting and intelligent questions regarding the Interfaces between science and culture came from the audience participation. The main theme that emerged from the conference was that even though someone has training in either a shamanic or scientific framework, the abduction or Interface experience fits into neither. No training provides all the answers to the abduction experience.

June 14, 1998

Here I am halfway across the world, having just given a five-day course to a group of gifted and enthusiastic New Zealanders. The course took place in Wellington, and now I have a few days of solitude at a century-old beach house at Paekakariki, about half an hour's drive from the city. I haven't explored the beach yet, because a huge storm rolled in with heavy winds and rain, but I was able to walk to the little village to buy food and a few souvenirs. There is a path down to the beach I will explore tomorrow.

In New Zealand my Interface experiences returned in full force, and I experienced a real dream about a medical device designed to test the eyes. I dreamed of a device that shone a series of vertical points of light simultaneously into the eye. The lights were reflected off the retina and back to the device. A photo or a series of photographs was taken from the interior of the eye and stored in a computer. By analyzing the reflected points of light, the computer could evaluate the health of the human eye in a noninvasive way. It is possible that both eyes could be evaluated at the same time. This appeared to be an elaboration of the current technology that simply takes a picture of the interior of the eye.

16

Searching for Answers

"The possibility of reduced-time interstellar travel, either by advanced extraterrestrial civilizations at present or ourselves in the future, is not fundamentally constrained by physical principles."

—Dr. Harold Puthoff, Director of Advanced Studies, University of Texas at Austin, in *Physics Essays*, vol. 9, no. 1, 1996.

March 15, 1999

In 1992 I discovered an artifact that had been left behind in my apartment. I want to recap here more of this event, because I have been able to uncover some important information related to this evidence.

On the afternoon of June 29, 1992, I flew back to New Jersey from California and Michael, my boyfriend at the time, picked me up at the airport. We drove back to my apartment, where we celebrated a romantic homecoming. The following morning, Michael was behaving very strangely. He was searching through the papers and books on the shelves by the bed. Then he was going through the magazines on the coffee table as if he was still looking for something. After that, he was in the bathroom and kitchen searching for something. I think I found what he looking for.

That evening after Michael had left, I settled down to watch

TV. I put my cup on the shelves by my bed and noticed a small gray piece of plastic, like the lid of a tiny box. It was a few centimeters long and attached to a piece of masking tape. It had the letters "TETRAD" on the top. The letters were long and thin. The cross section of the device or lid was designed so that it could slide over another small piece. The lid was open at both ends and manufactured from an Earth-type gray plastic. There were two rounded projections on the underside of the container with the letter *R* in the middle. Perhaps it contained two other things?

I recorded then that finding this artifact made me feel very nervous and paranoid. I hid the lid and planned to find out what the trademark "TETRAD" stood for. My guess was that it was something medical or electronic. Later I took the plastic lid to an electronics lab, and the technician identified it as the cover for a microchip, used to protect the microchip in transit. Someone had brought the microchip to my apartment—someone, perhaps Michael, got careless and left behind the cover and masking tape.

Since 1992 access to the Internet has become faster and more efficient. I decided to punch in "TETRAD" as a key word and see what came up. I was not expecting much. However, what I have uncovered both excites and scares me.

The first entries referred to dissection needles used in a laboratory process called tetrad dissection. These ultrafine needles were used in manipulating yeasts for dissection. The needles had nothing to do, however, with a TETRAD company or manufacturer.

Next I searched for "TETRAD Corporation" and my finding made me want to turn off the computer. I was treading on dangerous ground here. A Tetrad Corporation located in Englewood, California, came up several times as a medical research company having contracts with DARPA (Defense Advanced Research Projects Agency). Of particular interest was an ultrasound program that Tetrad was performing for DARPA.

I decided to go directly to the source and accessed the DARPA website. I did this with trepidation, worrying that I might open a "can of worms." However, I was reassured to see a notice on the first page assuring the reader that DARPA did not collect the e-mail addresses of those who accessed its pages. I hoped that was true. It also stated that all of the information contained on the site was unclassified. That was reassuring.

The information I accessed on Tetrad was related to research conducted in 1995 and was referred to as "Biological Sensors and Multiorgan Diagnostic Screening." The website posted this information:

> Many soldiers wounded in combat must be diagnosed and treated during the first hour after they are injured or their chances of recovery are poor. In fact, the percentage of wounded who survive this "Golden Hour" has not changed since the Civil War, partly because it is so difficult to get good diagnostic information on the battlefield. This focus area will improve the quality and timeliness of diagnostic information available both on the battlefield and in the field hospital by developing technologies that will provide information about where shrapnel is located in the body, the extent and nature of the wounds, and internal bleeding.
>
> The civil trauma care community has a very similar set of problems, creating an opportunity to work on technologies of interest to both the DoD [Department of Defense] and civil sectors. This will help ensure that emerging civil trauma care technology will meet the military's requirements for "far forward" devices such as low power consumption, portability, and ruggedness, and that the DoD will benefit from the interoperability, technological dynamism, and cost reducing economies-of-scale stemming from the civilian marketplace. The projects in this focus area should lead to commercially viable, militarily useful devices that will give corpsmen and physicians better diagnostic information much less invasively, particularly through the use of ultrasound.

Beneath this information was another section that read "Combat Surgical Ultrasound System & Probes with Multi-Modality Image Fusion for Front Line Surgical Guidance and Telesurgery." The name of the company developing this instrumentation was Tetrad Corporation. A description of this project followed:

> This project will develop a system that will allow field surgeons to use internal, ultrasound probes to rapidly assess internal organ damage far less invasively. These small, rugged, autoclavable probes will be inserted through wounds and other small holes. The ultrasound data they produce will be fused with other diagnostic data such as MRIs and laparoscopic video, in order to produce a more useable and versatile image for the surgeon. This project will develop the probes, ultrasound system, and data fusion techniques needed to integrate

> this system into a mobile surgery unit located near the front lines. Civilian applications for minimally invasive surgery and trauma care closely parallel the needs of the combat surgeons, creating an opportunity for this technology to be sustained by a larger marketplace. Eventually, these capabilities could become one of the building blocks for the remote combat surgery of the future.

The estimated cost of this project was $6,531,732 and the project was planned to be completed in twenty-four months. Another similar project was described as a "Low Power, High-Resolution, Portable Ultrasound Imaging System" at an estimated total project cost of $2,834,680 and a duration to completion of twenty-four months. However, these were projects that were being discussed in 1995. There was no information from the early 1990s, so I can only guess which Tetrad technology was left in my apartment.

This information has almost blown me away. Was this what Michael was into? Before I get too paranoid, let me recap the facts: Michael was just out of the army and was connected to a medical unit. He was still active in the military and wore his dog tags everywhere, even to the beach; he had an intense interest in medical devices and inventions. During the summer we dated, I experienced many real dreams involving medical procedures, and Michael was present in these real dreams. I awoke from them with real trauma such as needle punctures and bruises. I found the microchip cover after his visit, and Michael had been concerned about retrieving something that day in the apartment. What was puzzling then, but makes sense now, was that a short time after we parted, he was promoted to the rank of major, even though he had not undergone any weekend or longer tours of duty during the previous year or so. Was I his project? I hate to ask that question but it has to be asked. Finding answers to these questions has left me with even more questions.

One of the questions is this: Is there any evidence that DARPA or its civilian branch, ARPA (Advanced Research Projects Agency), ever had an interest in or concern with extraterrestrial matters, abductions, or UFOs? A literature search brought to light a reference to a May 1971 publication entitled *LDEs, Hoaxes, and the Cosmic Repeater Hypothesis*. The publication, while being sponsored by ARPA through the Office of Naval Research, was approved for public release and sale. Therefore, this knowledge was never classified. The authors of the document were

O. G. Villard Jr., A. C. Fraser-Smith, and R. P. Cassam of the Radioscience Laboratory of Stanford Electronics Laboratories at Stanford University in California. The principal researcher was Villard, and the scientific officer was the director of the field projects program at the Office of Naval Research located in Arlington, Virginia.

The paper refers to a phenomenon termed the "long-delayed echo," or LDE, known to radio amateurs whereby a delayed transmission is experienced. "In listening to a two-way station QSO, have you ever encountered the situation where one operator persistently begins his transmission before the other has completed his remarks and turned it over to him? If so, you may be hearing the interfered-with station via a delayed channel." This situation is relatively rare and imagination, hallucination, hoaxes, and practical jokes may account for some of the events. The summary refers to reports of LDE, or "long delay echoes," of more than two seconds, and concludes as follows: "In the author's view, the extraterrestrial-origin hypothesis in explanation of the very long delays is at the moment as plausible as any other."

What follows in the report is very exciting, remembering that this was written in 1971, almost thirty years ago. The section is entitled "The Cosmic-Repeater Possibility":

> When a physical phenomenon is encountered which appears to depart from previous experience as much as this one does, it is certainly wise—in seeking explanations—to be flexible and to investigate every possibility no matter how remote. . . .
>
> Consideration of the very large number of stars in the sky has led to a belief among astronomers that conscious life of the general type which has originated on Earth is probably not unique in the universe, and may well have also evolved elsewhere. However, consideration of distance and probabilities leads to the view that if another "Earth" exists somewhere, it is so far away that—unless there are physical laws which we don't now understand—personal visits would require so much transit time as to be out of the question.
>
> On the other hand, "visiting" by probes seems to be a possibility. Assuming that other civilizations share the same curiosity to support scientific research that we do, they could—in principle, at least—send out spacecraft which would be put into orbit around likely stars or preferably planets, to await some sign of civilized activity. Having found same in the form of Herzian waves, the probe would presumably report that fact

> back to its senders, while at the same time attempting to alert the discoverers of its presence.
>
> The probe, it may be assumed, will not know in advance exactly what form of electromagnetic communication to expect. Therefore, what more effective way to perform the alerting function than to repeat back to whomever might be listening, some fraction of a transmission that had just been sent?

If this paper had been written by amateur radio enthusiasts, the content could be dismissed as wild speculation, but, remember, this report was sponsored by ARPA and the navy, authored by distinguished scientists at Stanford University, and distributed to a long list of authorities, including the navy, air force, army, Department of Defense, NASA, ITT, RAND, Raytheon, Stanford Research Institute, Sylvania Electronics, MIT, Battelle Memorial Institute, the Arecibo Observatory, RCA, General Electric, and many Ivy League universities.

Another question that needs to be answered is how many people have experienced the same things I have. If so, what is being done about it and by whom? During my filing, I came across a letter I had received from an association in Silver Springs, Maryland, called the Association of National Security Alumni Electronic Surveillance Project. Here I found other citizens worried about government intervention in our lives. I found that the group was keeping records and investigating cases dating from the 1970s in which individuals had become targeted for surveillance and harassment. The letter states: "No one is exempt from the prospect of being targeted for harassment and experimentation. Once a base of operations is established, anyone within range of these directed-energy technologies becomes fair game. . . . It should be noted that the parties engaged in these surveillance and harassment activities do not respect 'niceties' where intrusions into privacy are concerned."

The letter was soliciting funds for the running of the organization. It is both reassuring and worrying that others feel there is sufficient cause to be concerned about these issues to form an association.

June 7, 1999

Back in 1993 I downloaded some interesting notes from the MUFON bulletin board system on the Internet and stored them in my files while searching for other pieces to the puzzle. Included in the notes was a speech presented by Norio F. Hayakawa, director of the Civilian Intelligence Network, on November 17 at the Los Angeles Whole Life Expo. These notes were then written up as an address that was entitled "UFOs: The Grand Deception and the Coming New World Order." Norio Hayakawa has been studying the extensive and remote place known as Area 51, and the article documented his findings. The article is a long one, so I am not going to repeat it in its entirety, only those points that have relevance to my own pursuit of information.

After going into a detailed description of the area, its location, and how well it is guarded, Hayakawa reveals information gleaned for Japanese television and aired on March 24, 1990, as "Saturday Super Special." According to Hayakawa, this program was seen by more than twenty-eight million viewers. According to Hayawaka:

> The U. S. Naval Research Laboratory seems to have a Parapsychology Research Unit that coordinates its research activities with DARPA (the Defense Advanced Research Projects Agency). It is my understanding that some of their activities conducted under the auspices of the Office of Naval Intelligence are being held at locations such as Area 51.
>
> ELF (Extremely Low Frequency) wave-emitting devices, scalar machines, electromagnetic beam weapons, and highly-defined hologramic projections are just a few examples of the many new types of mind-control "weaponry" that the government seems to have developed in the past three decades or so. Newest research on special types of hallucinatory and memory-tampering drugs are a growing arsenal that the Office of Naval Intelligence boasts to have developed in its own Parapsychology-Mind Control Unit.
>
> According to recent information provided to me by a highly reliable informant within a special operations group of the Department of the Navy, two of the widely used devices will be R.H.I.C. (Radio Hypnotic Intra-Cerebral Control) and E.D.O.M. (Electronic Dissolution of Memory). The first of the two, Radio Hypnotic Intra-Cerebral Control, calls for the implantation of a very small electronic micro-radio receiver. It acts as a stimulator which will stimulate a muscle or electronic brain response. This, in turn, can set off a "hypno-programmed" cue in the victim or subject, which would elicit a pre-conditioned behavior. The second one, Electronic Dissolution of Memory, calls for a remotely-controlled production within the brain of acetylcholine, which blocks transmission of nerve impulses in the brain, This results in a sort of

selective amnesia. According to this source, in the hands of certain units within the intelligence community both of these methods are already beginning to be used.

This information could readily be dismissed as the overactive imagination of a group of conspiracy theorists. However, this weekend I received interesting Internet links that refer to two patents granted, individually, to two inventors, Sidney A. Ross of Mission Hills, California (1974), and Robert G. Malech of Plainview, New York (1976). Mr. Ross applied for his own patent, while Malech's patent was submitted by a company called Dorne and Margolin, Inc., of Bohemia, New York. I will describe these individually:

The patent issued to Sydney A. Ross was issued on September 24, 1974, under the title "US3837331: System and Method for Controlling the Nervous System of a Living Organism." His abstract follows:

> A novel method for controlling the nervous system of a living organism for therapeutic and research purposes, among other applications, and an electronic system utilized in and enabling the practice of the invented method. Bioelectronic signals generated in specific topological areas of the organism's nervous system, typically areas of the brain, are processed by the invented system so as to produce an output signal which is some way analog of selected characteristics detected in the bioelectronic signal. The output of the system, typically an audio or visual signal, is fed back to the organism as a stimulus. Responding to the stimulus, the organism can be trained to control the waveform patterns of the bioelectrical signal generated in its own nervous system. The invention system comprises means for frequency filtering, rectifying, integrating and amplifying. In addition, the system includes means for transducing the processed signal and displaying it as an output to the subject.

Ross the inventor claims the following: "A method of controlling the nervous system of a living organism by altering the waveform pattern of a bioelectrical signal generated in its nervous system . . . causing said organism to concentrate mentally so as to affect the intensity or state of said sensory signal in a preselected way: whereby said organism is trained to alter the waveform pattern of said bioelectrical signal in a desired manner and thereby to control its nervous system."

In a separate section of the patent description is a diagram of how the device works, featuring a human head as the input and output for the signal. References are made to a paper in *Medical and Biological Engineering* (vol. 8, no. 2, pp. 209–11, 1970), and the *Washington Post* (April 30, 1972, Section D3).

The Malech device is titled "US3951134: Apparatus and Method for Remotely Monitoring and Altering Brain Waves." There are no references mentioned, although a schematic of the device function is provided. The patent was issued on April 20, 1976, and Malech's abstract follows:

> Apparatus and method for sensing brain waves at a position remote from a subject whereby electromagnetic signals of different frequencies are simultaneously transmitted to the brain of the subject in which the signals interfere with each other to yield a waveform which is modulated by the subject's brain waves. The interference waveform which is representative of the brain wave activity is re-transmitted by the brain to a receiver where it is demodulated and amplified. The demodulated waveform is then displayed for visual viewing and routed to a computer for further processing and analysis. The demodulated waveform can also be used to produce a compensating signal which is transmitted back to the brain to effect a desired change in electrical activity therein.

I have quoted this material here to support the idea that some abductees claim that ELF has been used to control them, either through microwave-generated sounds or influence of implants. I am not claiming this was used on me specifically.

June 11, 1999

Several people have sent me a reference to a website called "The Starchild Project" (www.starchildproject.com). The site is dedicated to information about two skulls that were discovered in Mexico, that may shed some light on the hybrid question. One of the skulls seems human but the other is very unusual. The two skeletons were found in an old mine tunnel. One of the skeletons, that of a woman, was lying on the surface. Sticking up out of the ground was a malformed skeletal hand, which turned out to belong to a much smaller skeleton. The smaller skeleton was reported to be short and malformed.

The two skulls were eventually passed on to an American couple. Anatomical analysis of the smaller skull revealed it to be from a "child" of about five years of age because of the closures of the skull sutures and the baby teeth in the upper maxilla. It is not clear whether the child was male or female. Several aspects of the skull generate questions as to its human origins. The skull bones are thinner than normal, although the dentition appears to have been normal with average wear for a small child eating solid food. The skull capacity is much larger than normal and the brain case is much wider than an average skull. There are other major differences in the facial bone structures between the two skulls. According to Lloyd Pye, the author of the website, the skull has many similarities that are reported by abductees and contactees who have claimed to have seen alien-human hybrids. Pye is now doing DNA testing on the skulls, and it will be seen whether this is another elaborate hoax or a vital link in the continuing quest for evidence. The starchild skull has since been determined to be nine hundred years old, male, and human.

The magazine *Electronics Now* (March 1999) had an interesting article on a new brain/computer interface. Written by Bill Siuru, it documents how surgeons have developed a "neurotropic electrode" that is implanted in the brain of paralyzed patients. "The neurotrophic electrode, which is housed in a tiny cone-shaped glass casing, is implanted in the motor cortex. The electrode is about 1.5 mm long and 0.1 to 0.4 mm in diameter. Nerve growth factors are implanted into the glass cone, and the cortical brain cells are induced to grow into the electrode's tip and form contacts."

The implant is mainly intended to provide a link between the invalid's brain and a computer in order for incapacitated patients to communicate. However, the article concludes: "The technique can also be used for basic research on understanding how the brain works. Never before have recordings been made from a human brain for so long and with such stability."

July 15, 1999

Thirteen years have elapsed since I started my quest. The journey has come to a temporary halt to evaluate what I have found. What conclusions can be assumed from all this accumulated information?

1. Basically, there is a real phenomenon that has been termed alien abduction (Abduction One).
2. At least one in fifty people reports some abduction experiences.
3. These are feasible numbers and occur worldwide.

4. More socially aware individuals ("The Influential Americans," according to the Roper Organization) report abduction experiences.
5. There seem to be two categories of abduction experience: the ongoing kind that commences in childhood, and the second, which occurs as a spontaneous one-of-a-kind abduction, usually from the roadside when a UFO is sighted.
6. Abduction seems to occur as an altered-state experience but may be accompanied by physical reactions: bruises, cuts, scoops, scars.
7. Experiencers of abduction events are not suffering from mental illness.
8. Abductees are not imagining or fantasizing their experiences.

However, a great deal of hype, myth, story-weaving, hypothesizing, speculation, and down-right denial, misinformation, disinformation, and ridicule has accompanied these stories. It is hard to find the truth when the phenomena have been buried in years of taboo.

How is it that an experience so pervasive as the abduction phenomenon can remain so hidden? There is a parallel. According to sociologists, in the nineteenth century doctors and social workers could not believe that parents had the capacity to hurt their own children. The concept of child abuse by parents was thought to be impossible. Even when the physical evidence was right before their eyes, physicians denied the possibility that parents could harm their children. It was not until the turn of the century that parental child abuse was considered and eventually accepted. Attitudes change over time.

Abduction Two is also a reality. How is it then, that the individuals involved in Abduction Two can carry out their activities without suffering from grievous guilt or misgivings? I understood the mind-set of these participants when I talked to a psychologist who had been employed in the government and military-sponsored LSD experiments during the 1970s. He was then a graduate student and about to be called up for military duty when he was approached by the CIA and offered a position as a research psychologist. He described his acceptance as "the patriotic thing to do." Little was known about LSD when he became involved in the research. Eventually, he left the program and devoted his life to offering therapy to clients who were overcoming alcohol and drug addiction. Appeals to patriotism, being "in the right theater," being "in the know," money, and power are all powerful incentives to belong.

Where does this leave me now? With many unanswered questions. However, I would not have missed Interfacing with the Visitors. Now that I am becoming older, contact with the Visitors has almost ceased. I thought that all contact had ceased with the Visitors. However, the other night I had a vivid real dream:

I asked to see the Visitors once more. I was asleep in my bed and I awoke. To my right was a tall, golden bag, which seemed as if it was made out of gold threads. The "bag" leaned over and lay next to me on the bed. Through the bag, I felt the form of a gray alien! I wondered why it was in the bag and I understood that this was so that I would not be scared. I felt its head, its hands, its body. I touched the gray alien all over, through the bag, and thanked him for being considerate and for not scaring me. I awoke in the morning, amazed and delighted that the Visitors had come once more.

July 18, 1999

What have I learned after thirteen years of investigation? First, that the abduction scenario is real. Nonhuman entities have been interacting with us for thousands of years and they will continue to interact with us. They are adept at traveling in and out of our dimension and Interfaces occur most often in an altered state of consciousness. However, Interfaces are real, depending on our interpretation of what is "real."

In 1994 *OMNI* conducted an interview with astronaut Brent Musgrave regarding the reality of extraterrestrial life. He replied that "there is no reality anywhere of anything":

> If dimensions exist that are beyond our conceptual ability, they define reality also. I do not impose my limitations on the system. I recognize that this room is not this room but only the way I perceive it. The signature a bat has of this room, seeing it in ultrasound, or a fly with that great big eye it has—neither looks upon my reality as I do. It's frightening to realize I'm in an environment that is nothing like the reality I perceive. My perceptions are there for one reason: I survive in this environment.

Reality is a consensual behavior. We agree as a society as to what is real. Over one hundred years ago meteorites were not thought to be real. It was thought impossible that stones could fall from the sky. Reality is a matter of terminology and consensus, rather than actuality. In the current climate of denial and ridicule, the reality of alien abduction has come under question. Acceptance of the phenomenon would have to involve a large-scale change of attitude. It would also have to involve a widespread change in worldview away from our current behavioristic and materialistic mind-set. It is interesting to note that other countries, such as France and Spain, have broken away from mechanistic tradition and have developed government agencies that openly collect and catalog information about UFOs and abductions in an effort to understand these phenomena.

Where do the Visitors come from? There is ample debate about the extraterrestrial origins of the aliens, but no definitive agreement has been reached. What is known is that the Visitors are adept at bending the rules of physics as we understand them. It is quite possible that they are able to transcend space and time. Abductees have reportedly given different versions of the aliens' origins. Rather than seeing this as evidence of error, it could point to the possibility that the Visitors are from more than one place. With the placement of the Hubble telescope in space, we are just now coming to understand the complexity of the universe.

A 1977 NASA publication entitled *The Search for Extraterrestrial Intelligence: SETI*, which was edited by Philip Morrison of MIT and John Billingham and John Wolfe of the NASA Ames Research Center, examines the "extraterrestrial hypothesis": the idea that aliens exist outside our planetary system, rather than originating from a different dimension. The preface by Philip Morison begins:

> Over the past two decades there has developed an increasingly serious debate about the existence of extraterrestrial intelligent life. More recently, there have been significant deliberations about ways in which extraterrestrial intelligence might in fact be detected. In the past two years, a series of Science Workshops has examined both questions in more detail. The Workshop activities were part of a feasibility study on the Search for Extraterrestrial Intelligence (SETI) conducted by the NASA Ames Research Center.

The publication mainly refers to the radio-telescopic quest for extraterrestrial signals, but the introduction gives intriguing insights into the mind-set behind the quest. The text indicates that the finding of large suns in the galaxy might yield planets like our own, and that "perhaps the intelligent life-forms existing on one of these planets may also be common and ubiquitous phenomena."

Why are they here? It appears that the Visitors have a fascination with humans. In 1990, after consciously interacting with the Visitors, I decided to carry out a meditative Interface to ask why they are visiting us. This began with a visual image of the portal, shaped like an iris shutter, with curved louvers that could open or shut the mind window. I requested an Interface and found myself in the virtual room with the Wise One. We briefly touched fingertips in greeting.

I asked why they were interacting with us. He answered that they were visiting us because we were like an exotic species. We were an aberration, a throwback, intent on destroying each other. However, the Visitors had no concerns about saving us if we chose to destroy ourselves. Theirs was purely an anthropological study. They were fascinated by our emotions. They chose some of their ranks, who had learned some of our emotional repertoire, to interact with us. They have no intention of any in-depth or long-term involvement with us in the future. They were here only as long as it took to do an adequate study. I suspect, though, that they will be interacting with us for a long time to come. We are a very complex species. However, this does not excuse the terror and horror they have exposed abductees to.

Are the Visitors interbreeding with us? I have to say "yes" to this, based on the anecdotal evidence from abductees of reproductive intervention, resulting in human/alien hybrids. Whether any of these hybrids are able to survive a normal Earth existence is debatable. We, as a modern species, have been fascinated with exploring and populating outer space. Perhaps we are already doing this as a hybrid species.

Is the government secretly monitoring abductees and abductions? Again, the answer is in the affirmative. It is obvious that "government," throughout all of its departments and agencies, knows less about Abduction One than we give them credit for. "Government" would never admit to having insufficient information, because that would lead to a loss of face and credibility. Therefore Abduction Two has been put into place to obtain information about Abduction One. Almost every person I have talked to who has experienced Abduction One reports some experience of Abduction Two.

Why do so many abductees report medical interventions and hospital dreams? I cannot speak for other experiencers, because dreams are personal. However, for me hospital dreams come under several categories: symbolic, veridical, and actual.

1. Symbolic hospital dreams occur as a way for my subconscious to make sense of the sterile and monotonous surroundings encountered during Interfaces.

2. Veridical hospital dreams are screen memories that may mask reproductive and medical interventions during Interfaces.

3. Actual dreams or real dreams of medical settings may reflect real memories of medical interventions during Abductions One and Two.

The evidence for actual hospital dreams comes from the physical trauma that is discovered the morning after such a dream. I call these real dreams. In real dreams, the dreamer shifts from an unconscious sleep state to one of partial or full consciousness and the individual knows she is awake during a real experience. By comparison, in a lucid dream, the dreamer knows she is still asleep and dreaming but able to direct the course of the dream. There is a real difference.

I have been able to use dreams as a tool to access information about my Interface experiences. Dreams have long been considered both a way of identifying and understanding traumatic experiences, as well as a way to deal with them. One of the conditions that has been thought to follow the abduction experience is post-traumatic stress disorder (PTSD). Dreams play a large role in PTSD, in identifying and dealing with experienced trauma.

There are certain criteria for PTSD that are referred to by the American Psychiatric Association's *Diagnostic and Statistical Manual of Mental Disorders, Third Edition, Revised* (1987). Many of these criteria are manifested in the abduction experience.

1. The person has usually experienced an event that is outside the range of usual human experience and that would be markedly distressing to almost anyone. This would certainly apply to abductions.

2. The traumatic event is persistently reexperienced in at least one of the following ways:

   a. Recurrent and intrusive distressing recollections of the event;
   b. Recurrent distressing dreams of the event;
   c. Sudden acting or feeling as if the traumatic event were recurring (includes a sense of reliving the experience, illusions, hallucinations, and dissociative [flashback] episodes, even those that occur upon awakening or when intoxicated);

d. Intensive psychological distress at exposure to events that symbolize or resemble an aspect of the traumatic event, even including anniversaries of the trauma.

3. Persistent avoidance of stimuli associated with the trauma or numbing of general responsiveness (not present before the trauma), as indicated by three of the following:

   a. Efforts to avoid thoughts and feelings associated with the trauma;
   b. Efforts to avoid activities or situations that arouse recollections of the trauma;
   c. Markedly diminished interest in significant activities;
   d. Feelings of detachment or estrangement from others;
   e. Restricted range of affect, for example, inability to have loving feelings;
   f. Sense of a foreshortened future, for example, not expecting to have a career, marriage, children, or a long life.

4. Persistent symptoms of increased arousal, not present before the trauma, indicated by at least two of the following:

   a. Difficulty falling or staying asleep;
   b. Irritability or outbursts of anger;
   c. Difficulty concentrating;
   d. Hypervigilance;
   e. Exaggerated startle response;
   f. Psychological reactivity upon exposure to events that symbolize or resemble an aspect of the traumatic event.

Following the discovery of my participation in the abduction scene, I decided I would explore my inner self through dream recall, personal memory search, meditational journeys, and journal keeping. These methods proved to be very successful in gently peeling away the layers of the Interface experience. These methods are not for everyone, and another person might prefer to undertake these exercises with the help of a therapist.

I am glad that I met and interacted with the Visitors. The Visitors have enhanced my being in many ways: physical, mental, social, emotional, psychical, and spiritual. I am sometimes asked why they chose me. I ask, why not? It has been estimated that one in fifty people experiences Interfaces with the Visitors. There is anecdotal evidence that many abductees have Celtic or Native

American ancestry and perhaps certain blood types. These theories have not yet been examined and verified.

Is there hope for the future of continued, full-consciousness interaction with the Visitors? I think this answer lies with children who have had Interface experiences. As mentioned earlier, I refer to these children as "enhanced children," because they appear to have a higher IQ than normal, feel a stewardship with the Earth, and show a social responsibility far beyond their years. Alice Bryant calls them "super children." She has observed that the children have a "light" in their eyes, enjoy projects that involve touch or feel, draw artistic outward swirls when doodling, and draw large eyes in stick figures of humans. There is often a sun in their artwork. Their "seeing" is different. There is a need for touch. They know they are different. They are filled with a knowledge that comes out as they mature. They have a passion and joy and they are often telepathic.

I have met many such children in my travels. They often talk about the "little doctors" who visit them at night. They may be found outside, at night, with the doors locked. They often draw pictures of UFOs, aliens, and their abductions. These children are unusually bright, wise, and self-confident, with a social responsibility beyond their years. These children are our future link with the Visitors; they are the citizens of the future, and we should be listening to them.

17

An Alien Threat from Outside This Earth

"I occasionally think how quickly our differences worldwide would vanish if we were facing an alien threat from outside this world."

—President Ronald Reagan, addressing the United Nations General Assembly in 1987.

July 1, 2000

There is a riddle that goes, "What is greater than God, more powerful than the Devil, the rich want it, the poor have it, and if you eat it you die?" Usually, the person trying to solve the riddle starts thinking of the things that it could be, instead of what it could not be. They reason that the solution must be something, when the actual answer is: nothing. So it is with the alien abduction enigma. The solution to the riddle is nothing like we have been led to believe.

During the past fifteen years, I have been fortunate to have come into contact with many top people in the UFO field who are also involved to some degree in the fields of parapsychology and remote viewing. Many of them hold key positions in the federal government, military, NATO, Department of Defense contractors, the aerospace industry, in top educational posts, or are leaders in pioneering engineering and physics research. No secrets have been told, but there have been veiled allusions made to those who have been "clued in," who have the ear of the president and his cabinet, who know much more than they are ever going to tell about the UFO and abduction phenomenon.

Because of my contact with these highly placed individuals, my own motives and actions have become suspect. There are some researchers within the remote viewing field who will not communicate with me for fear they will become suspect themselves. Anything I say in this last chapter will be looked upon with suspicion and distrust by them. There will be concerns that my whole book is disinformation, designed to lead the naive reader away from the truth. Therefore, I have decided to stick with the facts. However, I have also included in this book ideas generated from discussions with individuals who are knowledgeable regarding the mechanisms of government, and who claim to be "in the know" regarding the Visitors. What these discussions tell me is that the United States, if not the world, is at war with the Visitors. This is no *Independence Day* scenario, with mother ships hovering over the major cities of the world, but an ongoing, maybe centuries-long, battle with the Visitors.

First, despite all of the media denial, there has been substantial documentation that many of our military and governmental leaders believe we have been interacting with intelligent entities who visit our airspace. Throughout this book, I have quoted famous politicians, statesmen, and military leaders regarding the UFO and alien abduction phenomena. At least five presidents have commented publicly on UFO phenomena. President Harry S Truman, in 1950, assured the American public that flying saucers, if they exist, "are not constructed by any power on Earth." President John F. Kennedy, in 1963 (during the height of the cold war), proposed the United States and the Soviet Union join in a cooperative program of space exploration. President Gerald Ford, in 1966, strongly recommended that there be an investigation of the UFO phenomenon by the Armed Services Committee. He felt that the government owed it to the people to establish credibility regarding UFOs, and to produce the "greatest possible enlightenment on the subject." In 1987 President Ronald Reagan, while addressing the United Nations General Assembly, commented how quickly our differences worldwide would vanish if we were "facing an alien threat from outside this world." And, in 1999, President Jimmy Carter made the following remark on *ABC News*: "I don't laugh at people any more when they say they've seen UFOs. I've seen one myself."

In November 1985, following a summit meeting with Mikhail Gorbachev in Geneva, Switzerland, President Ronald Reagan reported on one part of their private discussions. Reagan said, "Just think how easy his task and mine would be in these meetings we held if, suddenly, there was a threat to this world from some other species from another planet outside in the universe. We'd forget all the little local differences that we have between our countries and we would find out once and for all that we are all human beings on this Earth together." In February 1987, Gorbachev confirmed this discussion when he said, "In our meeting in Geneva, the U. S. President said that if Earth faced an invasion by extraterrestrials, the United States and the Soviet Union would join forces to repel such an invasion. I shall not dispute the hypothesis, though I think it's early yet to worry about such an intrusion."

According to some political observers, that was a slow beat of the war drum by Reagan, and Gorbachev wasn't ready to march to it. In 1987, President Reagan, while addressing the United Nations General Assembly, repeated his statement of how quickly our differences worldwide would vanish if we were "facing an alien threat from outside this world." Did the Soviet Union know more about the "threat" than the United States? According to one political observer, who wishes to remain anonymous, his assessment is that the most consistent and persistent drumbeat comes from the camp of the Visitors, and doesn't sound like a war drum. He says that it has had his attention for years, and the attention of thousands of women and men around the world who are brave enough to admit to their encounters. "How frustrating this must be," he continues, "to the super-secret gatekeepers of this information." How baffling it must be for them that the Visitors have spent so much time with these individuals. They ask, "Don't the Visitors know who is in charge, or who and what are really important?"

High-ranking military leaders and statesmen have also been quoted maintaining the reality of the UFO phenomenon. General Nathan Twining, while he was chairman of the Joint Chiefs of Staff (1955 through 1958), stated that the reported phenomenon is "something real and not visionary or fictitious." In 1954, Air Chief Marshall Lord Dowding, commander-in-chief of the British Air

Force Fighter Command, was quoted in the *London Sunday Dispatch* as being convinced that "these objects do exist and that they are not manufactured by any nation on Earth." General Douglas MacArthur is quoted in the *New York Times* for October 8, 1955, as saying that the countries of Earth will have to unite and make a common front against attack by people from other planets. "The politics of the future will be cosmic, or interplanetary," he added.

Admiral Roscoe Hillenkoetter, the first director of the Central Intelligence Agency (1947–50), made the statement that it was imperative that "we learn where UFOs come from and what their purpose is." Then, in 1960, he added that behind the scenes, high-ranking military officers were "soberly concerned about the UFOs." And, Senator Barry Goldwater, in a letter dated 1975, wrote about his efforts to find evidence of the UFO phenomenon. He requested to see what evidence the air force was storing at Wright Patterson Air Force Base, and was denied this request. He added that this information was still classified "above Top Secret."

Persons in a position to have knowledge of the UFO phenomenon, because of their connections to government and the military, have also voiced their opinions. Dr. J. Allen Hynek, scientific consultant for Air Force Project Blue Book, is quoted in *The UFO Experience: A Scientific Inquiry* (1972) as saying that when the long-awaited solution to the UFO problem came along, he believed that it would prove to be not merely the next small step in the march of science, but a "mighty and totally unexpected quantum leap." Shortly before his death in 1985, he excused his actions in Project Blue Book by saying, "We had a job to do, whether right or wrong, to keep the public from getting excited."

Very few people have traveled outside of the Earth's atmosphere. One of those people is *Apollo* astronaut Edgar Mitchell, the sixth man to walk on the Moon. On a TV program entitled *UFOs: 50 Years of Denial*, which aired on the Learning Channel on March 4, 1999, he said that the evidence points to the fact that the UFO crash at Roswell in the late 1940s was a "real incident" and that material was indeed recovered from that crash site. Can it be that these highly placed people—some of whom we elected into office, or to whom our government has given positions of trust over the American people—are wrong?

Some powerful part of the U. S. government has been acting as if we are or should be at war with the Visitors. I realize that such a statement is impossible to prove, given the confused state of information available. But that "confusion" is itself part of the evidence.

If we were at war with another nation, what evidence would we see? Formally declared war has been out of vogue since the end of World War II for important legal and political reasons. Under international law, a host of conditions come into effect when war is formally declared. These conditions can have a great impact on trade, communications, financial intercourse, travel, and other relations for nations not party to the declared war. Additionally, it is easier to get into hostilities than to get out of them.

If war has not been formally declared, the option is open to make a face-saving statement, bring the bodies home, and, as quietly as possible, stop fighting. There are a number of examples within the memories of millions of people throughout the world today. In each case, there is a large body of printed and visual news reports, heroes and scapegoats fully identified, memorials and monuments erected. Thousands of engraved headstones silently and sadly mark the event. This is some of the normal stuff of war, declared or otherwise.

Where is the conventional evidence of war between the United States and the Visitors? It does not exist in any tangible form. But that does not prove that some level of hostilities has not been taking place. While "war" may not be a technically accurate term to describe what could be going on, the term is generally understood as the action taken to defend against a threat. I will continue using the word "war" because of its popular use and understanding in the United States.

There is a huge problem in trying to conceptualize such a war. Exactly who is the enemy? What is their war-making capability? What are their objectives, their intentions? From answers to these and other questions, a war strategy could be developed and supported.

If there is a war going on, it is an exceedingly bizarre war. There has been no effort to build public support. The secrecy, denial, and ridicule associated with the phenomena are abundant proof that the best minds available to develop a strategy have not been enlisted. We don't know who in government has assumed the responsibility to fight this war, and we certainly don't know whether we are winning or losing. For decades it has been reported worldwide that Visitors' craft appear and disappear in the blink of an eye. What does this mean? It suggests that we don't know where they came from, or when. The bizarre becomes the fantastic and, probably, in the hearts of the frightened few who are the keepers of these secrets, it becomes the grotesque.

One of the most important pieces of intelligence one needs to seek in war is the intention of the enemy. Unless you intercept a believable message that states the enemy's intentions, the vault that holds these secrets is in the mind of the enemy leader. Recall the repeatedly reported capability of the Visitors to influence the minds of those with whom they interact. Now, the war would appear to move from the grotesque to the hopeless. It is no wonder that those "in the know" have kept silent, if only to save face when the facts become known.

In conventional warfare, one of the first indications of war would be that one nation would be denied access to the countries or lands of the enemy. It appears that we have been denied ongoing access to two of our closest extraterrestrial neighbors, the Moon and Mars.

Let's look at the U. S. space program: where we were half a century ago, and where we are today, foundering in a near-space equivalent of the Bermuda Triangle. Is it possible that our many recent failures to revisit the Moon and record data from Mars are the result of action by unfriendly neighbors? The following information is taken from two Internet records of space exploration dates: "Time Line of Space Exploration" compiled by Randy Culp (see www.execpc.com) and "Chronology of Space Exploration," compiled by Calvin Hamilton (see www.solarviews.com).

NASA was founded on October 1, 1958, to take over for the National Advisory Committee on Aeronautics. The first man-made vehicle to impact on the Moon was *Luna 2*, a Soviet craft, which was launched on September 12, 1959. On April, 23, 1962, *Ranger 4* was launched, and made the first U. S. lunar impact. By July 31, 1964, the American *Ranger 7* had relayed the first close-range photographs of the Moon to Earth, and by March 1965, *Ranger 9* had transmitted high-quality images of the Moon, many of which were shown live on television. In July 20, 1969, Neil Armstrong and Edwin Aldrin, made the first manned soft landing on the Moon in *Apollo 11*. Between November 14 and 24, 1969, *Apollo 12* made another manned landing on the Moon with its crew Charles Conrad, Alan L. Bean, and Richard F. Gordon. *Apollo 14* also made a manned landing on the Moon on February 5, 1971. Its crew consisted of Alan B. Shepard, Edgar D. Mitchell, and Stuart A. Roosa. In July 1971, *Apollo 15* arrived at the Moon with crew David R. Scott, James B. Irwin, and Alfred M. Woorden. Scott and Irwin drove the first lunar roving vehicle.

Skylab, America's first space station, was launched on May 26, 1973, and was manned for 171 days by three crews until it was abandoned in February 1974. Since then, the U. S. space program hitched rides on the Soviet space station *Mir*. In January 1994, the U. S. launched *Clementine*, a new DoD satellite that performed a lunar mapping mission using advanced ballistic missile defense technologies. The official name for *Clementine* was the "Deep Space Probe Science Experiment" (DSPSE). It was a Department of Defense program used to test new space technology. *Clementine* was a new design using lightweight structures and propellant systems. It spent seventy days in lunar orbit in 1994. It used cameras and lasers to gather altimeter data. However, it suffered a malfunction on May 10, 1994, ending its mission.

Following *Clementine*, *Luna 23*, a Russian lunar probe, crashed into the lunar surface in late 1994, although *Luna 24* made a successful landing on the Moon. On January 24, 1990, Japan launched *Muses-A*, consisting of two small orbiters, but they failed to send back data from their orbit around the Moon. The people of the United States have not gone back to the Moon since. Is this just poor management, or has someone or something prevented us from returning?

Let's take a look at our interactions with the planet Mars. Launched on July 14, 1965, the American *Mariner 4* returned the first close-up images of Mars, and in November of 1971, *Mariner* 9 was the first spacecraft to orbit another planet, Mars. Over the next year, it mapped 100 percent of the Martian surface. On May 28, 1971, the Soviet *Mars 3* lander was launched and made the first successful landing on Mars. However, it failed after relaying twenty seconds of video data to the orbiter. *Mars 4* arrived at Mars in February 1974, but failed to enter orbit because of a malfunction of its breaking engine. *Mars 5* made it into Mars orbit, but both *Mars* 6 and 7 failed. In 1976, *Viking 1* and 2, both American Mars orbiter/landers, touched down on Mars: *Viking 1* on July 20, and *Viking 2* on August 7. Both landers had experiments on board to search for Martian microorganisms.

Then there was nothing more until the launch on July 7, 1988, of Russia's *Phobos 1*, a Mars orbiter/lander, which was lost en route. *Phobos 2* was launched on July 12, 1988, by the USSR as a flyby/lander, and entered Mars orbit on January 30, 1989. The orbiter then moved within eight hundred kilometers of the Martian moon, Phobos, and failed. The lander never made it to Phobos. At a Society for Scientific Exploration professional conference in 1991, photographs were presented that showed *Phobos 2* encountering a very large object, which seemed to engulf the craft. Then, nothing further was heard about a mission until the American *Mars Observer* was launched on September 25, 1992. Communication was lost with the *Mars Observer* on August 21, 1993, just before it was to enter Mars orbit. On November 7, 1996, the *Mars Global Surveyor* entered an elliptical orbit around Mars, and was designed to orbit Mars over a several-year period and collect atmospheric and surface data.

The *Mars Pathfinder*, an American lander and surface rover, arrived at Mars on July 4, 1997, in the *Ares Vallis* region. The area was renamed the Sagan Memorial Station. A six-wheeled rover named *Sojourner* rolled onto the Martian surface on July 6 and survived eighty-three days, analyzing rocks, winds, and other weather factors, and sending back images. The *Mars Surveyor* failed to communicate shortly after its landing.

It seems that the United States has suffered its share of failed landings and communication in landing on or orbiting Mars. In particular, it seems that anything that tries to approach Mars's moon Phobos seems to fail or disappear. There are future landings planned by NASA, including *Mars Surveyor 2002*, *Mars Surveyor 2003*, and *Mars Surveyor 2005*. Only time will tell if they will be successful.

If the preceding information is seen in the light of the suspicions voiced by Richard Hoagland, Stanley McDaniels, and Ingo Swann, then we must consider it possible that there exist, on both the Moon and Mars, artificial structures which may have been constructed by intelligent life forms. Hoagland pointed out to the American public the now famous "face" on Mars and other structures that resemble pyramids and other nonnatural shapes. McDaniels made precise measurements of these structures and deduced that they were more likely to have been made than to have evolved naturally. Ingo Swann has proposed that there are many nonnatural structures on the Moon, particularly on its far side. In his book *Penetrations,* he describes how he was taken to a secret location, where he was asked to remote view coordinate locations on the Moon. He described facilities and entities working there. Ingo Swann's propositions sound far-fetched, but untouched, early NASA photographs, shown to me by an ex-CIA pilot, show definite nonnatural elements, such as large pipes sticking up out of the ground. The pilot said that these photographs can be obtained from NASA but that the areas have been airbrushed to cover the anomalies. I have also carried out "blind" remote viewing sessions with my students, and they have described many of these same anomalies.

If we are at war, is there any evidence that the U. S. military and government are interested in the UFO and abduction phenomena? The answer to this is a resounding affirmative. Let's consider the Star Wars scenario. We have seen television footage taken from the space shuttle, where streaks of light come speeding up from the Earth's surface. There has been speculation that these result from technology developed by the Strategic Defense Initiative (SDI), ostensibly to keep our skies free of cold war missiles. SDI, first proposed by President Ronald Reagan in 1983, was instituted as a military research program, as an antiballistic missile defense system.

The goal of the SDI system was to intercept incoming missiles, high above the Earth, using space- and ground-based lasers, subatomic particle beams, and computer-guided projectiles, and electromagnetic railguns. A network of space-based sensors and specialized mirrors were to have been put in place to support these weapons and direct the laser beans toward targets. SDI was given a lower priority in 1993 and the management of the program was handed over to the Ballistic Missile Defense Organization (BMDO), a less costly program using ground-based antimissile systems. Was SDI developed to fight the cold war, or was it designed to deal with the Visitors? Why was the program kept in operation long after the cold war ended? Another question remains: is there evidence that the companies developing SDI programs have expressed interest in the UFO and abduction fields?

In October 1988, I attended the UFO Conference at North Haven, Connecticut. I shared a room there with MK from Maryland, whom I later learned was there "undercover" for Science Applications International Corporation (SAIC) in McLean, Virginia, a government contractor involved with SDI applications. MK made no secret of the fact that she was working on SDI-related projects. She also made no secret that she was gathering information from abduction researchers and abductees about their experiences. Later I was told by another employee (of an SAIC contractor in Palo Alto) that MK went on to become oversight manager of their parapsychology laboratory, which was doing work under the SAIC umbrella. SAIC and SDI research appears to have been closely intertwined with the abduction and parapsychology fields.

What other evidence is there that we may be at war with the Visitors? In wartime, laws and regulations limiting the contact that citizens can have with the enemy are put into place. There is a prohibition of fraternization with the enemy. Stiff penalties are imposed, such as fines and imprisonment, on individuals who breach these rules. UFOs and the Visitors have been deemed not to be a national security threat by the government and military, and the public has been assured for more than fifty years that UFOs are nothing more than hoaxes and delusions. Why, then, was there the need for the Extraterrestrial Exposure Law that was passed back in 1982?

This law is contained under Title 14, Section 1211 of the Code of Federal Regulations, adopted on July 6, 1969, before the *Apollo* moon shots. In 1982, Dr. Brian T. Clifford of the Pentagon announced at a press conference that contact between U. S. citizens and extraterrestrials or their vehicles is "strictly illegal" and anybody found guilty of such contact would automatically become a wanted criminal to be jailed for one year and fined $5,000. Dr. Clifford stated that this was "no joke." According to NASA spokesman Fletcher Reel, the law as it stands is not immediately applicable, but could quickly be made applicable in case of need. This law is probably unenforceable. By implementing this law on a public citizen, NASA would be overtly admitting the existence of extraterrestrial contact, something it and other agencies have worked for years to cover up.

There are many other conditions of war that could be covered in this chapter, but I wanted to point out a few of the most obvious ones. It is relevant here to cite the common excuse put forward as to why the government could not come forward with what they know about the UFO and abduction scenario—they do not want to "cause panic." They cite the incident of Orson Welles' radio play, *The War of the Worlds*, to support their position. However, this does not make sense. Polls and surveys of the public show that a wide spectrum of the population has seen UFOs or feel that they have experienced alien abduction. There is a public sense of curiosity rather than fear and panic regarding the topics. Perhaps the panic scenario is one that would become evident if the bigger picture were known.

Where do abductees fit into this picture? Abductees are basically pawns in the game. Yes, they were chosen by the Visitors, to be part of Abduction One, but not for any enlightened, New Age reasons. However much I would like to think that the Visitors chose me for my intelligence, intuition, and heritage, there are many other less intelligent, less intuitive abductees from other parts of the world out there who are no more special than I. My unsuccessful quest, searching for the time when I gave permission, makes sense now. I never did give permission. Abductees are prisoners of war in their own land with no Geneva Convention to ensure their rights.

Not only are we abducted by the Visitors, but we have become the unwitting research subjects for government and military groups trying to understand and deal with the Visitors: what I call Abduction Two. I have had to face this fact. Please remember that a lot of what I wrote in my journals is at odds with this final chapter. Throughout the journals, I experienced wide swings in my understanding of the situation, and much of what I wrote then would seem to contradict these conclusions. What is different about me is that I have a voice. I love to write, I am incredibly stubborn, and I stick with a problem, long after others would have given up. A lot of what I experienced during my lifetime makes sense now, as I view the alien enigma in a new light.

Why do so many people, women in particular, find that the Visitors lose interest in them as they enter their fifties? According to much of the anecdotal material, the Visitors have a definite agenda of hybrid reproduction in place. When the human capacity to reproduce is gone, so are the Visitors. The Visitors have used our bodies for their own ends. However, this cold reasoning does not ease the longing to see and interact with the Visitors again once they leave. I have heard abductees talk about the Visitors with longing in their voice, with nostalgia, as if they were talking about a lost love. I can identify with these feelings. When the Visitors stop coming, there is an empty hole that nothing earthly can fill.

What is the message of the Visitors' "drumbeat?" It may be simple, but it is probably more complex, and most of us hear what we want to hear. It is clear that some in government hear only fear, and with that deadly filter over their rational response, they are doing things that are as frightening to the public as anything they may have experienced with the Visitors. I echo one of my colleagues who declares that his options are few, but that he lives his life in truth with regard to the Visitors and that he remains open to listen, watch, and wait.

In concluding this final chapter, I would like to relate an anecdote that was given to me as an urban legend, one which might shed light on the Visitors' drumbeat. It is the story of a former U. S. president, who publicly acknowledged seeing a UFO before he became president. More than that, he pledged to look into the subject if he was elected. He did carry out this promise, and asked appropriate officials to check government records. Little of significance was reported to him, and this information was only made public years later.

However, the president was smart and realized that additional direct attempts to locate the suspected information would be easily defeated by a team that had kept all previous presidents ignorant. With his military and engineering background, he was unique, and far different from the typical resident of the White House. Quietly and effectively, he worked the Pentagon system. One day the Chairman of the Joint Chiefs of Staff asked for a private meeting. In that meeting, the president was told that there was a program that addressed UFO/ET phenomena. The president thanked the chairman and said that he had no desire to be treated differently than previous presidents on this subject, but if any other president had been introduced to the program, he expected this also. He had passed the first test. The gatekeepers put away the briefing that they had prepared for any president who insisted upon knowing "everything the government knows about this subject." The bottom line of that long briefing was that: "This is a very complex scientific problem, that additional time and work eventually will solve. Until we have achieved breakthroughs that are currently beyond our improving science, the policy of secrecy on the subject is completely justified. The potential of public panic and global economic disruption warrants continuation of the sophisticated counterintelligence program that has been successful, albeit with some unfortunate and unavoidable minimum loss of life and liberty."

The president quietly waited, and a decision was made to give him what no previous president had ever received: full disclosure.

The plan was elaborate. The president's family went on a skiing holiday, and it was announced that the president was going to Camp David to prepare for an upcoming foreign visit. A presidential double boarded a helicopter from the White House South Lawn, and later that night, a closed van drove to Andrews Air Force Base with the president in disguise. The small executive air force jet flew the president to a military base in Florida. Under the cover of night, he was driven into a hangar and ushered into a small, but well-appointed briefing room. There, the schedule was explained to him.

The first hour was a threat briefing; the second hour was a defensive briefing; then, after a short break, he was to be taken to a lower-level chamber where he was to see the recovered alien hardware and preserved alien bodies that had been collected since 1947. From every perspective, the briefings went well. The president asked intelligent questions. The well-prepared briefer responded fully, and quickly admitted when there was no information to answer a particular question.

When the small party went down the ramp to the display area, the evening unraveled. The outside guards opened the massive double doors to a completely empty chamber. The custodial personnel were staggered and confused. Some recall that the president's reaction was a slight smile. All agreed that he quickly said, "Gentlemen, it is obvious that the program is over. I am ready to return to Washington."

A week later, the president was informed that every item was now back in its previous place. He was asked if he wanted to make a second visit to the site. He answered, "I cannot imagine a more complete briefing than the first one. A second visit is not necessary. I learned everything that I need to know."

Following this, the custodians were nervous every hour the president was in office. They took extreme and effective steps to ensure that he would not be reelected. The former president has never talked about this incident, and probably never will. What he learned remains his secret, but since he left office, his determined efforts to resolve global conflicts, to model a life promoting democracy, and to nurture hope and freedom are well known and respected. He continues to wage peace, and thus perhaps reveals the secret that he learned in the empty chamber.

All urban legends are romanticized myths, and this one is no exception. Could it be true? Possibly so, most probably not. Is it unsettling to think that the president of the United States does not know what government custodians know about Visitor phenomena? If he does not know, who is leading the war against the Visitors? Equally important, is there a concurrent parallel diplomatic track, and who is leading it? I assume that someday we, the public, will have answers to these questions. What is not clear is who will eventually provide them: the Visitors, or our government? Is it a pious hope to speculate that it might be a friendly, joint presentation? At present, there are no data.

As my friend Maria asks, "What can we learn from this?" First, that we have close neighbors in our solar system, and they have been interacting with us for centuries. They are interested in us biologically, as a species. They are not necessarily anthropologists, as the Wise One said, but something close. The Visitors are a fact of life for a great many people. Second, the world, and in particular the United States, considers itself at war with the Visitors and has put in place all of the conditions that accompany war: secrecy, penalties, regulations, and subterfuge.

What is needed is an open dialogue between abductees and those charged with the authority to understand these phenomena—to begin to understand Abduction One, without resorting to Abduction Two. This would involve a new paradigm, a change in mind-set from the militaristic thinking of the current leadership to one that is more open and trusting. This would be a huge undertaking; it would involve a risk of losing face, but it could be done. It is time that it is done.

Index

About the Author

Angela Thompson Smith was born in Bristol, England. She is now an American citizen and lives in Las Vegas, Nevada with her husband David A. Smith and her stepsons David B. (21), Daniel (17), and Johnathan (15). Angela's professional background has been in nursing and social work, and she recently completed her Ph.D. in Psychology. She plans to continue her career as an experimental psychologist, focusing on identifying the "footprints of consciousness." Angela likes to read, and writes books and poetry. She is very interested in outdoor activities such as camping, nature, and exploring the ghost towns and scenery of the American Southwest. Angela Thompson Smith's previous book was *Remote Perceptions: Out-of-Body Experiences, Remote Viewing, and Other Normal Abilities* (Hampton Roads, 1998).